MARVEL

COOKING WITH

DEADPOOL

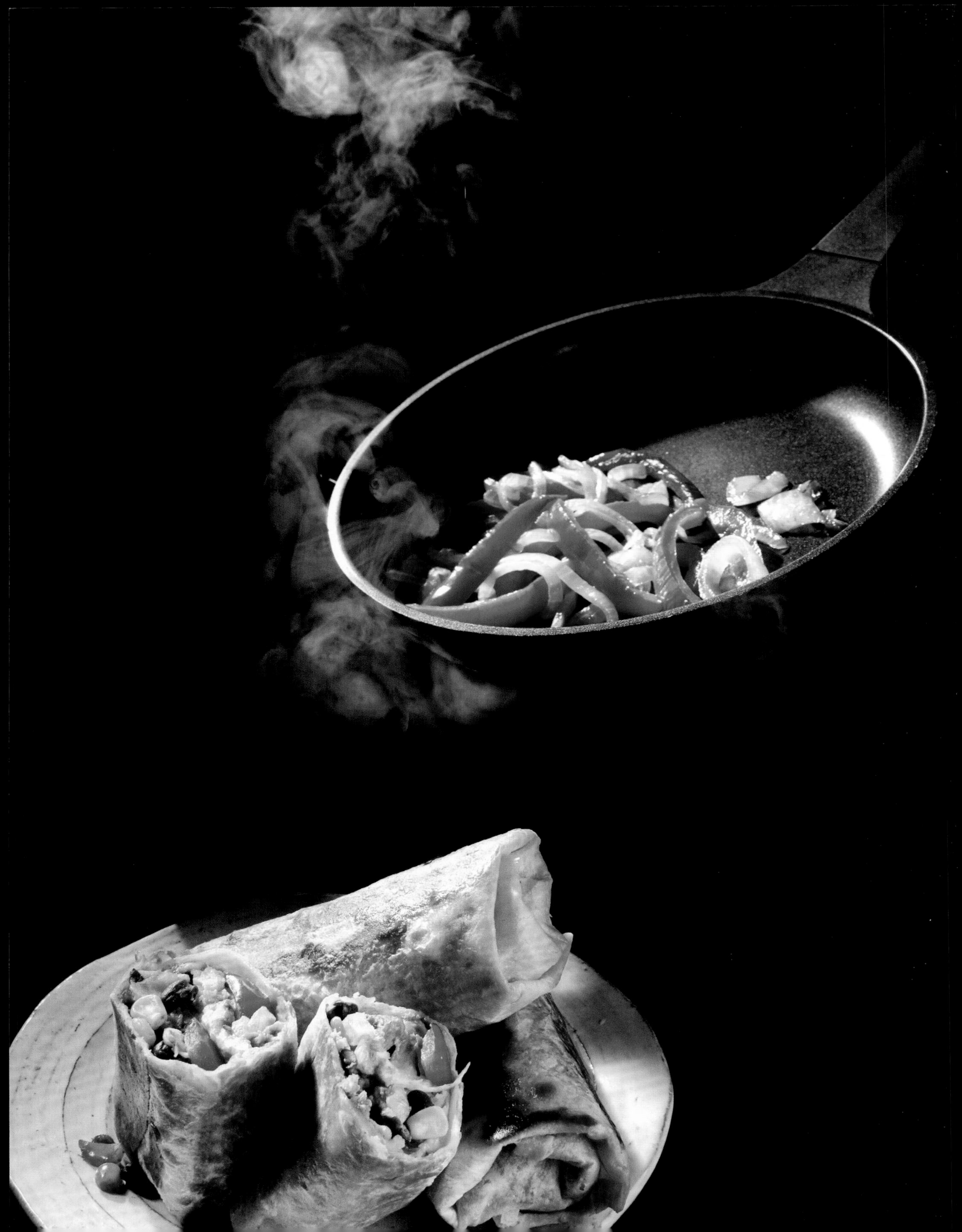

MARVEL

COOKING
WITH
DEADPOOL

DON'T WORRY! I GOT THIS.

WRITTEN BY MARC SUMERAK
RECIPES BY ELENA P. CRAIG
PHOTOGRAPHY BY TED THOMAS

INSIGHT
EDITIONS

SAN RAFAEL · LOS ANGELES · LONDON

CONTENTS

THIS IS MY BEST IDEA EVER!

Hey there, 'pool pals!

It's ya boi Wade Wilson, aka Deadpool. The Regeneratin' Degenerate. The Merc with a Mouth. And now: the Cook with a Book!

That's right, after years of trying to earn fame and notoriety through my regular activities as a mercenary and (occasional) super hero, I was somehow still unable to locate the elusive secret ingredient that would propel me to superstardom. If I wanted to take my brand to the next level, I needed to diversify. But how? My own line of skin-care products? An exclusive collection of designer pouches? A multimillion-dollar feature-film franchise? Nah. Those would never work.

Then, one day after blowing up a restaurant full of henchmen, it suddenly hit me like a chunk of unusually delicious debris. If I really wanted to up my game, I needed to be like every other B-list celebrity and write my own cookbook! I figure if professional wrestlers and talk show hosts can convince you to fork over a bunch of dough to learn how to make their mom's mac and cheese, then you must be easy targets, right?

Given my extreme personality, one might fairly assume that this culinary journey will be filled with nothing but bacon-wrapped cupcakes and hamburgers that use grilled cheese sandwiches for buns. And while those definitely sound like things I would put in my mouth-hole after a hard day of merc-ing, I've decided to defy expectations and focus on some more traditional dishes, each with a distinctly Deadpoolian twist. You heard me! I'm going full-on Julia Child here (only slightly more attractive).

I know you might not think of me as a culinary genius yet, but give me a chance and I promise I won't disappoint. After all, when you're in my line of work, every single meal could be your last, so I've learned to make each one the very best it can be. Plus I've developed some serious chops when it comes to chopping.

So what will you find in these pages? Everything from appetizers to entrées to breakfast to dessert, that's what! Whether you're prepping a multicourse holiday menu for an entire team of your favorite mutants or you're just heating up a pizza for one, this book has got something for absolutely everyone. In fact, I've force-fed these dishes to countless hostages, and they've all given me universal praise. Some even wept openly! What can I say—when you cook with this much joy, folks can taste it in every bite.

Now, I realize there's a significant chunk of my audience whose experience in the kitchen peaked at microwaving a burrito. If you fall into that category and only bought this book to keep it in mint condition as the collector's item it is, I totally respect that. But to give you a fighting chance when it comes to making these meals, I've included some skill pages so you can figure out how the hell you're supposed to do some of the ridiculous things I'm talking about (unless you happen to be the one jerk on the planet who already knows how to spatchcock a chicken). So not only do you get to cook, you get to learn. How's that for added value?!

Now if you don't mind, I've got meals to cook and people to kill. Hope you'll join me for at least one of the two . . .

Love and snuggles,

♡ Deadpool! ♡♡

XOXO

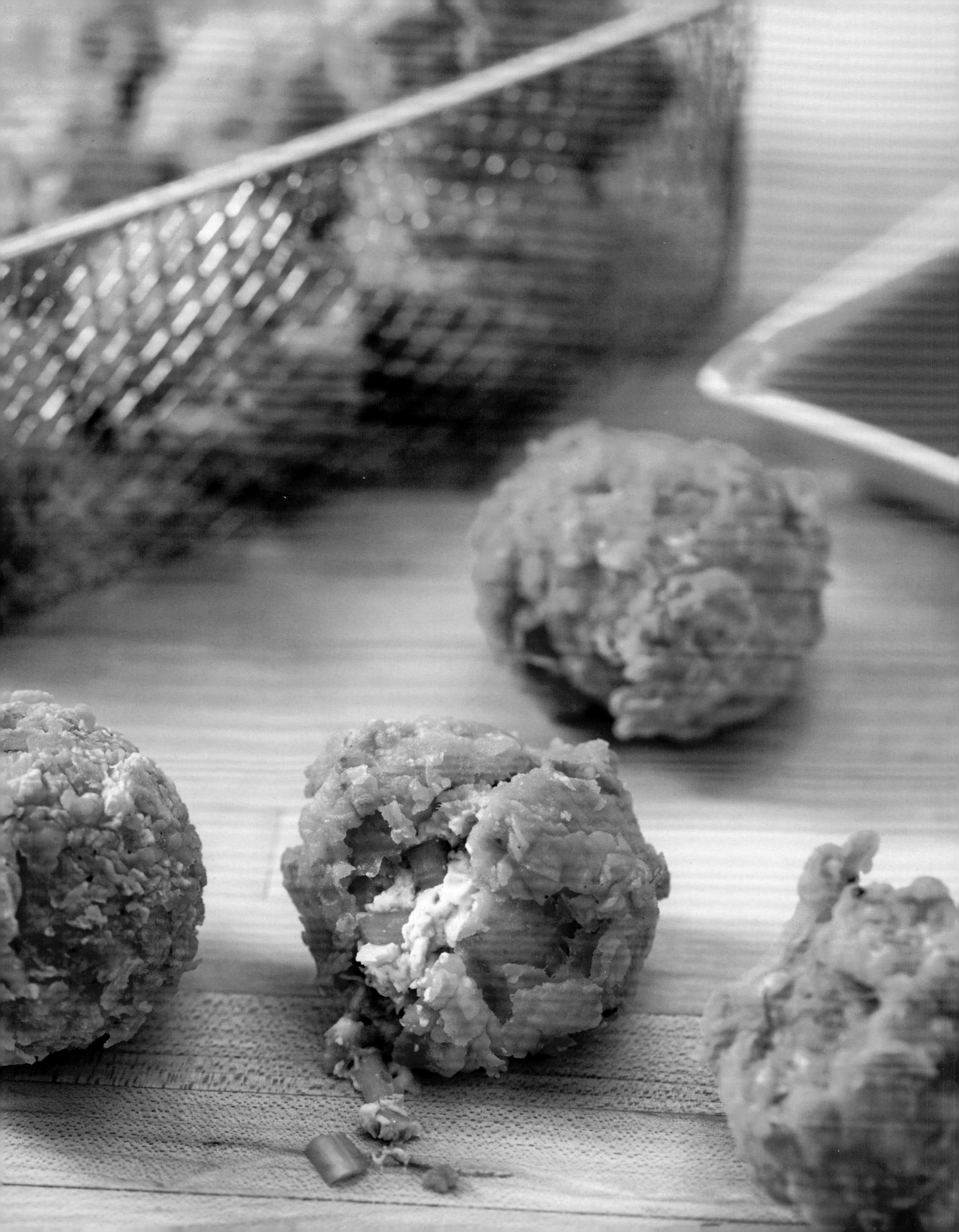

SMALL BITES FOR
BIG MOUTHS

When I was first starting out as a mercenary, I was determined to go straight for the biggest jobs I could find. The kinds of gigs that would make me an instant legend in the community, that would earn me piles of cash and some serious street cred. But looking back on those early days now, I'm not afraid to admit that I occasionally bit off more than I could chew. And with a mouth as big as mine, that's really saying something.

If Cable would let me borrow his time travel tech for once, I'd . . . Well, first, I would go back to last Thursday night and remember to set my DVR to record the hockey semifinals. But after that I'd pay a little visit to a young, eager Wade Wilson and remind him that it's okay to start out small. While one big hit might seem like the best way to set himself up for life, he might actually be better off easing in with a few smaller jobs that expand his range of skills and eventually add up to the same awesome result. That's a hard-learned lesson I now apply to a lot of things in my life, including cooking.

That's why we're kicking things off with a selection of savory snacks and starters aimed to please a wide variety of palates. Whip up one of these surefire hits for your next shindig and I guarantee everyone will be begging you to cater their next event. And then, my friend, you'll finally be ready to move on to the big score!

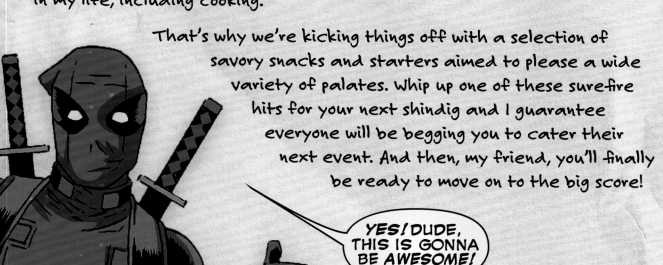

YES! DUDE, THIS IS GONNA BE AWESOME!

POOL-TINE

Oh, Canada! My home and native land! If you're in the mood for some authentic cuisine from the Great White North, look no further than poutine—the semiofficial national dish of a nation that, for some unknown reason, still refuses to acknowledge me as its most valuable export. Poutine, which roughly translates to "face full of yum" in Saskatchewanian, consists of a heaping pile of golden brown *pommes frites* (French fries to you Yankees), smothered in a rich brown gravy and a topped off with cheese curds. If that sounds like a heart attack on a plate to you, you're right. But if your internal compass is set to deliciousness, then poutine is true north! (If you can't find quality cheese curds, you can sub in mozzarella pearls instead, but your visa will instantly be revoked. Sorry.)

FOR THE POTATOES:

3 pounds russet (or other baking) potatoes, cut into wedges

Scant ¼ cup olive oil, to coat

Salt

FOR THE GRAVY:

2 cups vegetable broth

2 cups water

2 teaspoons beef bouillon

4 tablespoons (½ stick) salted butter

4 cloves garlic, minced

1 shallot, minced

6 tablespoons all-purpose flour

1 tablespoon Worcestershire sauce

½ teaspoon salt

Fresh black pepper, to taste

TO SERVE:

One 8-ounce package fresh mozzarella pearls or cheese curds

Fresh parsley, for garnish (optional)

1. Line 2 rimmed baking sheets with parchment paper and place them in the oven. Preheat the oven to 450°F.

2. To make the potatoes: Rinse the potato wedges to remove the excess starch, and pat dry. In a large mixing bowl, coat the potatoes in olive oil and salt to taste. Carefully add the potatoes to the baking sheets in a single layer, being careful not to overcrowd the pan.

3. Bake the potatoes for 20 minutes. Remove the sheets from the oven, shake them to turn potatoes, and bake another 10 to 15 minutes, until crisp and brown.

4. To make the gravy: Combine the broth, water, and bouillon in a medium bowl, and set aside.

5. In the meantime, melt the butter on medium heat in a medium saucepan. Add the minced garlic and shallot, and cook until translucent. Add the flour, and continue to cook, stirring continuously until the roux turns a deep golden brown.

6. Slowly add the broth mixture, stirring until smooth. Add Worcestershire sauce and salt, and continue to cook on medium heat until the gravy thickens.

7. To assemble your Pool-tine, place your crispy fries in a bowl, sprinkle with mozzarella pearls or cheese curds, top with gravy, season with pepper to taste, and top with parsley, if desired.

TIP:
FOR THOSE OF YOU BELOW THE 49TH PARALLEL, THIS GRAVY IS EQUALLY DELICIOUS ON YOUR FAVORITE FROZEN FRIES OR EVEN A CLASSIC BAKED POTATO!

I'M A REAL FUNGI

As you may have noticed, I wear a mask. Why is that, you ask? Am I trying to hide my true identity to protect the people I love? Nah. All the people I love are totally capable of protecting themselves. It's because my face has been so ravaged by disease that my healing factor can barely keep it in check! Still hungry? Good. If you still have an appetite after that disgusting truth, then you'll probably enjoy these less-than-lovely little mushrooms. They may be wrinkled and ugly, like my face, but they're also buttery and irresistible, like my soul. It's what's on the inside that matters these days, right, ladies? So time to stop judging a book by its cover (unless it's this book, which you already bought, so I trust your judgment), and give these fungi a chance!

2 tablespoons olive oil

3 tablespoons salted butter

8 cloves garlic, minced

1½ pounds whole mushrooms, cleaned and stemmed (stems reserved)

Salt, to taste

¼ to ½ teaspoon red pepper flakes, depending on heat preference

¼ cup vermouth

Crusty bread, for serving

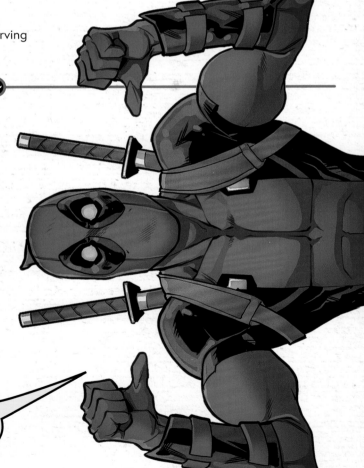

1. In a large sauté pan on medium heat, combine olive oil and butter until the butter begins to foam. Add garlic, and sauté until just translucent. Add the mushroom caps and stems, and cook, stirring only occasionally, until the mushrooms are brown and have absorbed most of the butter. Add the salt, red pepper flakes, and vermouth, using the liquid to deglaze the pan.

2. Cook for about 5 minutes, then remove from heat. Serve hot with crusty bread for sopping up the sauce.

OKAY, FOLKS SAY... ...DEADPOOL IS THE GREATEST OF ALL TIME!

JUST THE TIPS:
MISE EN PLACE

The French have a word for everything. Probably because they have their own language. But some of their words sound so much better than ours. Like *pantoufles*. Or *pamplemousse*. Or mise en place, which is just a cool way chefs say "everything in its place." Turns out that staying organized in the kitchen is the key to pulling off difficult recipes. It helps ensure that your timing isn't off and you don't miss steps or ingredients. Here are some tips:

1. Read the recipe. This shouldn't be too hard, since it's right here in the book. Pay special attention to cooking times and make sure you have all the required equipment. No one wants surprises when they're elbows deep in raw meat.

2. Gather your stuff. Ingredients, tools, pans, towels, emergency contact numbers. Whatever you might need during the cooking process, now's the time to find it!

3. Ready, set, chop! Prep time! Slice and dice all the ingredients into the proper sizes and portions, then place them into adorable little bowls so you'll have easy access when it's time to add them to the mix.

4. Stay organized. Put your little bowls onto one baking sheet for easy portability. (But don't put that baking sheet straight into the oven and expect your recipe to come out complete. This is cooking, not magic, got it?)

5. Keep it clean. Once those bowls are all empty, stack them up and set them aside until your meal is complete. Then it's time to wash them up. Or, if you're like me, time to move them to the sink and forget they're there until one of your enemies shoots a laser beam straight into your kitchen. Either way, no more dirty dishes!

Banh Mi Buckshot

YIELD: THIRTY 1-INCH BALLS

The island nation of Madripoor is world-famous for being the kind of place where you can get anything you want—for a price. For some people, that means high-tech weapons or enhanced powers. For me? It's a sandwich I've only ever been able to find in a little bodega deep in the heart of the island's seedy Lowtown district. It reminds me of a twist on the traditional Vietnamese banh mi, so like everything in Madripoor, the recipe was probably stolen. Still, it's so scrumptious that I've routinely found myself fighting my way through a horde of Hand ninjas just to get my hands on one. Eventually, I realized I could just buy the stupid recipe. Best $1.2 million I've ever spent. Since I still haven't figured out how to fit a baguette in my pouches, I came up with these little buckshot-sized balls as a variation on the sandwich's trademark filling. Now I can have a taste of Madripoor wherever my missions take me.

FOR THE MEATBALLS:

1 tablespoon fish sauce

1 tablespoon seasoned rice vinegar

1 tablespoon soy sauce

½ teaspoon curry powder

¼ teaspoon cayenne

¼ teaspoon garlic powder

1½ tablespoons minced fresh ginger

Juice and zest of 1 lime

1 tablespoon minced fresh mint

2 tablespoons minced white part of the scallion (greens reserved)

¼ cup finely minced carrot

1 pound ground pork

FOR THE SRIRACHA MAYONNAISE:

½ cup mayonnaise

2 tablespoons sriracha

1 teaspoon seasoned rice vinegar

1 teaspoon minced green of the scallion

1. Preheat the oven to 425°F. Line a rimmed baking sheet with parchment paper, and set aside.
2. To make the meatballs: Combine the first eleven ingredients in a medium bowl. Add ground pork, working the mixture with your hands until everything is well incorporated. Form the mixture into 1-inch balls, and place them on the baking sheet so they are close together but not touching. Bake for 15 to 20 minutes, until cooked through and beginning to brown.
3. To make the sriracha mayonnaise: Mix all the ingredients together, and chill until ready to serve.
4. Serve the balls hot with the sriracha mayo, and enjoy.

TIP:

CAN'T EAT 30 OF THESE BABIES IN ONE SITTING? NO WORRIES! JUST POP YOUR BALLS IN THE FRIDGE AND REHEAT 'EM IN A 350°F OVEN FOR TEN MINUTES WHEN YOU'RE READY! (THAT DID NOT SOUND RIGHT. . .)

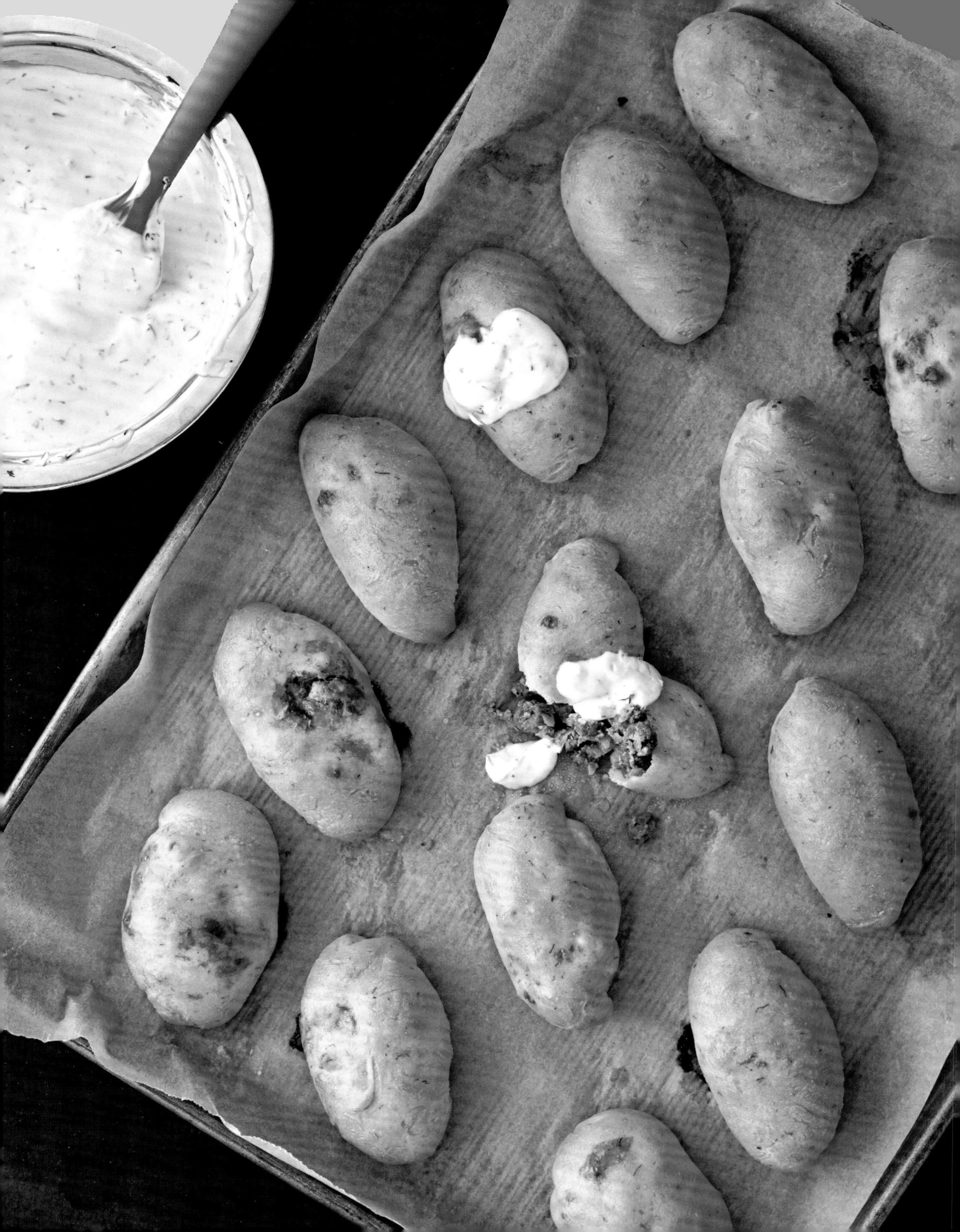

PETE'S MEAT PIES

Most folks who find themselves face-to-face with Colossus have trouble seeing anything beyond his massive metallic muscles. But my pal Piotr is more than just a paragon of platinum perfection. I love it when he decides to embrace his softer side, especially when he cooks up these traditional piroshki his mama used to make back on the Ust-Ordynsky Collective in Siberia. They're soft and delicate on the outside, with a powerful dose of meaty goodness in the middle . . . almost like a reverse Colossus!

FOR THE DOUGH:

1 package (2¼ teaspoons) active dry yeast

½ cup milk, room temperature

3 tablespoons unsalted butter, melted

1 egg, room temperature

½ tablespoon sugar

½ teaspoon salt

¼ teaspoon dried dill

2½ cups all-purpose flour

FOR THE FILLING:

1 to 2 tablespoons oil, for pan

1 onion, finely chopped

1 shallot, finely chopped

1 pound ground beef

2 eggs, plus 1 for egg wash

3 tablespoons sour cream

1 tablespoon red wine vinegar

1 tablespoon Worcestershire sauce

2 tablespoons minced fresh dill (or 1 tablespoon dried)

2 teaspoons salt

Fresh black pepper, to taste

FOR THE SAUCE:

1 cup sour cream

2 tablespoons fresh dill (or 1 tablespoon dried)

1 tablespoon Worcestershire sauce

1 teaspoon salt

1 teaspoon garlic powder

¼ teaspoon paprika

1. To make the dough: Dissolve the yeast in ¼ cup of water, and let stand for 2 minutes. Combine the yeast mixture with the rest of the dough ingredients in the bowl of a stand mixer (or large bowl if mixing by hand), and mix with dough hook on low until a soft dough is formed. Turn the dough out onto a lightly floured surface, and knead until elastic, about 5 minutes. Place the dough in a lightly greased bowl, cover with a towel, and put in a warm place to rise for about 1½ hours or until doubled in size.

2. While the dough is rising, make the filling: Coat a sauté pan with oil, and heat on medium. Add onion and shallot, and cook until just starting to brown, 5 to 7 minutes. Add the ground beef, and cook, stirring to break up the meat, until brown, about 5 minutes more. Move the mixture to one side of the pan and crack 2 eggs into the space. Let the eggs cook briefly before using your spatula to lightly break them up and mix them with the beef. Continue stirring until the egg is cooked through. Remove the pan from heat, and add the remaining filling ingredients. Stir until well combined.

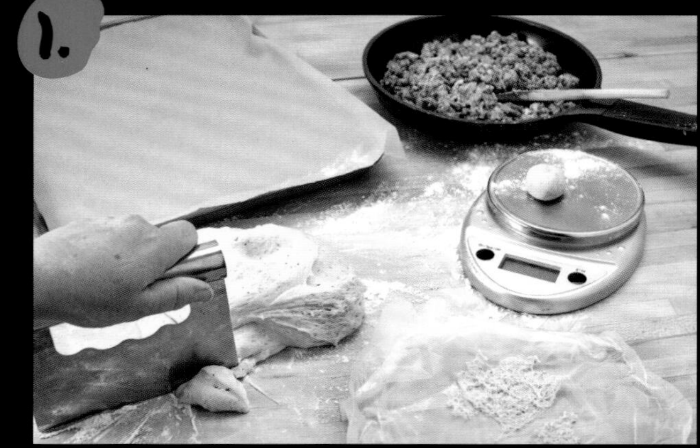
1.

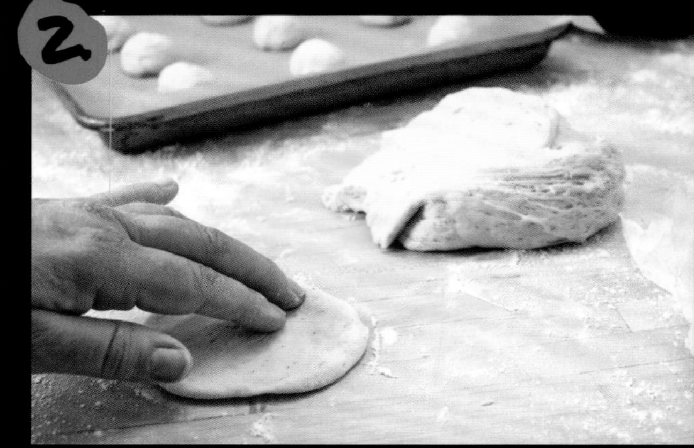
2.

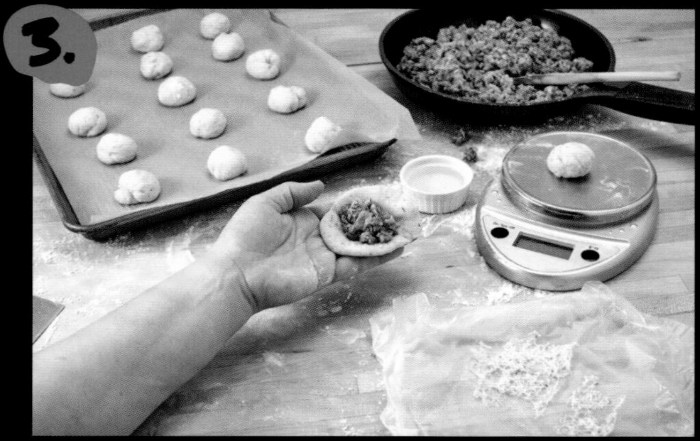
3.

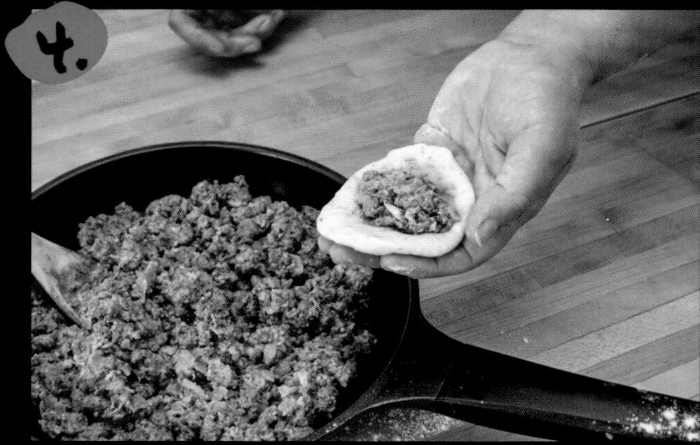
4.

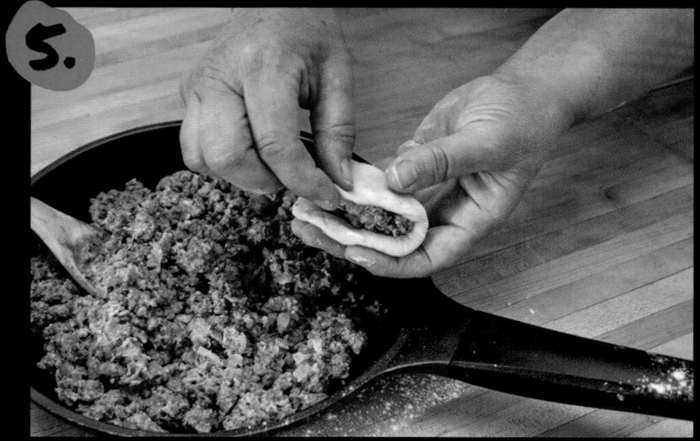
5.

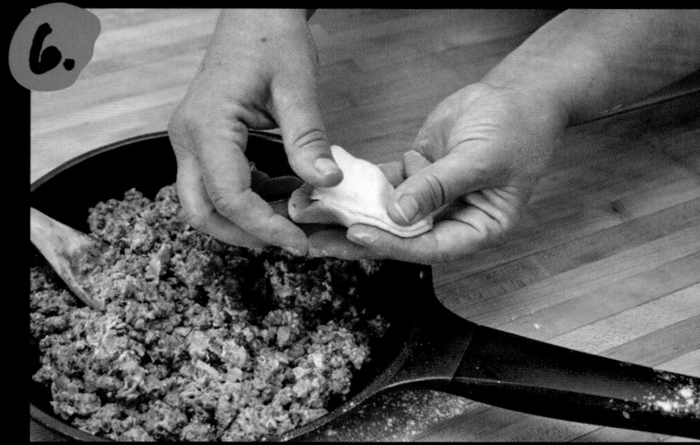
6.

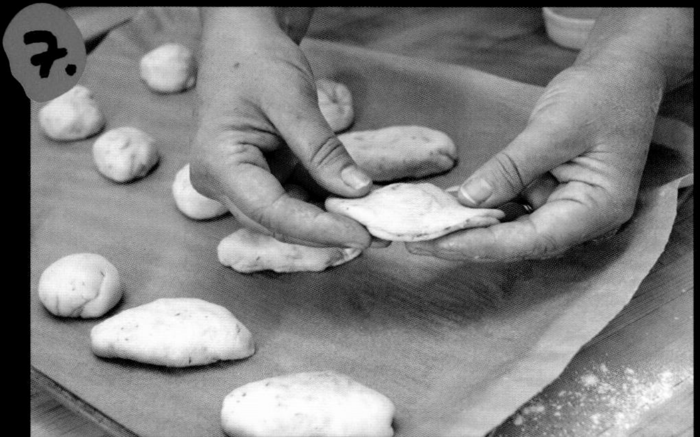
7.

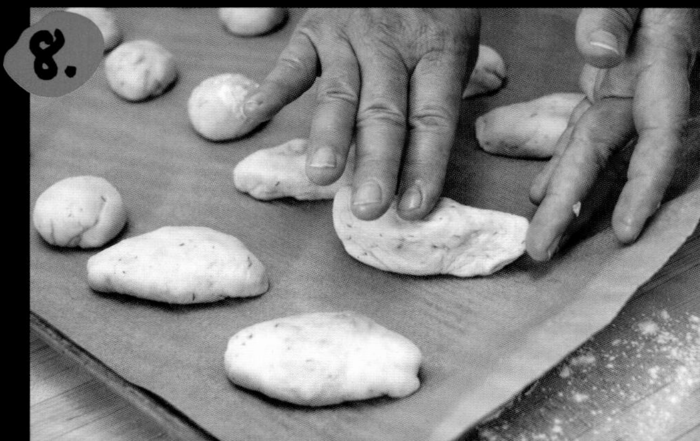
8.

3. To assemble: Line 2 baking sheets with silicone mats or parchment paper. Using your hands and a scale, if you have one, form 24 equal dough balls, and place them on the baking sheets. Cover the sheets with a cloth while working. Use the palm of your hand to flatten each dough ball into a 3- to 3½-inch circle, and fill with 2 mounded tablespoons of filling. Moisten the edge of each dough circle, fold over the filling, and pinch closed.
4. Place back on the baking sheet, seam side down, and gently form into an oval rather than a half moon. Repeat with remaining pies, covering each tray with a cloth when done. Let the pies rise until puffy, 30 to 40 minutes. Midway through the rise, preheat the oven to 350°F.
5. Beat the remaining egg with 1 tablespoon of water, and brush each pie completely with egg wash. Bake until golden brown, about 20 minutes.
6. To make the sauce: Mix all the ingredients together until well blended.
7. Serve the meat pies warm or at room temperature with sauce on the side.

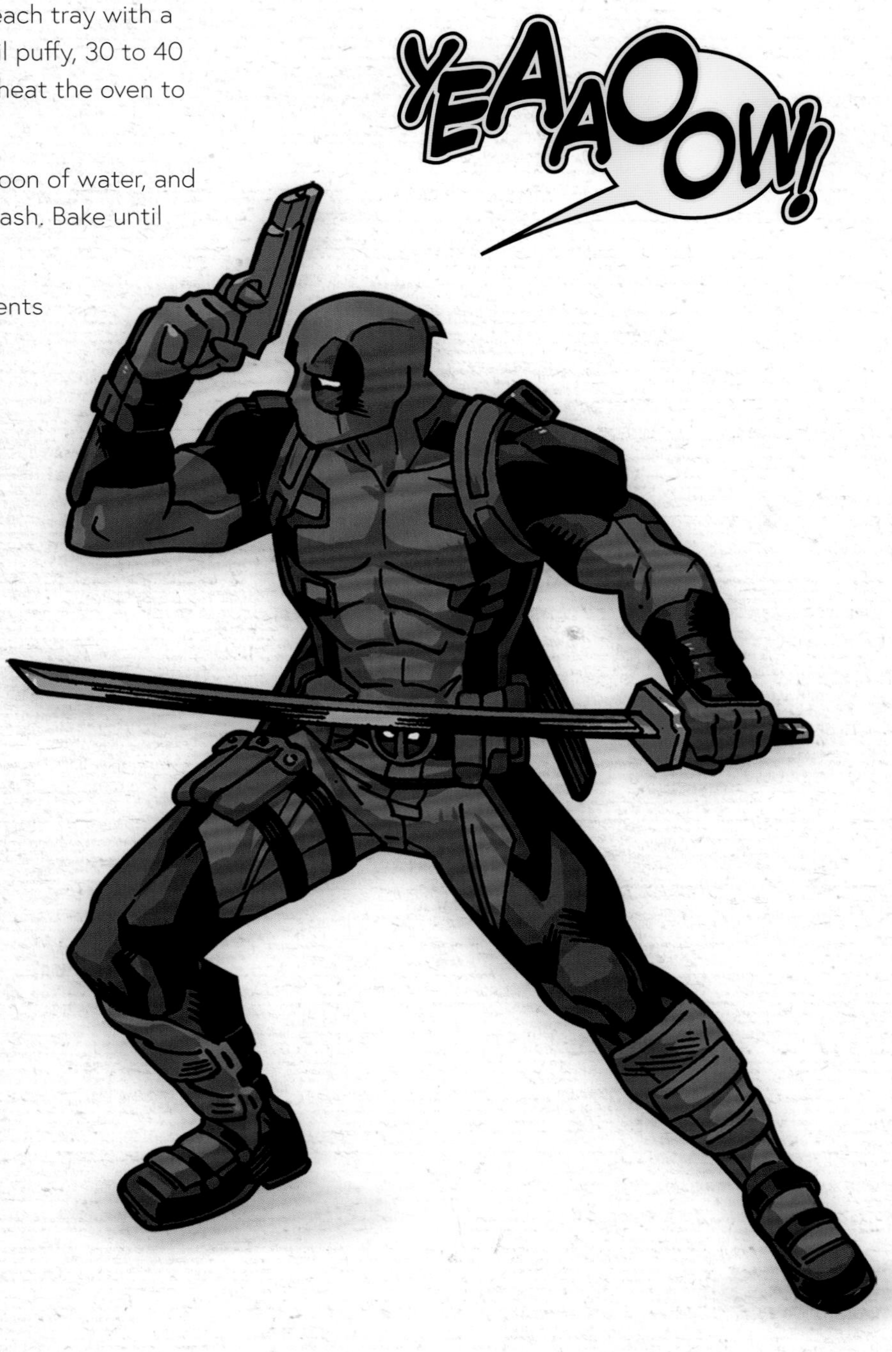
YEAAAOOOW!

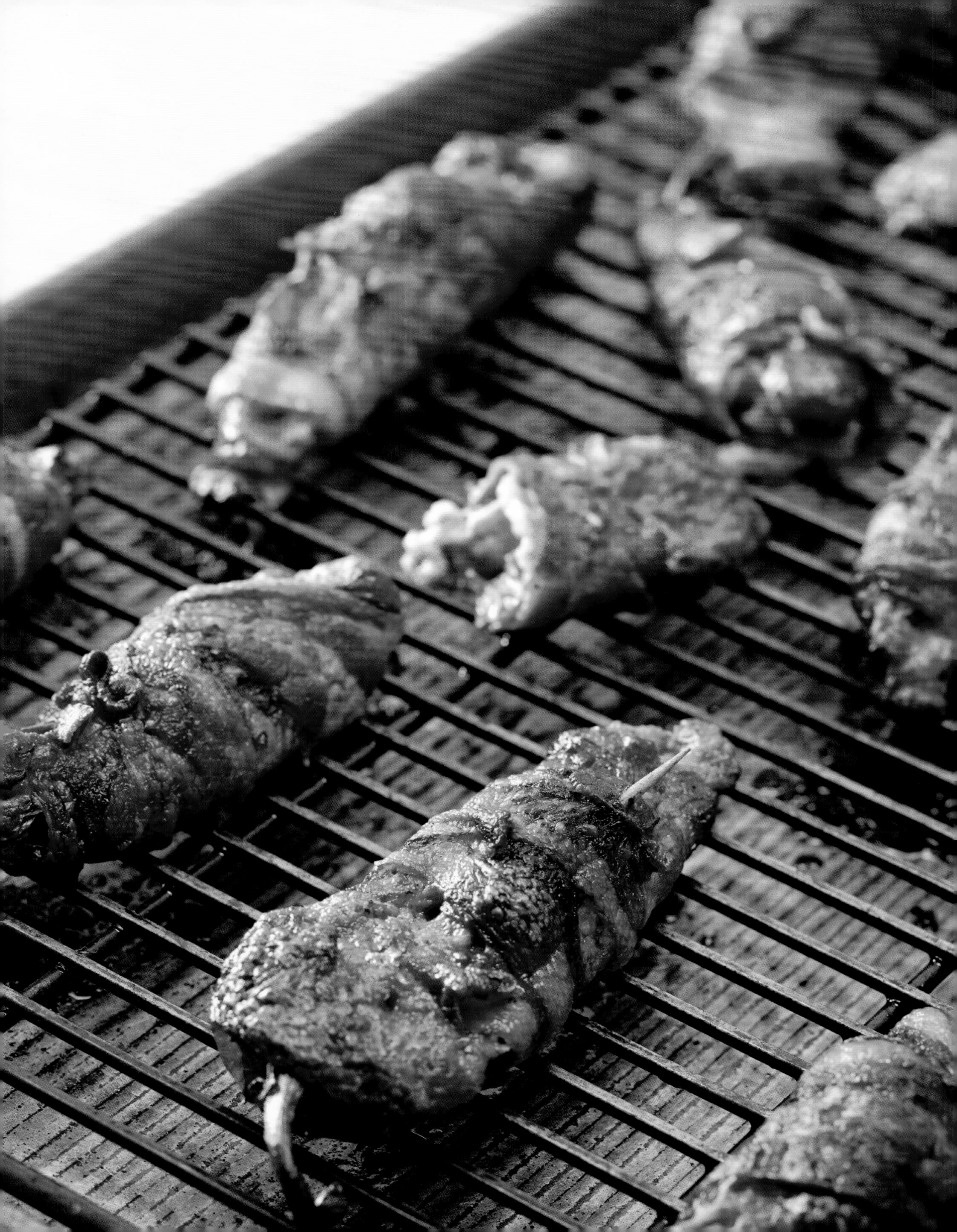

NEGASONIC WARHEADS

YIELD: 20 PEPPERS

Do you ever get tired of this thing we call life? Ever wonder why we bother when nothing we do actually matters? Well, put away the black eyeliner, Nietzsche, because Uncle Wade is about to get all X-istential on you. See, we're not all players in some big cosmic game, no matter what the Watcher tries to tell you. We all carve our own paths in this miserable existence, and mine happens to be an extremely lucrative one based entirely on making mayhem for money! But that doesn't mean I don't find myself getting a little numb to the world every now and then. On those occasions, I pop a few of these blazing hot bacon-wrapped stuffed jalapeños—named in honor of my favorite emo mutant, Negasonic Teenage Warhead—into my world-famous word-hole. Because I'm human(-ish), too, and sometimes I just need to feel something real.

1 cup (8 ounces) cream cheese, softened

1 cup grated pepper Jack

1 teaspoon chili powder

½ teaspoon cayenne pepper

2 shallots, minced

10 straight, similarly sized jalapeños, halved lengthwise and seeded

20 cocktail sausages

20 bacon slices (about 2 packs)

YES!

CRAP. I'M TALKING TO MYSELF AGAIN.

1. Preheat the oven to 375°F. Set a wire rack over a baking sheet.

2. In a small bowl, mix the cream cheese, pepper Jack, spices, and minced shallots until well combined.

3. Spread 1 tablespoon of the cheese mixture on each jalapeño slice until it is completely covered and top with a mini sausage. Wrap a slice of bacon around the filled jalepeño, covering it from end to end so the bacon overlaps slightly. If necessary, secure with a toothpick.

4. Place the jalepeños on the rack in the baking sheet. Bake for 35 to 40 minutes, until bacon is crisp and jalepeños are soft.

BULGING MUSSELS

If you happened to be a super-powered individual in the '90s, you saw your fair share of impressive muscles. And I'm not talking about your typical, everyday, super-hero-wrapped-in-a-form-fitting-spandex-costume muscles. No, no, no! I'm referring to hulking physiques so overexaggerated that you could make out every strained strand of sinew through a full suit of body armor! It was a weird time, kids. Thankfully, anatomy seems to have toned itself back down a bit in the decades that followed, and we're all better off for it. But while the days of giant muscles on the battlefield may be far behind us, the days of giant mussels, steamed and served in a vegetable broth and cream sauce, will hopefully never end.

1 to 2 tablespoons oil, for pan

2 tablespoons salted butter

2 garlic cloves, minced

½ cup fine bread crumbs

½ cup vegetable broth

2 pounds fresh mussels, cleaned and debearded

½ cup cream

Salt and fresh black pepper

1 cup loosely packed parsley leaves, roughly chopped

Crusty bread, for serving

1. Select a medium stockpot with a tight-fitting lid, and heat on medium. Once the pot is hot, lightly coat the surface with oil, and add butter. When the butter begins to foam, add the garlic, and cook until just translucent.

2. Add the bread crumbs to the pot and cook, stirring constantly, until crumbs are lightly brown. (Be careful—they burn easily.) Transfer bread crumbs to a serving bowl.

3. Return the pot to the stove, add vegetable broth, and bring to a simmer. Add the mussels and half the bread crumb mixture, stir once, and cover. Cook 6 to 8 minutes, until the mussels have opened, discarding any that remain closed.

4. Use a slotted spoon to transfer the mussels to the serving bowl. Add the cream to the pot and cook for 2 to 3 minutes, scraping up the remaining bread crumbs and garlic from the bottom, until cream is slightly thickened. Add salt and pepper to taste.

5. Pour the sauce over the mussels, top with remaining bread crumbs and parsley, and serve immediately with warm crusty bread.

FIREBALLS

While I've somehow become known for carrying a wide variety of weapons, I'll be honest: For a guy with a job as deadly as mine, I actually prefer to play it safe. I mean, who needs an Infinity Gauntlet when the classics—like guns and swords—get the job done in a much simpler and less world-shattering way. But on the occasions when I do have to pull out the heavy artillery, there are few weapons more singularly satisfying than a flamethrower. After a long day of scorching the eyebrows off Hydra agents, I find myself craving something that will make me sweat as much on the inside as I do on the outside. That's where these little Buffalo chicken meatballs come in. While the blue cheese center cools them down a bit, you should still use caution. These balls have some real kick!

FOR THE FILLING:

⅓ cup (2 ounces) crumbled blue cheese

¼ cup finely diced celery

FOR THE BALLS:

4 tablespoons (½ stick) salted butter, melted

4 tablespoons hot sauce of your choice

½ teaspoon salt

Fresh black pepper, to taste

1 teaspoon baking powder

1 pound ground chicken

½ cup all-purpose flour

FOR DREDGING:

2 eggs

2 tablespoons hot sauce

1 cup all-purpose flour

1 teaspoon salt

Fresh black pepper, to taste

Peanut or canola oil, for frying

FOR THE SAUCE:

½ cup hot sauce

3 tablespoons honey

2 tablespoons ketchup

4 tablespoons (½ stick) salted butter

1. Line a baking sheet with foil or parchment, and set aside.

2. To make the filling: Combine blue cheese and celery in a small bowl, and set aside.

3. To make the balls: In a medium bowl, mix melted butter, hot sauce, salt, pepper, and baking powder. Add ground chicken to mixture, and work it with your hands until well combined. Sprinkle flour over the mixture, and work again until incorporated. Using a spoon or your fingers, scoop 2 tablespoons of chicken mixture and make an indent in the meat with your thumb. Add a pinch of the filling to the indent and form the meat into a ball around the filling. Set on baking sheet, and repeat until all the mixture is used. Place the baking sheet in the refrigerator to chill for at least 1 hour.

4. To prepare your dredging stations and fry: Beat the eggs with 2 tablespoons of hot sauce in a small bowl, and mix the flour, salt, and pepper in a separate one. When you're ready to fry, heat about 2 inches of oil in a large heavy-bottomed skillet or frying pan to 365°F (a deep fryer can be used as well). Working in small batches, dredge each ball in the egg mixture, followed by the flour mixture, and then add to the hot oil. Fry each batch until the balls are a deep golden brown color and cooked through, 3 to 4 minutes. Drain on a wire rack or paper towels.

5. To make the sauce: Combine all the ingredients in a small saucepan on medium heat until smooth and hot.

6. Serve the Fireballs with the sauce on the side for dipping.

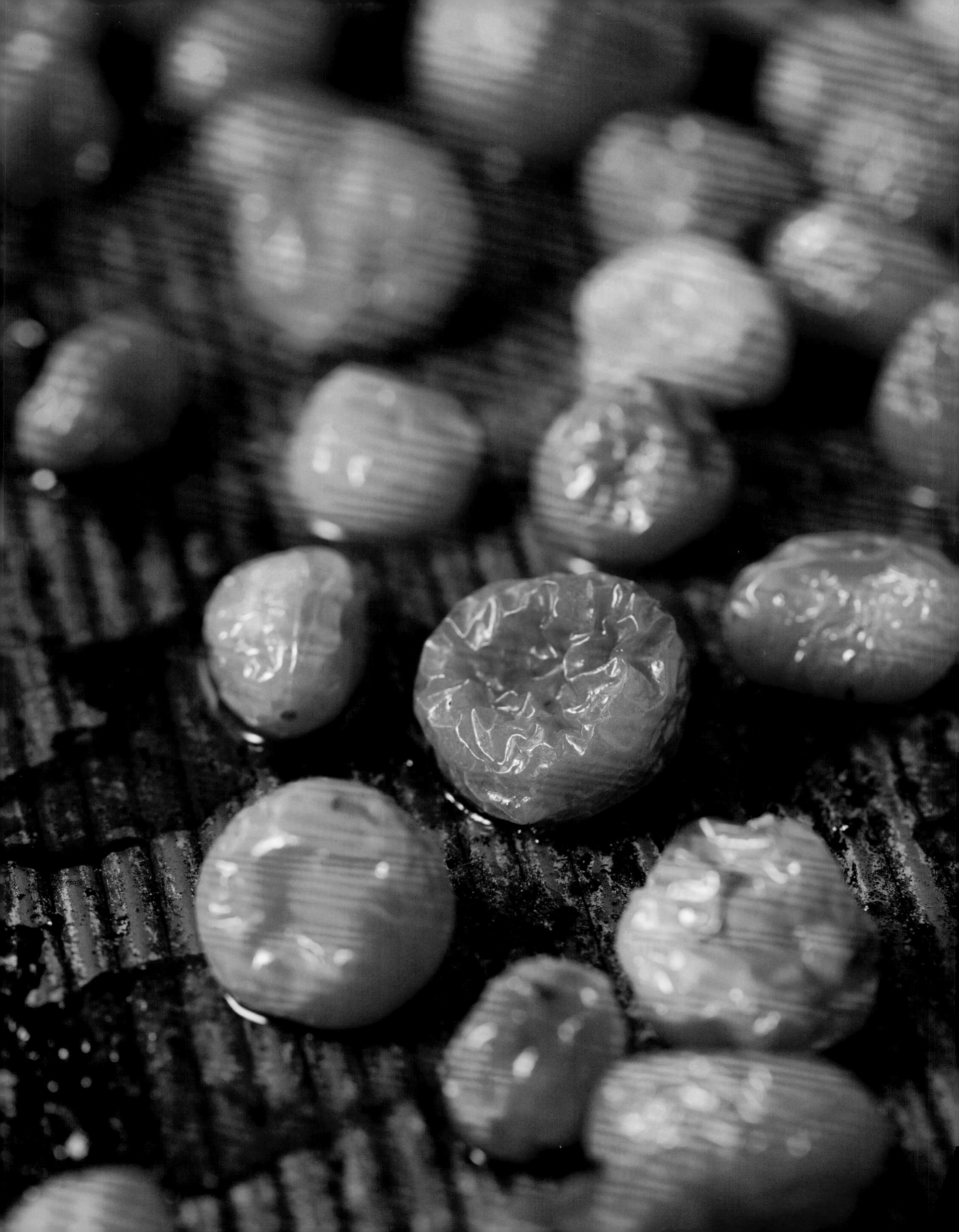

Side Jobs

Being a mercenary isn't an easy gig. There are times when I've got more on my plate than I can possibly handle, and then there are times when I spend weeks just sitting around the house eating expired cereal straight out of the box. "Feast or famine," as they say. When things get a little lean, I like to pick up a few side jobs to fill in the gaps. Stuff that'll keep me excited and offer a bit of variety while I prepare to dive back into the big game. That same philosophy carries over to when I'm cooking a meal.

While an Apocalypse-sized slab of meat may sound like all you need to keep your body going, cooking up a few diversified options alongside the main attraction helps to keep things fresh and exciting. Don't worry, it's not like I'm cooking up a bunch of random junk and throwing it on a plate. (I'm not an animal!) These sides are perfectly crafted to complement and enhance my favorite entrées.

LET'S **DO** THIS CRAZY BAD THING!

Plus, if you do happen to be going through one of those aforementioned periods of famine and a fancy main course is outside your budget, I've got good news. You can assemble a few of these sides into one dish and still have yourself a hell of a feast!

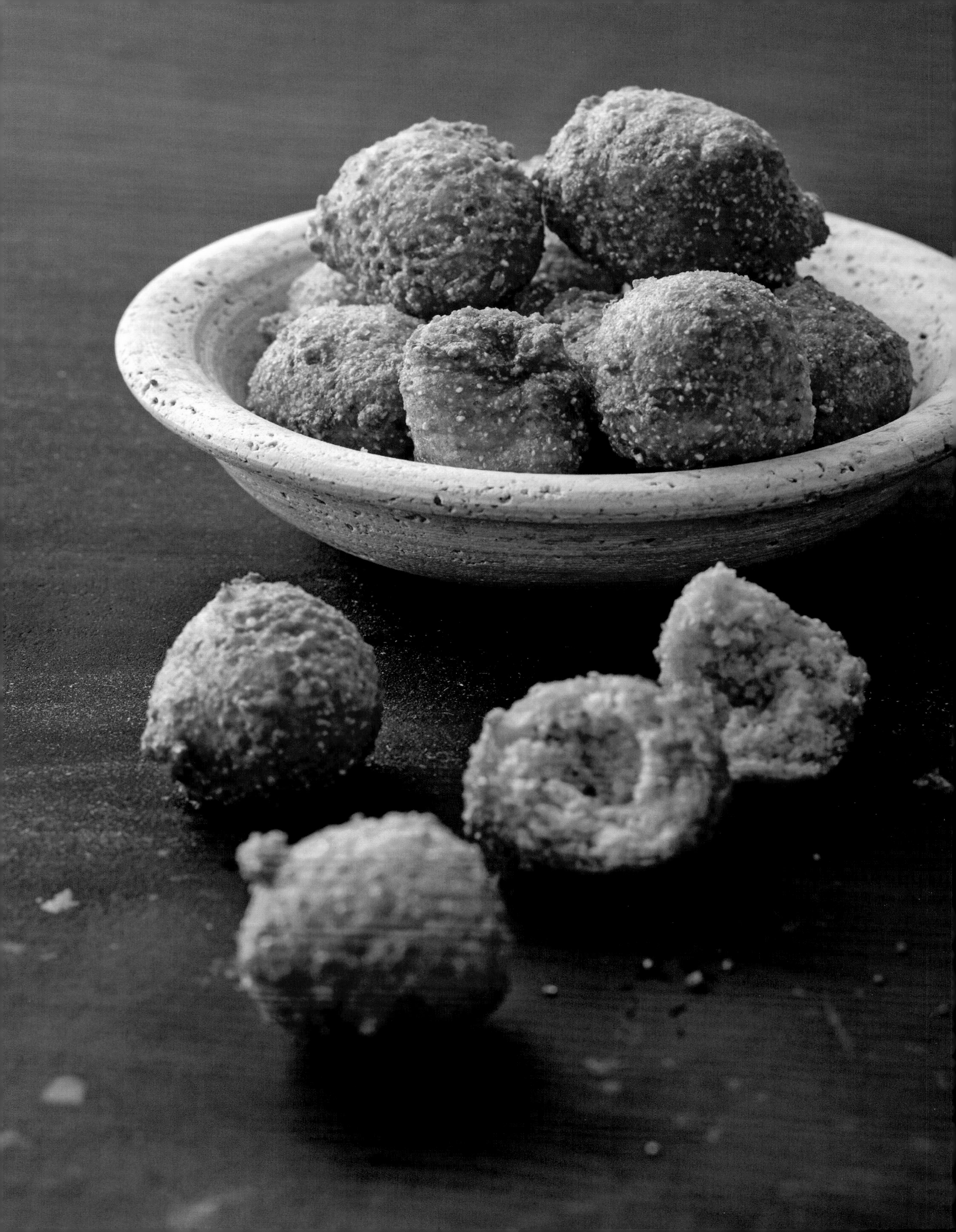

Look at Them Puppies!

Yield: About 20 Puppies

So I was an Avenger for a while. No, really, true story: I was drafted by Captain America himself to serve on a Unity Squad devoted to fostering peace between humans, mutants, and Inhumans. During that time, I also had a brief romantic encounter with the Southern belle known as Rogue. And by "romantic encounter," I mean we made out. A lot. Unfortunately, her ability to absorb other people's attributes meant she also absorbed my memories, which are not anything a lady should ever have to see. Then an old boyfriend came back into the picture, things got awkward, the squad disbanded, we lost touch, she married Gambit, and my invitation to the ceremony apparently got lost in the mail. But if she asks, I'm doing fine. Just fine. Now, if you need me, I'll be eating the hush puppies she taught me to make by the handful as I cry myself to sleep.

1⅔ cups yellow cornmeal

⅓ cup all-purpose flour

2 teaspoons baking powder

½ teaspoon baking soda

1 teaspoon sugar

1 teaspoon salt

¼ teaspoon cayenne pepper

2 teaspoons onion powder

2 eggs

1 cup buttermilk

2 quarts oil, such as peanut or canola, for frying

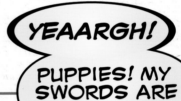

1. In a large Dutch oven or deep fryer, heat oil to 365°F. In a large bowl, whisk together all the dry ingredients.
2. In a separate bowl, beat the two eggs with the buttermilk until well combined. Add the buttermilk mixture to the dry ingredients and stir until just combined.
3. Preheat the oven to 200°F. Using a tablespoon or a 1½-inch cookie scoop, portion the batter. Drop the scoops of batter into hot oil and fry until deep golden brown on all sides. Transfer to oven to keep warm until ready to serve.

YEAARGH!
PUPPIES! MY SWORDS ARE USELESS!

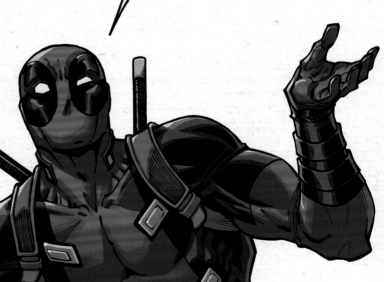

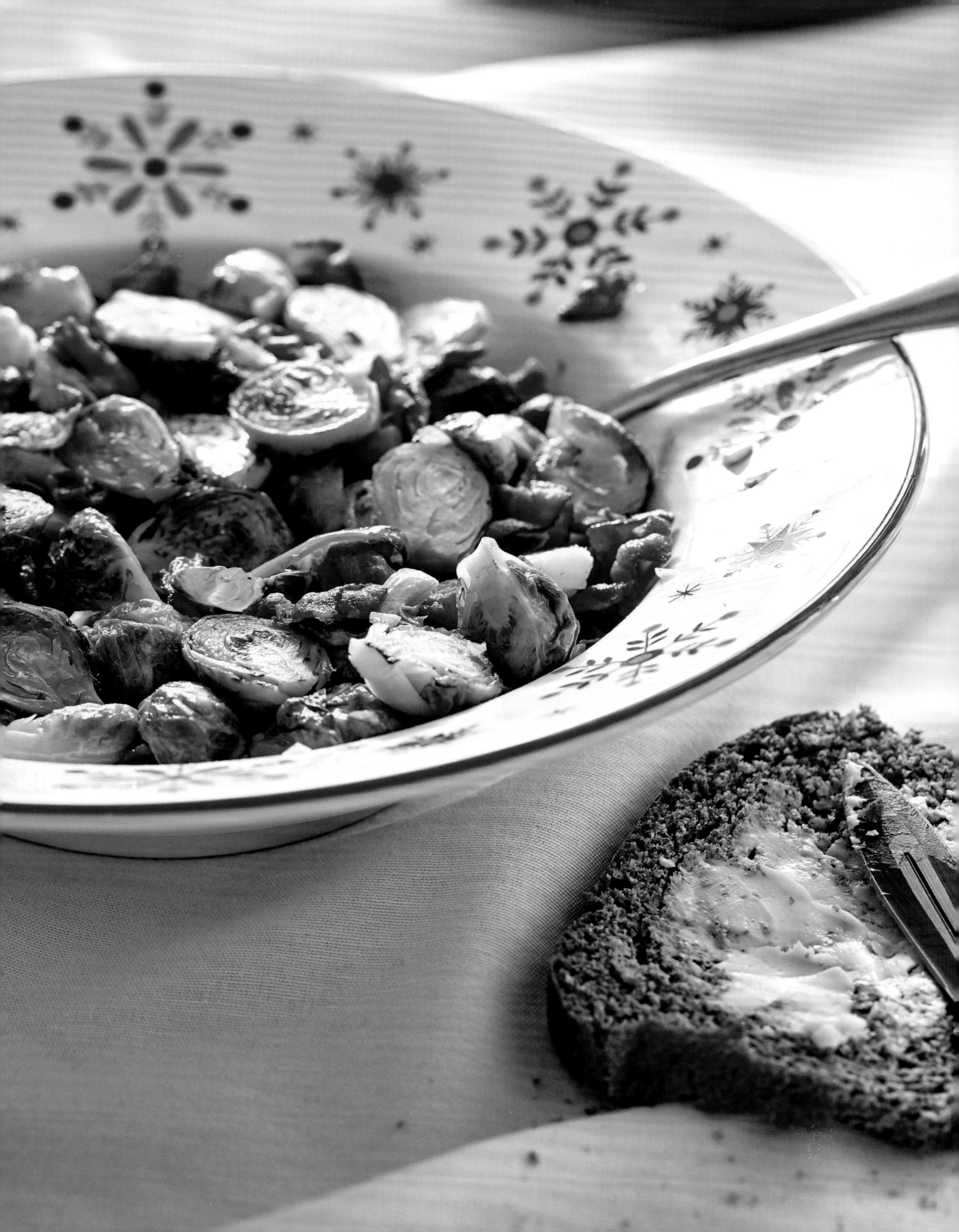

Brussels Sprouts Cockaigne

Yield: 8 servings

Okay, I'll admit I was initially drawn to this recipe because the name had me giggling like a middle school girl. I had to look up what "Cockaigne" meant and, after a few very unfortunate internet searches, I discovered that it's a medieval word meaning "mythical land of plenty." Obviously, that's not nearly as funny as I what I originally thought, but what's in a name anyway? What really matters is what's in my stomach, and this simple, savory side dish is always an acceptable answer. Recipes like this actually make me wonder if the joy of cooking might be almost as gratifying as the joy of merc-ing. But then I remember a brussels sprout has never given me a briefcase full of cash to make its corporate rival "disappear." Oddly enough, the guy who did pay me to do that happened to be from Brussels. Kinda funny . . . but still not as hilarious as the word "Cockaigne." Heh.

1 pound brussels sprouts, trimmed and halved

Salt and fresh black pepper

8 ounces (about 8 slices) bacon

4 tablespoons (½ stick) salted butter

5 cloves garlic, minced

1. Prepare an ice bath by filling a large bowl with ice and water, and set aside. Blanch the brussels sprouts by bringing a large pot of water with a pinch of salt to a boil. Add the sprouts, and boil for 2 minutes. Drain the sprouts, and immediately submerge them in the ice bath to stop cooking. Drain again, and set aside.
2. Cut the bacon into 1-inch pieces, and cook in a sauté pan or skillet on high heat until all the fat is rendered and bacon is crisp. Using a slotted spoon, remove the bacon pieces to a plate, leaving a coating of bacon fat and brown bits. Turn the heat to low, and melt the butter in the pan, using it to scrape up the brown bits from the bottom. Add garlic, and cook until just fragrant. Raise the heat to medium, and add the brussels sprouts, cut side down. Cook for 3 to 5 minutes, until brown. Return bacon to the pan, shake pan to turn over the sprouts, and cook another 3 to 5 minutes, until tender. Salt and pepper to taste.

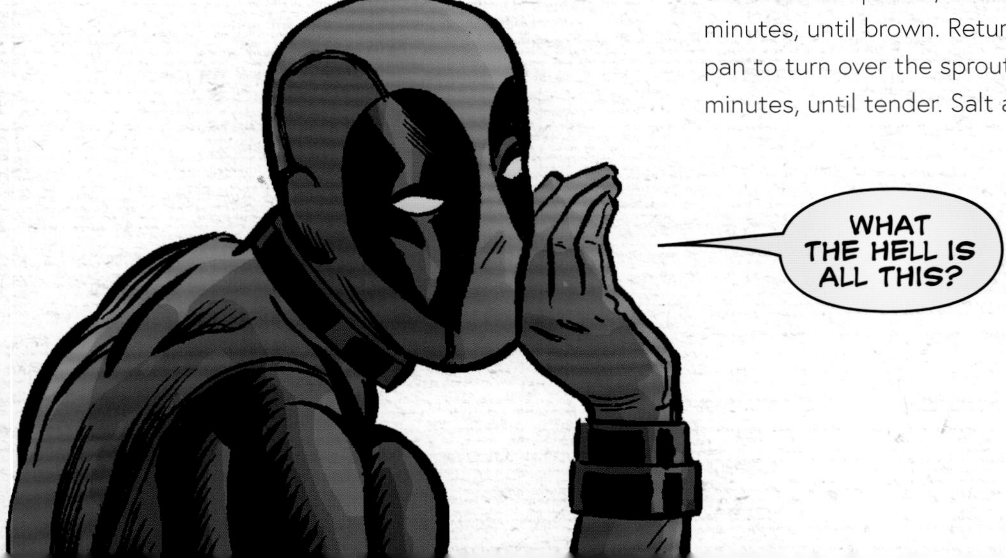
WHAT THE HELL IS ALL THIS?

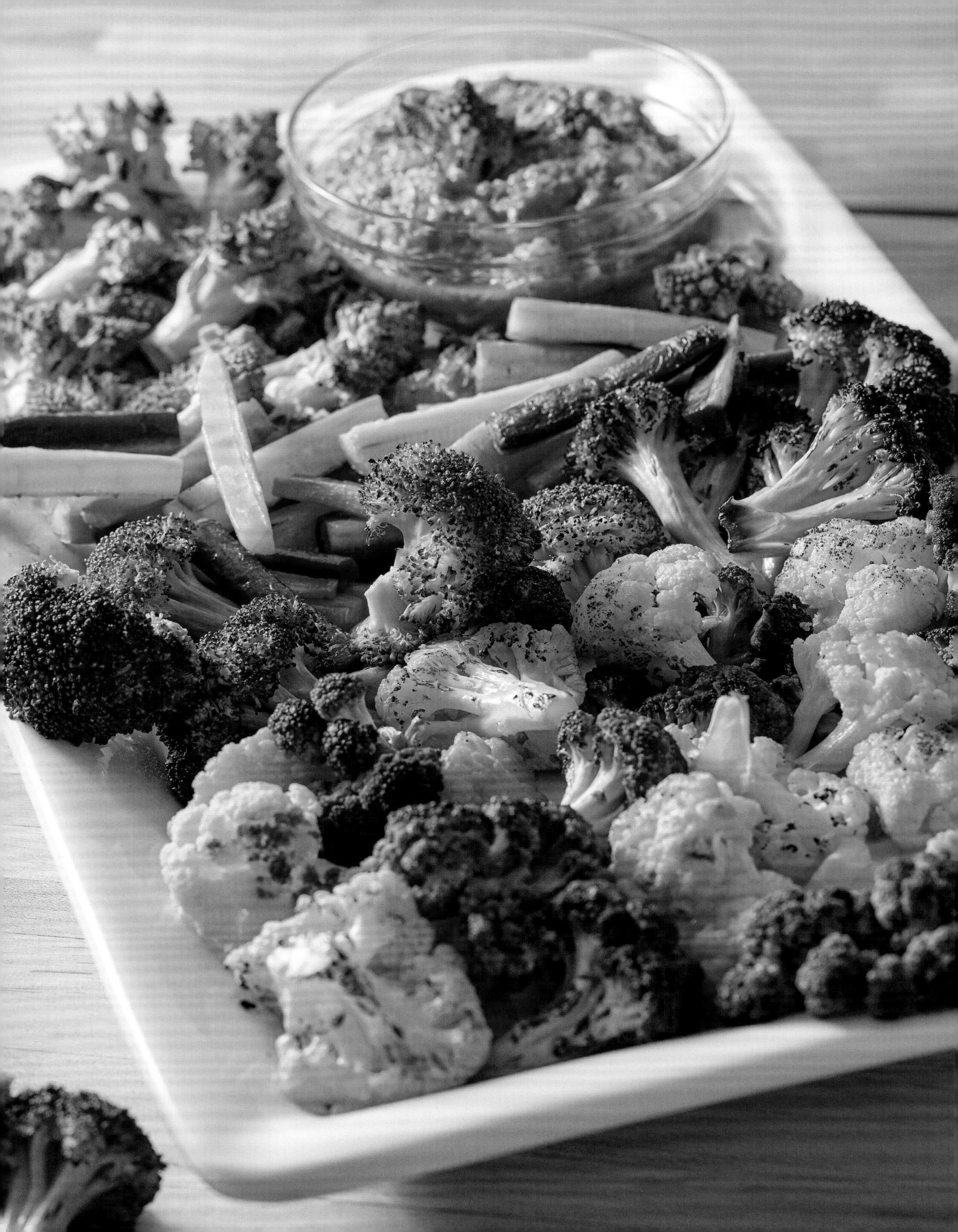

CONTROLLED BURN

YIELD: 8 SERVINGS AS A SIDE DISH AND IS AS AN APPETIZER

How do you like to celebrate Arbor Day, kids? Personally, I like to carefully arrange some broccoli and cauliflower on my plate and then pretend I'm Galactus devouring a planet covered in tiny, nutritious trees. (Hey, we've all got our things.) But while I may be famous for being crude, I've never had the stomach for *crudités*. So when it comes to my forest of flavorful florets, I like to roast 'em first. Don't leave 'em in the oven for too long, though, unless you want start an adorably tiny wildfire in your kitchen. Served with a nice romesco sauce, this is one sumptuous side dish that will have you wishing every day was Arbor Day!

FOR THE ROMESCO SAUCE:

4 cloves garlic, peeled

3 ounces manchego cheese, rind removed

1 cup sliced almonds, lightly toasted

One 16-ounce jar roasted red bell peppers

¼ cup olive oil

1 tablespoon red wine vinegar

½ tablespoon fresh thyme leaves

FOR THE ROASTED VEGETABLES:

3 heads cauliflower in different varieties, such as classic white, cheddar, graffiti, or Romanesco

2 bunches broccoli

1 bunch rainbow carrots, optional

¼ cup olive oil, to coat vegetables

Salt and fresh black pepper, to taste

1. To make the sauce: Starting with garlic, add the ingredients for the sauce to a food processor in the order listed, pulsing after each one. Continue to pulse until sauce is well combined and the consistency of pesto. Chill until ready to serve.
2. Preheat the oven to 425°F. Break each head of cauliflower and broccoli down to florets. Scrub the carrots, and cut into long trunks about an inch wide. In large bowls, toss cauliflower and carrots separately in olive oil, salt, and pepper, and add to a rimmed baking sheet in a single layer, keeping the vegetables separate. Roast for 20 to 25 minutes, until fork tender.
3. Prepare an ice bath by filling a large bowl with ice and water, and set aside. In a large stockpot, blanch the broccoli florets in boiling water for 1 minute, then drain, and immediately submerge in the ice bath to stop cooking. Drain broccoli, and spread on another rimmed baking sheet in a single layer. When the carrots and cauliflower are done, pop broccoli in the oven, and roast for 5 minutes or until fork tender.
4. Plate veggies together and serve warm or at room temperature with romesco sauce.

MASHED STUFF

Americans think they've got the market cornered when it comes to Thanksgiving, but they're not the only ones who know how to celebrate the bounty of the season with style. Whether you observe American Thanksgiving at the end of November or *real* Thanksgiving in the middle of October, what's really important is embracing the true meaning behind the day: gluttony, my third favorite sin. For those of you who crave the taste of Thanksgiving all year long and don't want to wait for a turkey to receive a presidential pardon it probably doesn't deserve, this recipe features all your favorite parts of the big meal in one exceptionally lazy side dish. Mashed potatoes? Check! Stuffing? Check! Uncle Albert's opinions about politics? None of that here! See? You really do have something to be thankful for!

FOR THE MASHED POTATOES:

3 pounds Yukon gold potatoes or other potatoes suitable for mashing

½ cup (4 ounces) cream cheese

4 tablespoons (½ stick) salted butter

½ cup vegetable broth

FOR THE STUFFING:

Butter, for pan

2 cups seasoned croutons

½ cup chopped fresh parsley

2 tablespoons snipped chives

½ cup half-and-half

Salt and fresh black pepper

1. To make the mashed potatoes: Peel and quarter the potatoes. Bring a pot of lightly salted water to a boil, add potatoes, and boil until very tender, about 25 minutes. Drain potatoes and return them to the pot on low heat. Gently mash the potatoes with a potato masher until steam stops rising from them. Remove pot from heat, and add cream cheese, butter, and broth. Continue mashing until mixture is mostly smooth and ingredients are incorporated. Scrape the mashed potatoes into a large bowl, and let cool slightly.

2. Preheat the oven to 350°F. Butter a 9-by-9-inch baking dish, and set aside.

3. Pulse croutons in a food processor until just crumbly (they should not be as fine as bread crumbs). Add 1 cup of the crouton crumbles plus the parsley, chives, and half-and-half to mashed potatoes, along with salt and pepper to taste. Stir until combined, then add mixture to the buttered baking dish and top with remaining 1 cup of crouton crumbles. Bake for 30 to 40 minutes, or until top is golden brown and potatoes are slightly puffed.

> **TIP:**
> EASY ON THE SALT THERE, PILGRIM! THE CROUTONS ALREADY HAVE MORE THAN ENOUGH, SO DON'T GO CRAZY, OKAY?

BOXING DAY BREAD

As I mentioned earlier, I'm a proud Canadian, born and raised. But when it comes to holidays, I'll admit, sometimes it feels like we got the short end of the hockey stick. When all the American kids were setting off fireworks on the Fourth of July, I was . . . well, also setting off fireworks, actually. Just not to celebrate anything in particular. (I like watching things explode.) But while President's Day and Memorial Day may not be on our calendar, at least we have Boxing Day: a special bonus day after Christmas originally designed to celebrate the hired help. As a mercenary, being hired to help is literally my job description. So when December 26 rolls around, you can usually find me kicking back with a loaf of this hearty holiday bread baking in the oven.

1 package (2¼ teaspoons) active dry yeast

¼ teaspoon sugar

1½ cups all-purpose flour

1 cup whole wheat flour

½ cup buckwheat flour

½ cup milk

½ cup hot water

4 tablespoons (½ stick) salted butter, melted, plus more for pan

1¼ teaspoon salt

¼ cup maple syrup

Oil, for pan and hands

1. Dissolve the yeast in ¼ cup of water with the sugar, and let stand for 2 minutes. Combine yeast mixture and all other ingredients in the bowl of a stand mixer (or a large bowl if mixing by hand), and stir on low until the dough comes together and begins to pull away from the sides of the bowl. Cover the dough, and let it rest in the bowl for 20 minutes before kneading.

2. Transfer the dough to a lightly oiled surface, oil your hands, and knead for 6 to 8 minutes, until the dough is elastic. Place the dough in a lightly oiled bowl, cover again, and let rise for 1 to 2 hours (this will depend on the room's temperature). The dough is ready when it is puffy and yields easily when pressed but is not necessarily doubled in size.

3. Butter a 9-by-5-inch loaf pan. Gently deflate the dough by pressing it with your hand and pulling it away from the bowl. Transfer to an oiled surface, and shape into an 8-inch log. Place the dough in the pan, cover loosely, and let rise for about 1 hour or until the center of the dough has risen to about an inch over the edge of the pan (be careful not to over-proof).

4. Preheat the oven to 350°F. Bake the bread until the internal temperature is 200°F, 30 to 40 minutes. Let rest in the pan for 5 minutes, then remove to a cooling rack.

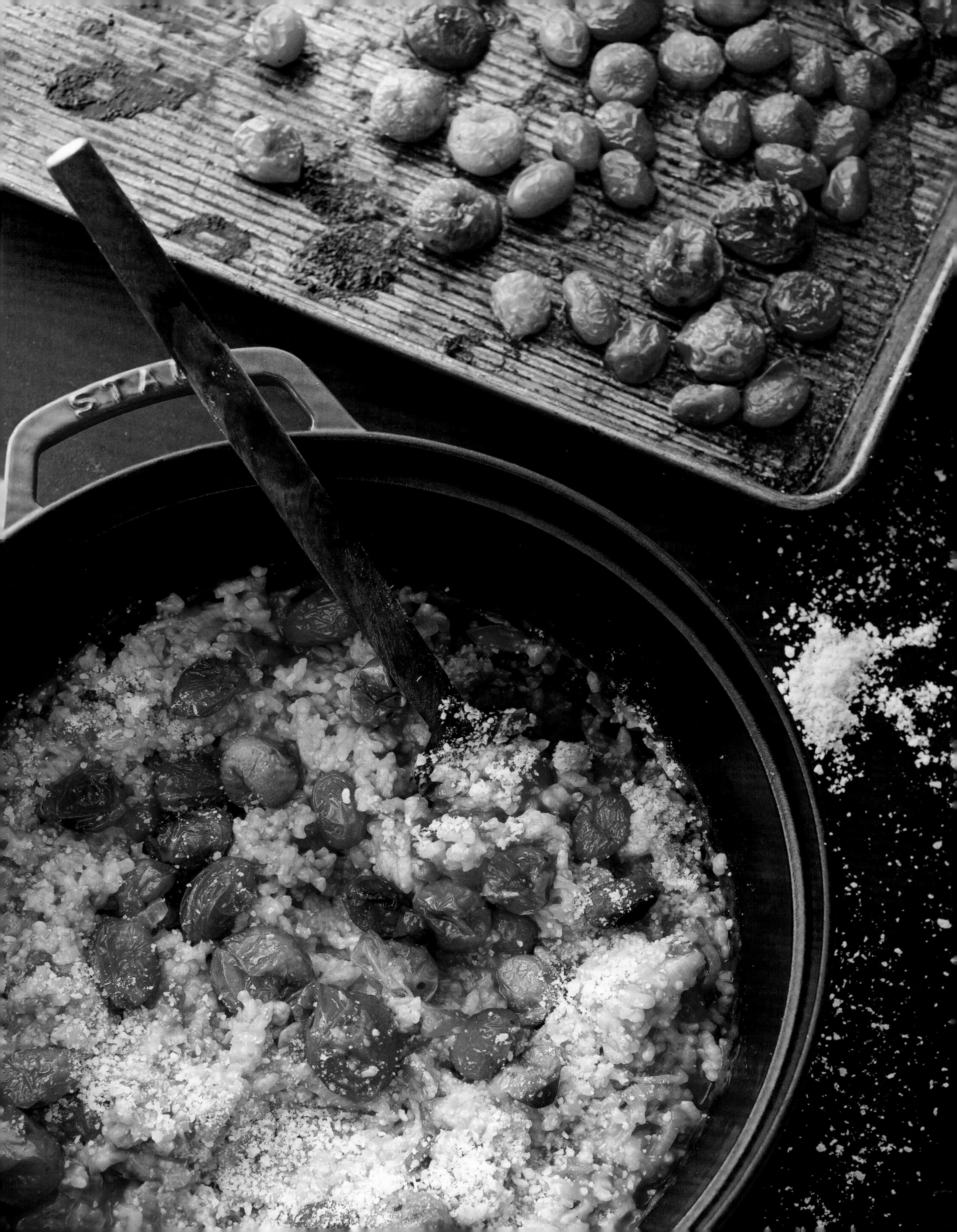

TOMATO, TAMAHTO, RISOTTO, RISSAHTO

YIELD: 8 SERVINGS

Spend enough time with mutants and you get used to double-checking your pronunciation. For instance, Magneto may have the powers of a magnet, but for some weird reason, he pronounces his name Mag-NEAT-o (which is especially odd, because "neat-o" is the last word I'd use to describe that geezer). Some foods have the same problem (looking at you, sriracha and tzatziki!). But fortunately for everyone, the only thing you need to call this side dish is delicious! Honestly, once you've got a mouth full of this perfectly cooked blend of rice and tomatoes, you won't be doing much talking anyway. And that's probably a good thing, particularly if you can't remember whether Xavier sounds like it starts with an X or a Z.

1½ pounds cherry or grape tomatoes, in a variety of colors, halved

3 tablespoons olive oil, plus more for pan

Salt

1 tablespoon balsamic vinegar

6 cloves garlic, minced

1 shallot, minced

1 pound Roma tomatoes, chopped

2 tablespoons salted butter

2 cups arborio rice

6 cups vegetable broth, plus up to 1 cup more

5 ounces grated Parmesan, plus more for serving

---

1. Preheat the oven to 300°F. Coat the cherry tomatoes in olive oil, and sprinkle with a generous pinch of salt. Spread the tomatoes out on a roasting pan, cut side up, and roast for 45 minutes to an hour, until tomatoes are reduced by half and caramelized. Remove from oven, and toss with balsamic vinegar. This can be done up to 3 hours ahead.

2. Preheat the oven to 400°F. Heat a large Dutch oven on medium, and coat with olive oil. Add butter and allow to foam. Add the garlic and shallot to the pan, and sauté until just translucent, 2 to 3 minutes. Add the Roma tomatoes, and continue to sauté until most of the liquid from the tomatoes has cooked off, 10 to 15 minutes. Add the rice, and sauté until the rice has translucent edges, 3 to 5 minutes.

3. Add 6 cups of the vegetable broth to the pan, cover with lid, and transfer to oven. Bake risotto for 30 minutes. At that point the broth should be mostly absorbed, and the rice should be just tender. If the rice needs more cooking time or liquid, add up to 1 cup more of broth, and cook in the oven for another 10 minutes.

4. Remove risotto from oven, and add the roasted tomatoes and the Parmesan. Stir until everything is well combined, and serve with additional Parmesan, if desired.

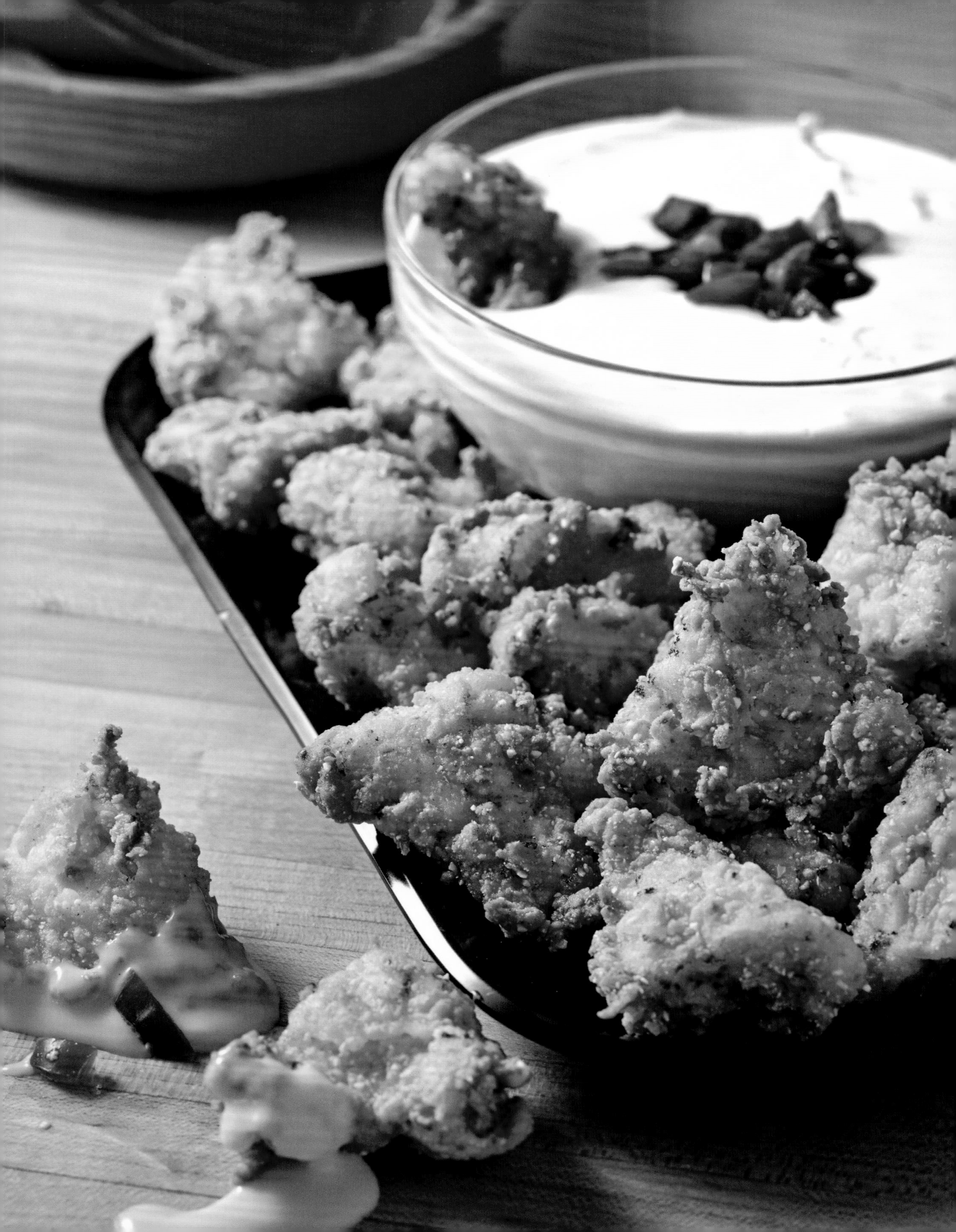

CHICK-ARRONES

Anyone who's ever met me knows I tend to push everything in my life to the extreme. My fighting style. My sense of humor. My complete and utter lack of social graces. But even I'm self-aware enough to admit that, after a while, "extreme" doesn't seem quite so extreme anymore. When you've expected to push boundaries all the time, suddenly pushing boundaries becomes the expected. And that's the opposite of edgy. Luckily, your old pal Deadpool wasn't about to be left in the dust as a new generation of trendsetters and tastemakers pushed the envelope in different directions. So I locked myself in a motel room for three weeks and tried to think of the most over-the-top idea to help me reclaim my rightful place as the champion of excess. The answer came to me in a moment of pure cosmic awareness. Chicken nachos—but get this: The nachos are the chicken. Mind. Blown. To the extreme!

2 boneless, skinless chicken breasts

1 teaspoon paprika

¼ teaspoon cayenne pepper

Salt and fresh black pepper

½ cup milk

½ cup sour cream

1½ cups all-purpose flour

1 cup yellow cornmeal

4 tablespoons cornstarch

1 teaspoon garlic powder

Oil, such as peanut, vegetable, or canola, for frying

1. Holding a knife parallel to the cutting board, slice each chicken breast in half lengthwise. Place a piece of chicken between two pieces of parchment paper, and pound with a mallet until about ½ inch thick. Cut the chicken into "chip"-sized triangles. Repeat with remaining pieces of chicken.

2. Whisk paprika, cayenne pepper, salt and pepper (to taste), milk, and sour cream in a large bowl, and add chicken to marinate while you work on the next step.

3. Prepare the dredge by whisking flour, cornmeal, cornstarch, 1 teaspoon salt, and garlic powder together in a shallow dish. Set aside.

4. In a large, deep skillet, heat 2 inches of oil to 365°F (you can also use a deep fryer). Working in small batches, remove the chicken pieces from the marinade, letting the excess drip off before rolling each piece through the dredge until completely coated. Fry the chicken "chips" in the hot oil, turning regularly, until all sides are golden brown. Place on a wire rack or paper towel to drain, and sprinkle with more salt if desired. Serve warm with Nacho Average Cheese Sauce (page 44).

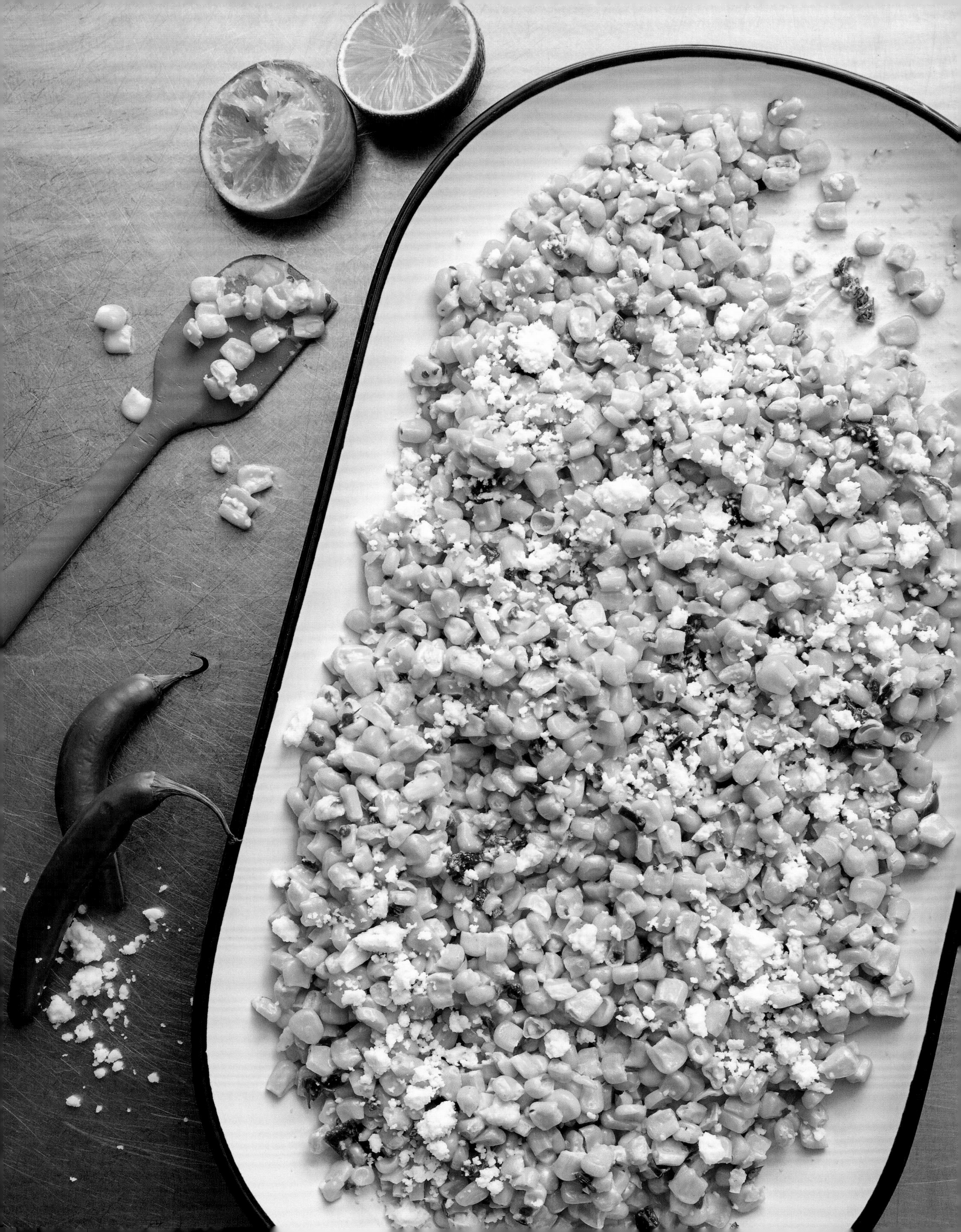

Street Corner Street Corn

YIELD: ABOUT 8 SERVINGS

When you're in a line of work like mine, danger lurks around almost every corner. But on the corners where danger doesn't lurk, hopefully there's some sort of food cart selling local specialties. Eating street food is a lot like being a mercenary, actually. One wrong choice, and you could end up crawling your way into the nearest hospital with a hole in your gut. One dish that never did me wrong was the Mexican street corn sold just across the street from the hidden Hydra warehouse near the docks. (You remember the one.) Unfortunately, after I burned the warehouse down with everyone inside, it really put a damper on the daily lunch rush, and the cart went out of business. Fortunately, I was able to whip up this off-the-cob variation in memory of the fallen.

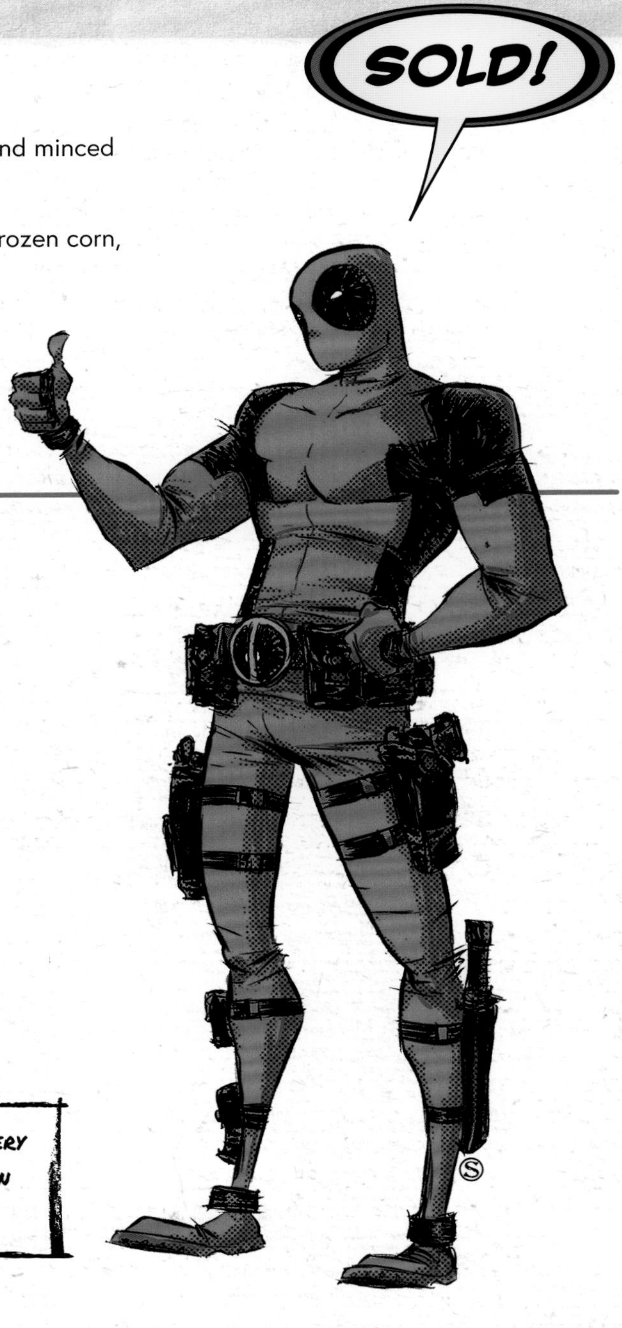
SOLD!

FOR THE DRESSING:

½ cup mayonnaise

2 tablespoons chopped chipotle peppers in adobo sauce

1 cup crumbled cotija cheese, divided

FOR THE CORN:

2 tablespoons olive oil

2 tablespoons unsalted butter

3 cloves garlic, minced

1 serrano chile, seeded and minced

2 teaspoons salt

One 32-ounce package frozen corn, defrosted

Juice of 1 lime

1. To make the dressing: Combine the mayonnaise, chile, and ½ cup of the cotija in a small bowl. Set aside.
2. Heat a large sauté pan on medium, and add olive oil, swirling to coat the pan. Melt butter in the pan. When the butter begins to foam, add garlic, serrano chile, and salt, and sauté until tender. Add corn and cook, stirring constantly, for about 5 minutes or until warmed through. Add the lime juice and stir to combine.
3. Transfer the corn to a large bowl, and mix in the prepared dressing. Sprinkle with the remaining cotija before serving.

TIP:

CAN'T FIND COTIJA CHEESE? TIME TO YELL AT THE LOCAL GROCERY STORE STOCK BOY UNTIL HE CRIES! AFTER THAT, I GUESS YOU CAN USE FRESH FARM CHEESE OR FETA AS AN ACCEPTABLE STAND-IN.

JUST THE TIPS: CHOOSING A KNIFE

There's a knife for every occasion, both in the field and in the kitchen. I like to keep mine sharp and clean, so they're ready to go whenever I need them. Some of my most favoritest blades include:

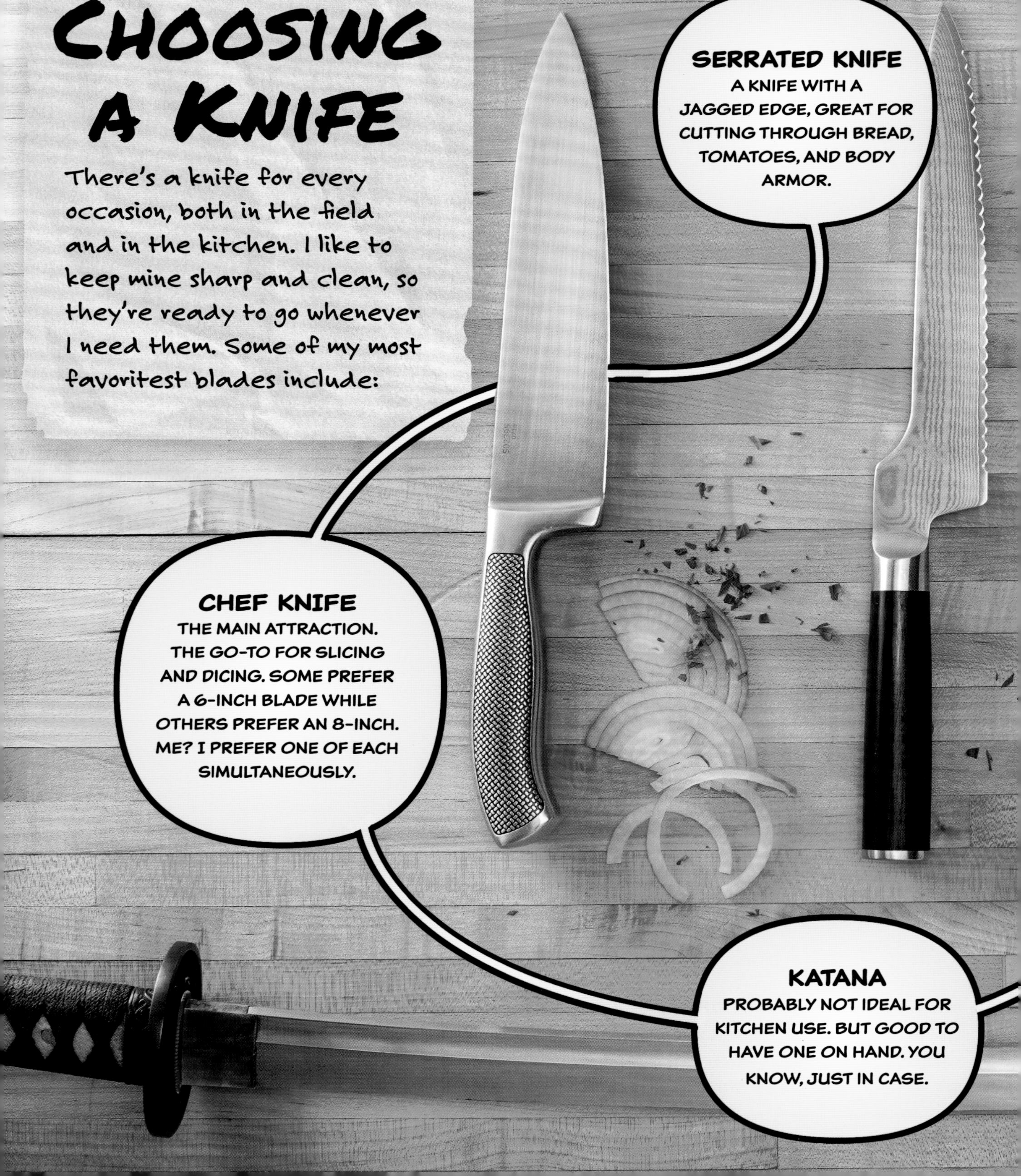
SERRATED KNIFE
A KNIFE WITH A JAGGED EDGE, GREAT FOR CUTTING THROUGH BREAD, TOMATOES, AND BODY ARMOR.
CHEF KNIFE
THE MAIN ATTRACTION. THE GO-TO FOR SLICING AND DICING. SOME PREFER A 6-INCH BLADE WHILE OTHERS PREFER AN 8-INCH. ME? I PREFER ONE OF EACH SIMULTANEOUSLY.
KATANA
PROBABLY NOT IDEAL FOR KITCHEN USE. BUT GOOD TO HAVE ONE ON HAND. YOU KNOW, JUST IN CASE.

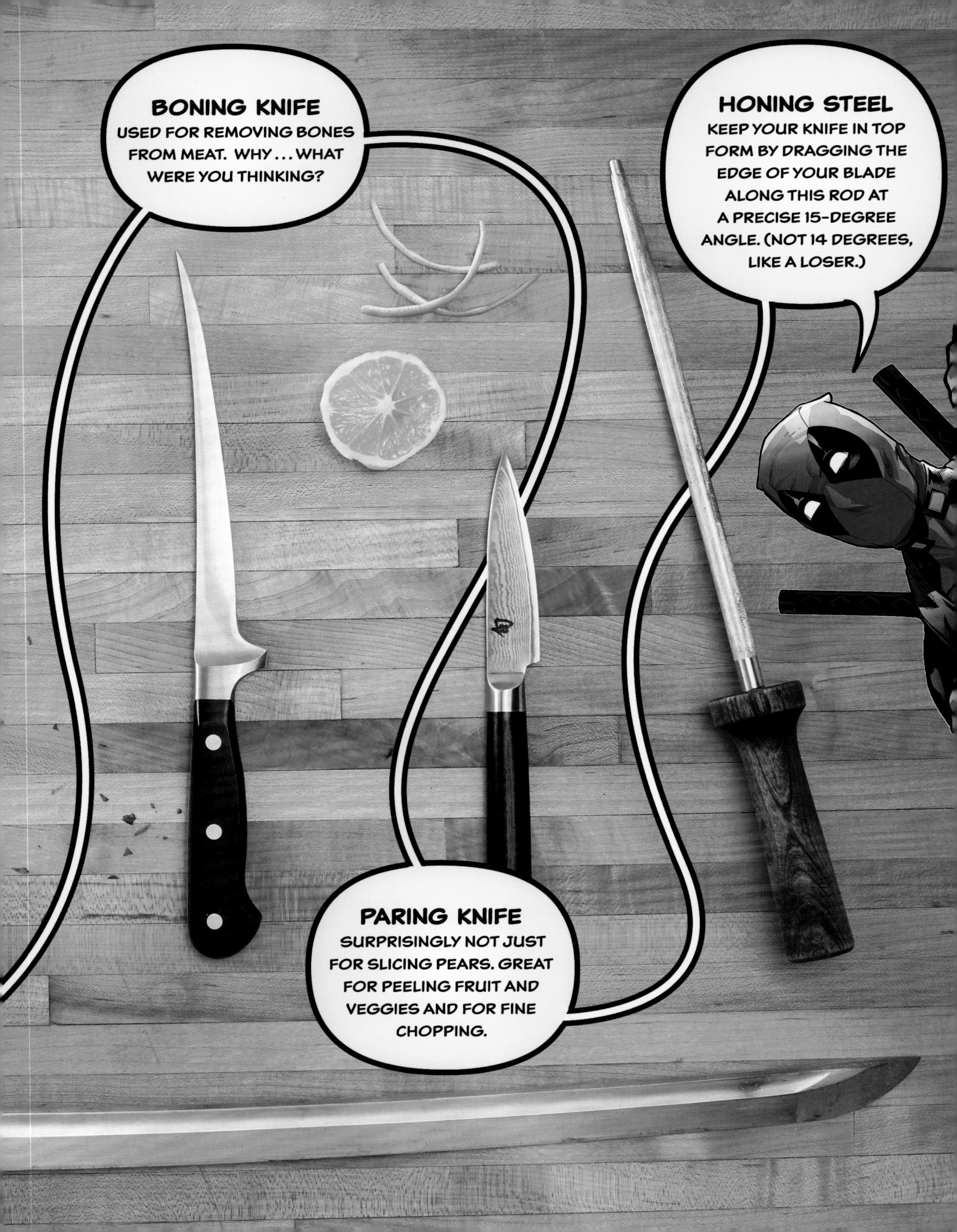
BONING KNIFE
USED FOR REMOVING BONES FROM MEAT. WHY... WHAT WERE YOU THINKING?
HONING STEEL
KEEP YOUR KNIFE IN TOP FORM BY DRAGGING THE EDGE OF YOUR BLADE ALONG THIS ROD AT A PRECISE 15-DEGREE ANGLE. (NOT 14 DEGREES, LIKE A LOSER.)
PARING KNIFE
SURPRISINGLY NOT JUST FOR SLICING PEARS. GREAT FOR PEELING FRUIT AND VEGGIES AND FOR FINE CHOPPING.

Krakoan Salsa

The X-Men have lived in a lot of unusual places over the years, but the Pacific island known as Krakoa might be the weirdest. See, Krakoa isn't actually an island. It's a living, breathing mutant organism, and it's decided to form a symbiotic relationship with the rest of its species. Since the X-folk moved in, they've found all sorts of uses for the unique foliage that grows within the Krakoan biosphere, like opening teleportation gates and manufacturing high-end pharmaceuticals. But me? I raid their garden to grab the ingredients for this tasty salsa.

2 ripe avocados, peeled and pitted

Juice of 1 lime

One 10-ounce can green chiles

½ tablespoon kosher salt

½ teaspoon garlic powder

½ tablespoon olive oil

½ tablespoon hot sauce

Fresh black pepper, to taste

¼ cup loosely packed fresh cilantro leaves

HEHEH

NOW... WHAT WAS I DOING?

1. In a food processor, blend the avocados and the lime juice. Add the rest of the ingredients, except cilantro, and continue to blend until smooth.

2. Add cilantro leaves and pulse until combined. Refrigerate until ready to serve.

Pictured on pages 94–95

Black Ops Salsa

For a guy who claims to be a solo act, I've been on a lot of teams. From X-Force to the Thunderbolts, I've collected a hefty stack of membership cards over the years, most of which have been permanently revoked. But one team I'll always be a member of, like it or not, is Weapon X—run by the mysterious organization that gave me my healing factor. Despite their sinister purpose and brutal methods, the folks at Weapon X know how to throw one hell of an office party. In fact, last time I tried to murder their director, I tortured him first until he gave me the recipe for his famous black bean salsa! Trust me, this one is to die for. (And he did!)

1 teaspoon salt

½ teaspoon garlic powder

¼ teaspoon ground cumin

¼ teaspoon paprika

1½ tablespoons olive oil

2 tablespoons rice vinegar

Juice of 1 lime

Two 15-ounce cans black beans, drained and rinsed

½ red onion, diced

1 small red bell pepper, diced

3 ounces dried mango, diced

½ cup loosely packed fresh cilantro leaves

1. To make the dressing, mix the spices, oil, vinegar, and lime juice in a small bowl. Set aside.

2. Pour the beans into a medium bowl. Add the onion, pepper, and dried mango. Add dressing, and mix until well combined. Refrigerate until ready to serve.

3. Just before serving, roughly chop the cilantro leaves and add to the salsa. Enjoy!

DP DIP

YIELD: ABOUT 2 CUPS

Whenever I find out that my friends are having a party, the first thing I do is whip up a batch of my world-famous dip. Okay, actually, the first thing I do is bombard them with text messages asking why I wasn't on the guest list until they come out with some weak story about my invitation getting lost or my voicemail being full. When they finally realize that I won't leave them alone until I'm offered an invitation and a formal apology, *then* I whip up a batch of my famous dip! This creamy concoction provides a perfect pairing for just about anything (particularly my signature Crab Rangoon Chimis, page 88).

3 cloves garlic, peeled

4 scallions, white and light green parts only, diced

1 cup fresh cilantro leaves

½ cup fresh parsley leaves

2 tablespoons fresh oregano leaves

3 tablespoons snipped chives

1 teaspoon salt

½ teaspoon cayenne pepper

Juice of 1 lime

1 teaspoon rice vinegar

2 cups (16 ounces) sour cream

Fresh black pepper

1. In the bowl of a food processor, pulse the garlic until well minced. Add the scallions and fresh herbs and continue to pulse, scraping down the sides of the bowl, until a pesto-like consistency is reached.

2. Add the salt, cayenne, lime juice, and vinegar, and pulse to combine. Add sour cream and blend until just smooth. Add pepper to taste. Refrigerate for at least 1 hour to let the flavors meld.

Pictured on pages 94–95

Make 'Em Sweat

YIELD: 6 WITH SOME LEFTOVERS FOR KNUCKLE SANDWICHES

There are plenty of things in this world I like raw. Steaks. Emotion. Comedy. Wounds. But when it comes to onions, no thanks. Those balls of stink used to drive me to tears, and that was before I'd even started to cut one. But then I discovered this magical method of cooking called "caramelizing." The process of sweating the onions brings out all the natural sugars inside and, through some sort of culinary voodoo, turns them from smelly to sweet. Add a touch of butter and brown sugar, and I'll be first in line to heap these babies onto anything, from sandwiches to main courses (see What a Ham, page 49).

1 to 2 tablespoons oil, for pan

4 to 5 pounds sweet yellow onions, thinly sliced

2 teaspoons salt

2 tablespoons salted butter

⅓ cup brown sugar

If making with What a Ham (page 49), substitute the brown sugar with ⅓ cup reserved ham glaze and 2 pineapple rings.

1. Heat a very large sauté pan on medium. Coat the surface of the pan with oil, and add onions and salt. Sauté until the onions sweat down and reduce to a manageable pile, about 10 to 15 minutes. Add the butter and continue to cook stirring occasionally, until the onions begin to brown.
2. Add the brown sugar or reserved ham glaze and pineapple rings and continue to cook, 20 to 30 minutes, or until the onions have reached a deep caramel color and a jam-like consistency.

TIP:

YOUR PAN MAY SEEM WAY TOO FULL AT FIRST, BUT DON'T PANIC. IN NO TIME FLAT, THOSE ONIONS WILL BE SHRINKING FASTER THAN MY REPUTATION AFTER PEOPLE REALIZE I WROTE I COOKBOOK.

Pictured on pages 140–141

Nacho Average Cheese Sauce

YIELD: ABOUT 3 CUPS

Ever feel the urge to go to a gas station, put your face directly under the nacho cheese dispenser, and just start pumping? You and me both, kid. But that's one dream you might want to cross off your list, because along with a mouthful of week-old orange goop, you'll also wind up with hideous burns all over your face and about a 90 percent chance of some sort of food poisoning. All those risks can be avoided by learning to make your own delectable nacho cheese sauce in the comfort of your own home. This liquid lactose goes great on nachos, chimis, or even by itself on a comically oversize spoon.

One 12-ounce can evaporated milk

1½ tablespoons cornstarch

2 cups shredded medium cheddar

1 cup shredded Monterey Jack

1 teaspoon salt

½ teaspoon garlic powder

¼ teaspoon turmeric, for color (optional)

1. In a large microwave-safe bowl, whisk the evaporated milk and cornstarch together until well combined. Microwave on high for 1 minute. Remove from microwave, whisk thoroughly, then return to microwave for another minute. Remove, whisk again, and microwave for 30 seconds to 1 minute more, until the mixture is scalding. Carefully remove from microwave, and whisk until most of the steam is gone.
2. Slowly add cheese, whisking or blending with an immersion blender, until all the cheese is melted and smooth. Add salt and spices. Serve immediately or refrigerate. The sauce can be reheated gently in the microwave 30 seconds at a time.

TIP:

STEER CLEAR OF PRESHREDDED CHEESES FOR THIS ONE, KIDS. THEY'RE FULL OF ANTICAKING AGENTS THAT PREVENT THE CHEESE FROM BLENDING WELL.

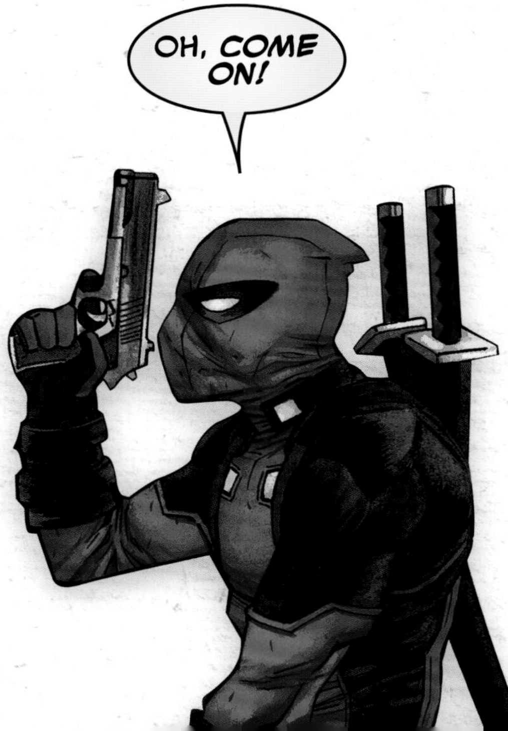
OH, COME ON!

VARIATIONS:

- Add 1 teaspoon ancho chili powder or paprika for smoky heat.
- Add 1 teaspoon cayenne pepper for more intense heat.
- Cheese can be swapped for different combinations of cheddar, Monterey Jack, and pepper Jack.

Pictured on page 86

LONGEVITY NOODLES

Whether it's Chinese New Year, your birthday, or just a random day on which you need a little extra love, these traditional stir-fried Asian noodles are the perfect way to celebrate. Not only do they have a great chewy texture, but legends say they can make your life longer (hence the name). And in my line of work, I'll take every extra day I can get! I've found that a quick bowl of these babies is particularly good for keeping my stamina up between missions. The fact that they're pretty easy to make is also a major plus for those nights I'd rather reduce my longevity in the kitchen.

8 ounces lo mein or linguine noodles, fresh if possible

2 teaspoons sesame oil

½ cup vegetable stock

3 tablespoons soy sauce

¼ teaspoon five-spice powder

½ tablespoon honey

6 tablespoons any oil, divided

½ teaspoon red pepper flakes, divided

1 pound mushrooms, cleaned and thinly sliced

Salt and fresh black pepper

1 cup scallions, thinly sliced, dark green parts reserved for garnish

1½ tablespoons minced fresh ginger (from about a thumb-size knob)

5 cloves garlic, minced

3 carrots, thinly sliced

2 zucchini, thinly sliced

½ head napa cabbage, shredded

2½ tablespoons fresh lemon juice

1. In a large stockpot, cook noodles according to package directions, drain, and rinse with cool water. Return noodles to the empty pot, and toss with sesame oil.

2. While noodles are cooking, whisk together vegetable stock, soy sauce, five-spice powder, and honey in a small bowl, and set aside.

3. Add 2 tablespoons of oil to a large frying pan on medium-high heat. When oil is hot, add ¼ teaspoon of the red pepper flakes and half the mushrooms to the pan. Sprinkle the mushrooms with salt to taste, and stir to coat. Spread the mushrooms in an even layer, and let cook until they lose moisture and start to sear, 4 to 5 minutes. Repeat with another 2 tablespoons of oil and the remaining ¼ teaspoon of red pepper flakes for the remaining mushrooms. Remove mushrooms from pan, and set aside.

4. Using the same pan, add the remaining 2 tablespoons of oil, white and light green scallions, ginger, and garlic. Cook, stirring constantly, until fragrant, about 30 seconds.

5. Add carrots and zucchini; cook while stirring until veggies are softened, 2 to 3 minutes. Add the cabbage, stirring until wilted, about 1 minute.

6. Reduce heat to medium, and add mushrooms and noodles. Add stock mixture, salt and pepper to taste, and toss until noodles and mushrooms are heated through, about 3 minutes.

7. Drizzle lemon juice over noodle mixture. Plate, garnish with reserved scallions, and serve.

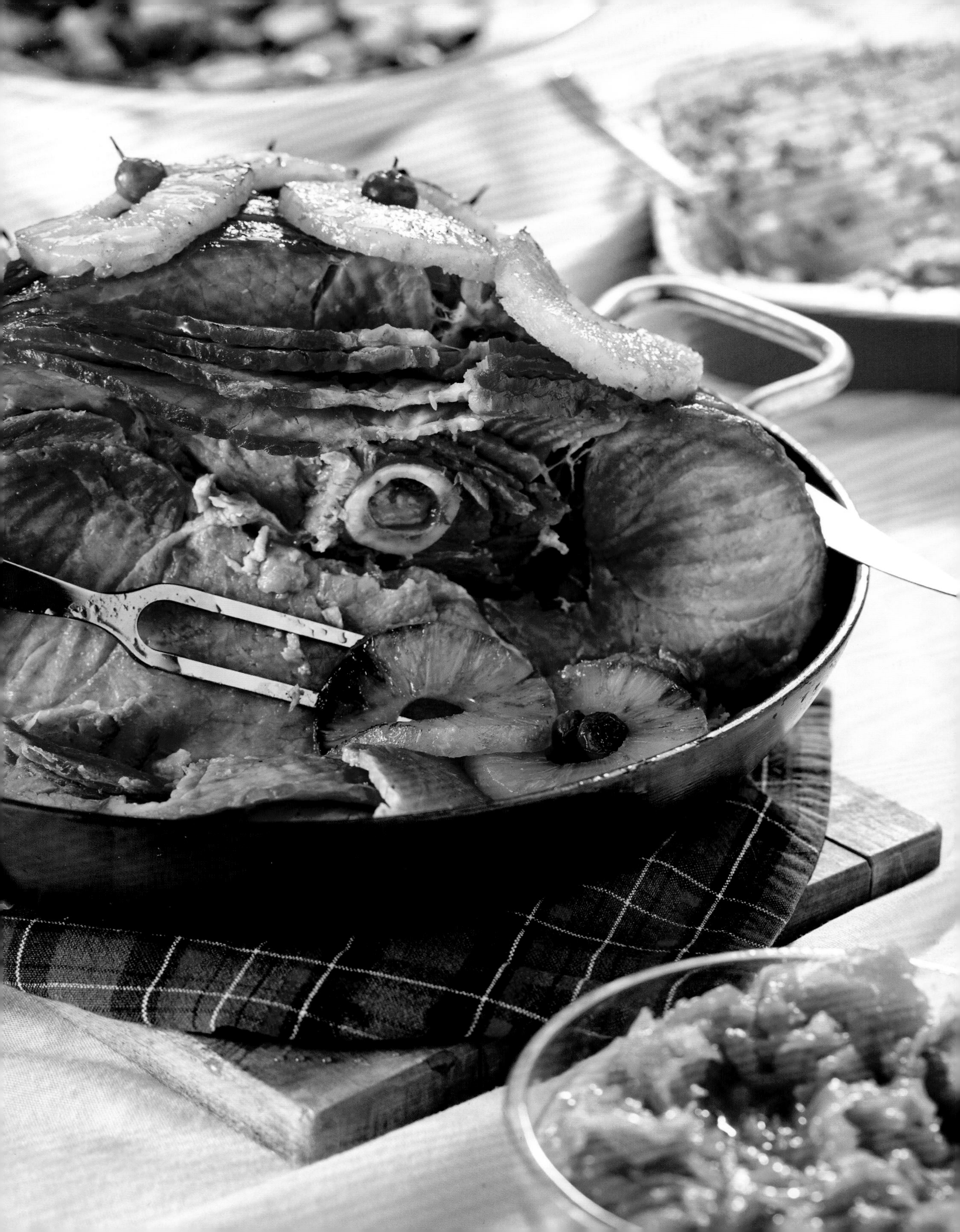

MAXIMUM EFFORTS

All right, kids. If you're cooking every single dish in this book in proper sequential order, which I assume you are, that means you've already figured out how to whip up quite a spread of starters and sides. Nice work! But sometimes it takes more than just an appetizer to amuse my bouche. That's where these bad boys come in. That's right, the entrées have arrived! Welcome to the main event!

Each of these massive meals is more than a mouthful, even for a merc with a mouth as big as mine. And because these dishes are the stars of the show, they naturally take a bit more effort and attention to successfully execute. (Trust me, I know a thing or two about successful executions!) Though they may take maximum effort, they also have an impressive payoff—if you can get the job done.

ADVANTAGE-- DEADPOOL!

This is it. Time to prove you've got what it takes. So clean off your knives—seriously, who knows where those things have been— and get ready for the culmination of your culinary crusade. And if you do happen to fail spectacularly, don't worry. You can always order takeout and claim you made it from scratch.

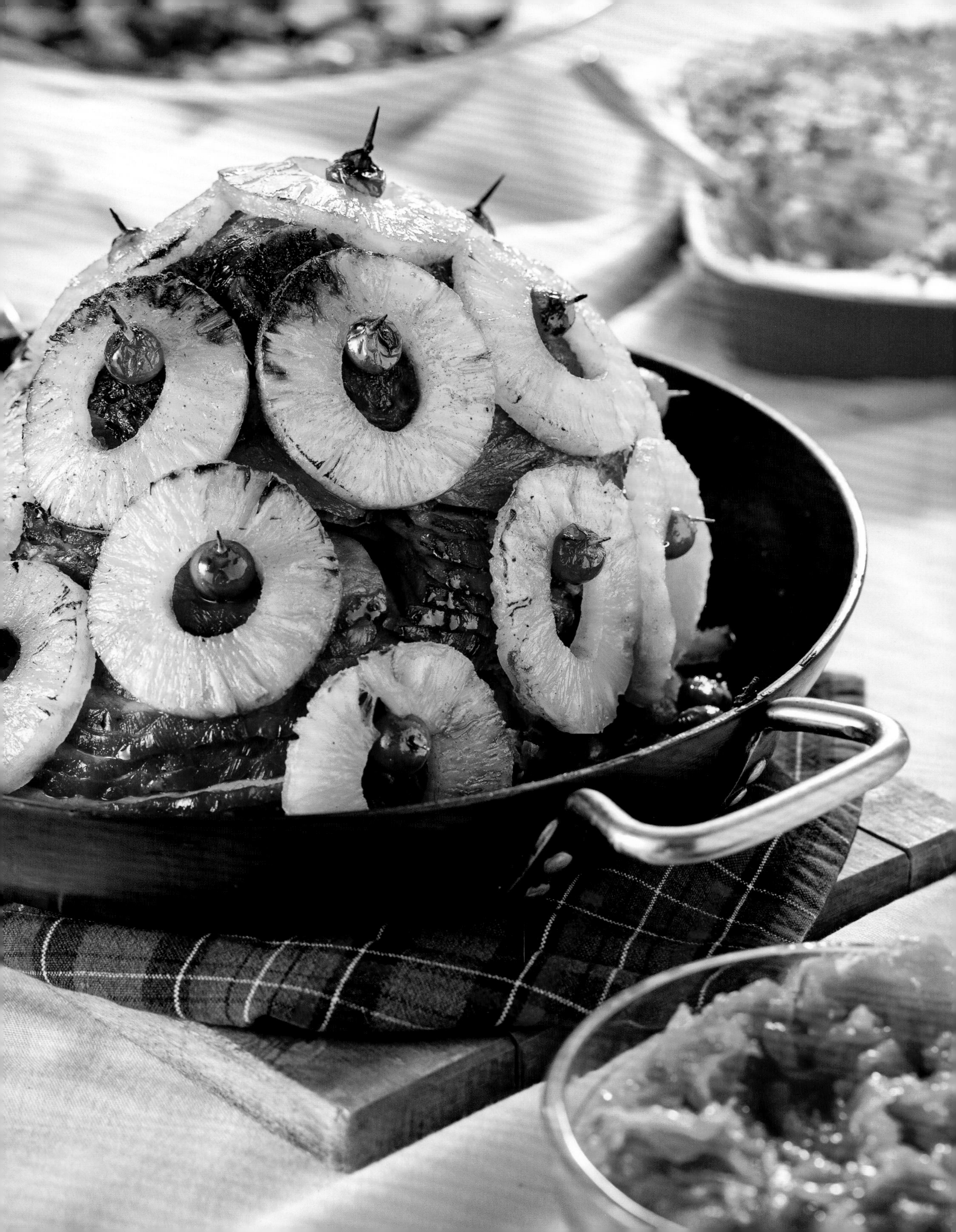

What a Ham

YIELD: 10 TO 12 SERVINGS WITH LEFTOVERS

Sometimes I wonder what it would be like to have a traditional family holiday around the dining room table. The kind of idyllic scene you'd find in an old-school Norman Rockwell painting. Then I remember that my "family" is a dysfunctional group of mutants and mercenaries who would likely blow one another to smithereens before I could even get the yams out of the oven. Still, a merc can dream. So if that magical day ever arrives, I plan to be ready with this classic glazed ham recipe. This one's straight out of your grandma's recipe box. (Literally. Someone paid me big money to steal it from your grandma.) Enjoy it with family and friends while you awkwardly avoid talking about politics.

FOR THE HAM:

One 9- to 10-pound bone-in ham, fully cooked, preferably spiral cut

Two 20-ounce cans pineapple rings, juice reserved

1 bunch red seedless grapes

¼ cup water

FOR THE GLAZE:

Reserved pineapple juice

1 cup honey

1 cup brown sugar

¼ teaspoon allspice

¼ teaspoon five-spice powder

TO SERVE:

Make 'Em Sweat (page 43) (optional)

SPECIAL SUPPLIES:

Toothpicks

1. To prepare the ham: Preheat the oven to 325°F. Place the ham cut side down in a roasting pan. Arrange pineapple rings all over the ham, as close together as possible, securing each ring with a grape skewered on a toothpick. Add the water to the bottom of the pan. Slice remaining pineapple rings in half, and add to bottom of pan, along with any extra grapes.
2. Tent the ham with foil, and bake until a thermometer inserted into the thickest part reads 130°F, about 2½ hours, or 15 minutes per pound.
3. While the ham is baking, prepare the glaze: Combine all glaze ingredients in a small saucepan on medium heat. Simmer, stirring occasionally, until glaze has reduced and achieved a syrupy consistency, 20 to 25 minutes. Set aside.
4. When the ham has reached 130°F, remove from the oven. Increase oven temperature to 425°F. Brush the ham with about ⅓ of the glaze, re-tent, return to the oven, and bake for 10 minutes. Repeat this process and bake another 10 minutes, then check the internal temperature. Continue to glaze and bake the ham at 10-minute intervals until the internal temperature reaches 140°F.
5. Tent with foil, and let rest for 10 minutes before carving. Any extra glaze can be poured over the ham slices when serving. Serve with the roasted grapes and pineapple rings.

TIP:

THIS RECIPE PAIRS PERFECTLY WITH MAKE 'EM SWEAT (PAGE 43), SO BE SURE TO SET ASIDE ⅓ CUP OF HAM GLAZE AND TWO EXTRA PINEAPPLE RINGS FOR YOUR CARAMELIZED ONIONS!

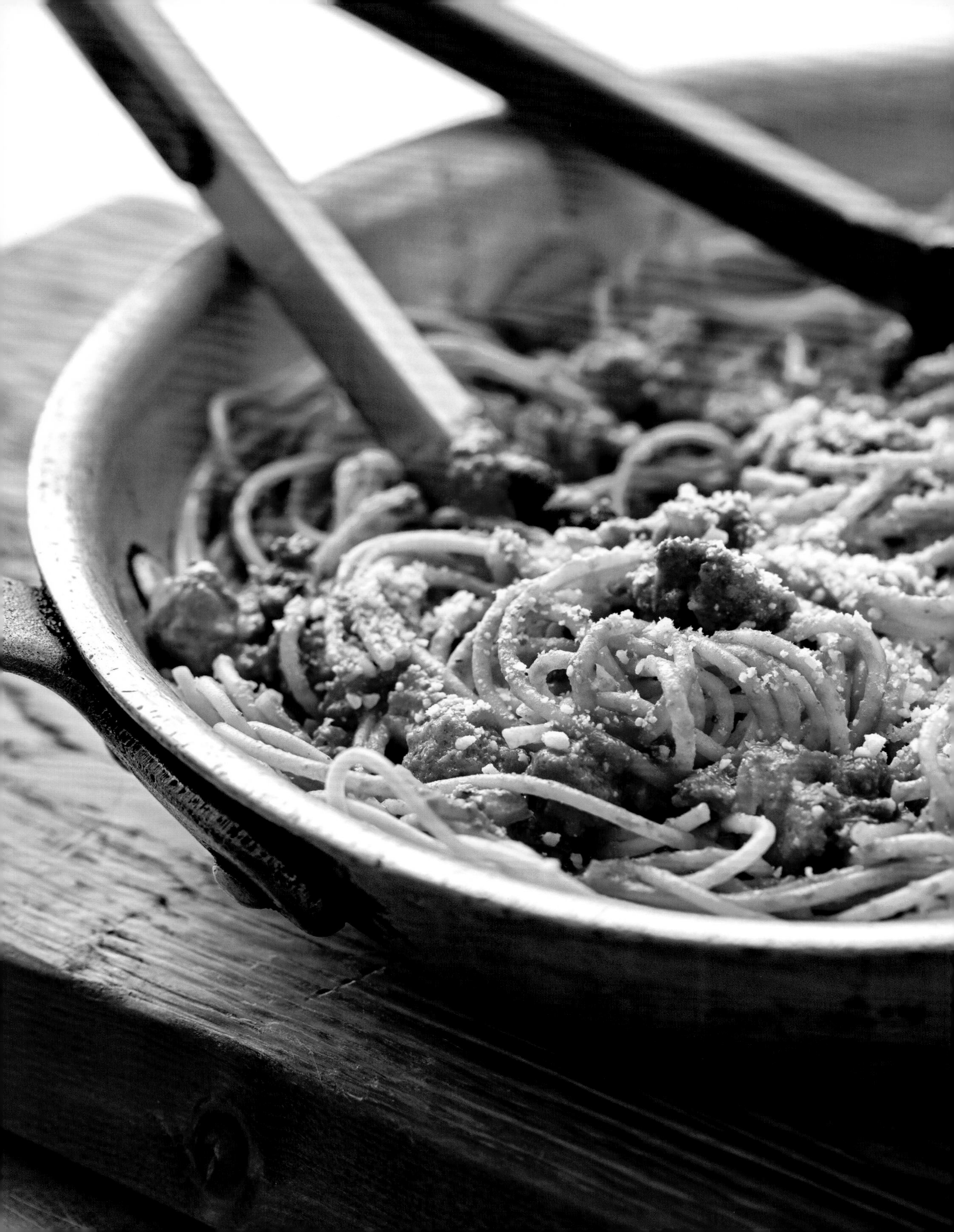

CABLE'S CUISINE: SPAGHETTI

Cable here. Deadpool asked me to share some of my favorite recipes, but he seems to have forgotten that I was raised on the battlefield of an apocalyptic future. We didn't eat for pleasure. We ate to survive a nightmarish hellscape. When I traveled back in time, I suddenly found myself with a bit more time on my hands for enjoying the simple things, like the occasional decent meal. So for the nights that my fellow X-Men force me to cook, I've taken a few of the more palatable MREs (Meals Ready to Eat) I've ingested over the years and adapted them into something a bit more suited for civilian consumption. The way I see it, if these are good enough for a soldier on the front lines of the war for mutantkind, they're good enough for you.

1 to 2 tablespoons olive oil

2 tablespoons salted butter

1 yellow onion, finely diced

6 cloves garlic, minced

1 tablespoon dried oregano

1 teaspoon red pepper flakes

1 teaspoon salt

1 pound ground beef

One 14-ounce can diced tomatoes

One 14-ounce can tomato sauce

2 tablespoons balsamic vinegar

½ cup heavy cream

½ cup finely grated Parmesan, plus more for garnish

Fresh black pepper

1½ pounds spaghetti or favorite pasta

1. Add oil and butter to a large sauté pan on medium heat. When butter begins to foam, add onion and garlic, and cook until translucent. Add oregano, red pepper flakes, and salt, and cook 2 more minutes. Add ground beef, and cook until brown.

2. Add diced tomatoes and tomato sauce, rinsing the sauce can by filling halfway with water and adding to pan. Add balsamic vinegar, and simmer on medium until reduced, 20 to 30 minutes.

3. Make a slurry with the cream and Parmesan by mixing them together in a small bowl or measuring cup until combined. Add slurry to sauce and simmer on low while pasta is prepared. Add pepper to taste.

4. Cook pasta according to package directions. Drain, and toss with pasta sauce in a large serving bowl.

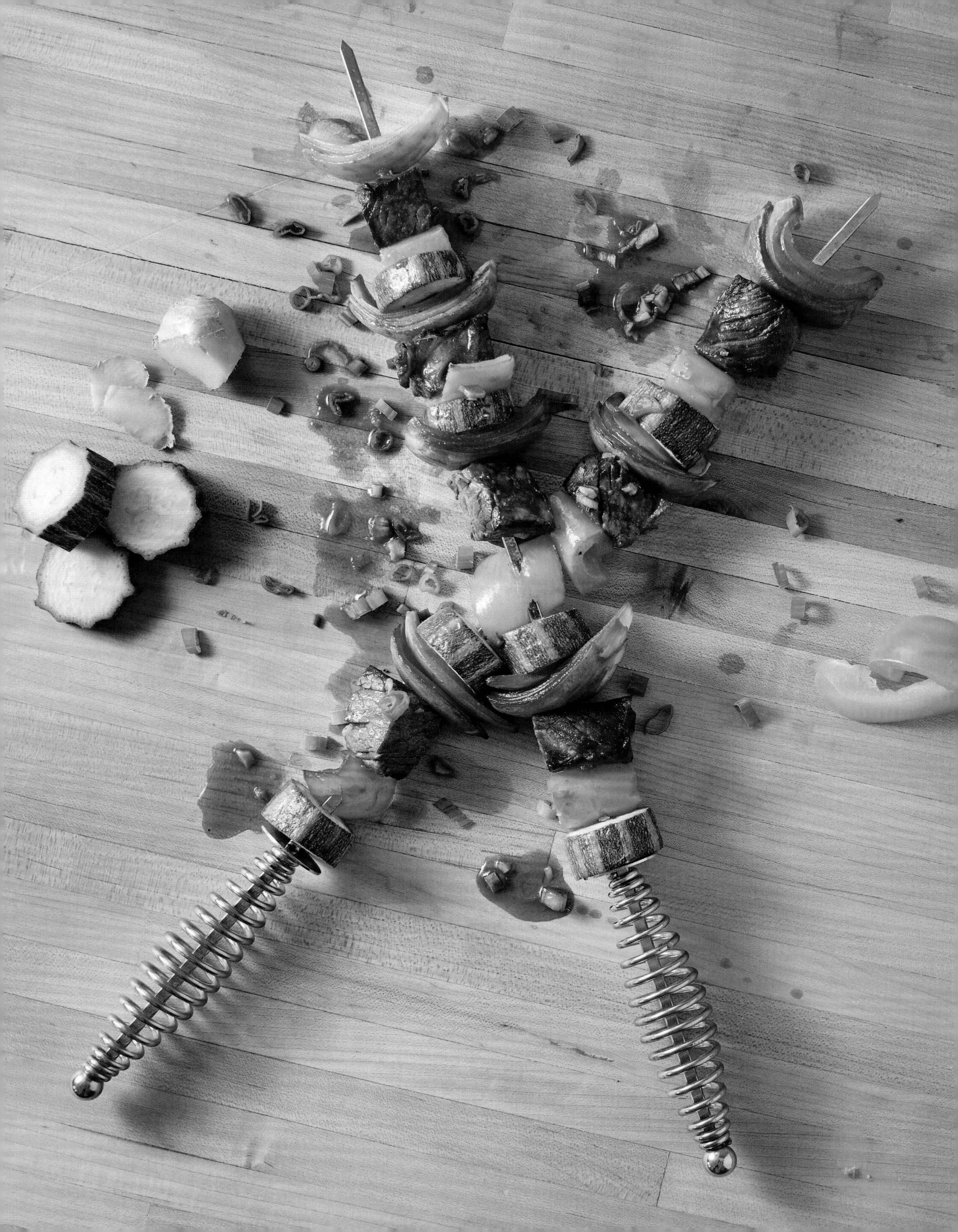

Stabby Meat Sticks

YIELD: 4 SERVINGS

There are two things I love more than anything else in the world: good food and stabbing things. That's why the humble skewer is my best friend in the whole world. (Don't tell Cable.) It's a sharp, pointy stick designed specifically for grilling up all sorts of meaty goodness. While this recipe is a classic kabob, you can always get creative with your combos of meats and veggies. But no matter what you're cooking up, just remember to take it off the skewer before trying to eat it . . . unless you've got a healing factor, too.

½ cup soy sauce

2 tablespoons olive oil

2 tablespoons seasoned rice wine vinegar

2 tablespoons light brown sugar

4 scallions, thinly sliced, divided

2 teaspoons minced fresh ginger

2 cloves garlic, minced

Four 32-ounce rib eye steaks (porterhouse or top sirloin will work too), trimmed and cut into 1-inch cubes

2 medium red onions

3 zucchini

2 yellow or orange bell peppers, stemmed and seeded

2 cups cooked rice, for serving

SPECIAL SUPPLIES:

12 skewers

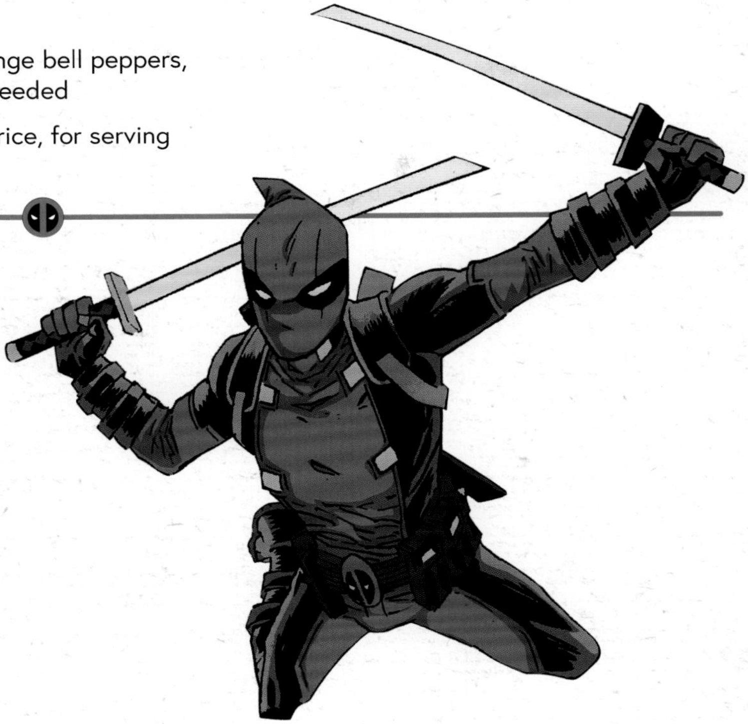

1. In a large bowl, whisk together soy sauce, olive oil, rice wine vinegar, brown sugar, white and light green scallions, ginger, and garlic. Add steak cubes, and marinate at least 15 minutes.
2. While steak marinates, cut the onion, zucchini, and bell pepper into 1-inch pieces, matching the size of the meat as much as possible. Preheat the oven to 450°F. Line 2 baking sheets with foil.
3. Thread marinated steak (do not discard marinade), onion, zucchini, and bell pepper onto the skewers, alternating between ingredients and dividing all the ingredients evenly across the 12 skewers. Arrange 6 skewers in a single layer on each baking sheet. Pour remaining marinade over skewers. Turn skewers to coat vegetables in marinade.
4. Roast in oven until steak is brown and medium rare, reading 145°F on a meat thermometer, about 8 minutes. Sprinkle with reserved dark green scallions, and serve over rice.

TIP:

DON'T HAVE ANY SKEWERS? USE YOUR SWORDS INSTEAD! DON'T HAVE ANY SWORDS? THIS MIGHT NOT BE THE COOKBOOK FOR YOU . . .

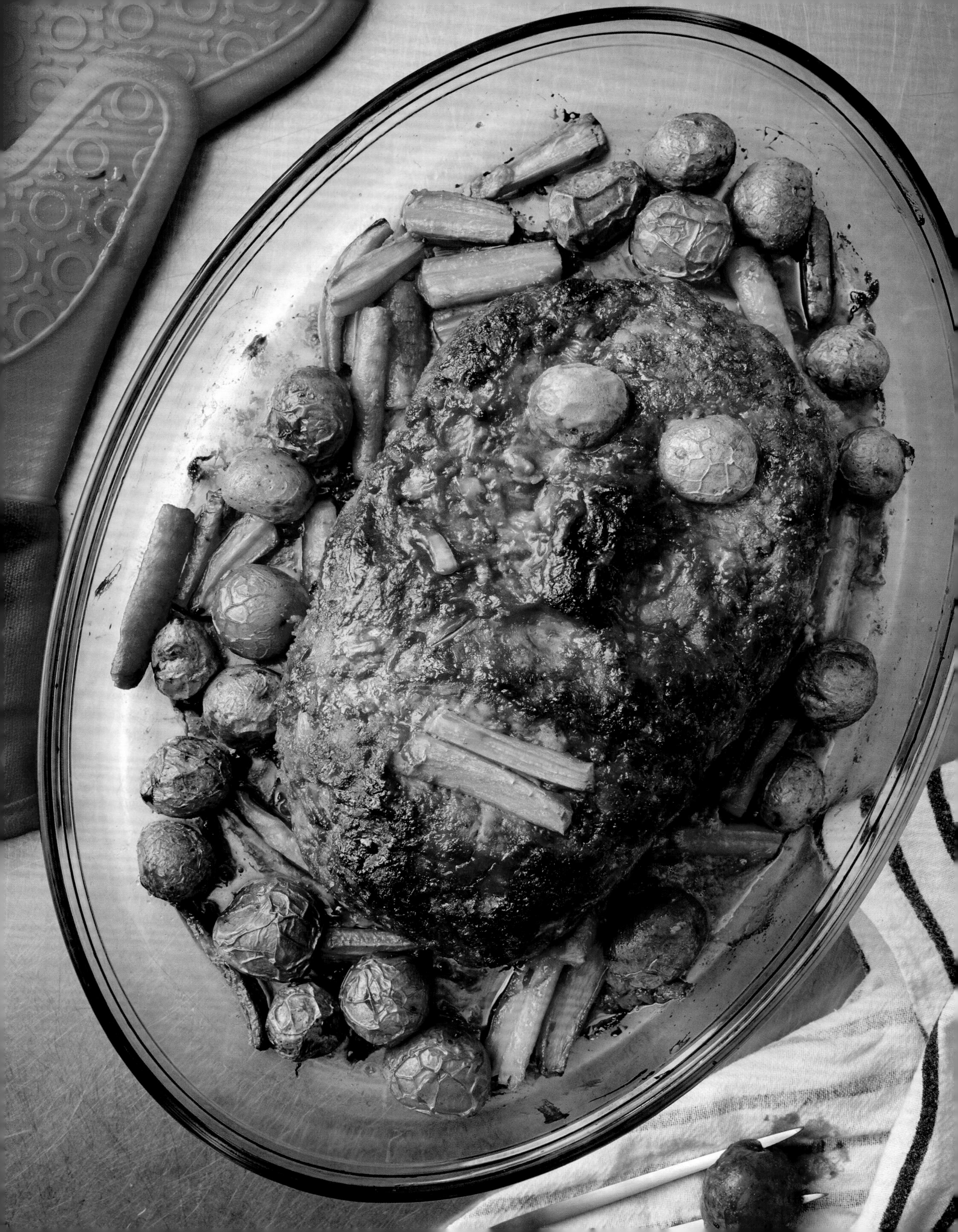

A Self-Portrait in Meat

YIELD: 6 SERVINGS WITH SOME LEFTOVERS FOR SANDWICHES THE NEXT DAY

It's been said that a good meal is the perfect reflection of the chef's soul. I'm not entirely sure who said it. In fact, there's a fairly decent chance I just made it up right now. Whatever the origin of that little nugget of wisdom, we can all agree that there's certainly some truth to it. But why stop at reflecting the soul? Personally, I want my food to reflect all of me—even my jacked-up face! And what better way to celebrate a guy with a face that looks like a meatloaf than to make a meatloaf that looks like his face? One aphorism I know I didn't make up is "we are what we eat." So this might be your best chance to be more like Deadpool, and the perfect opportunity for me to unironically utter yet another of my favorite sayings: "Eat me!"

FOR THE MEATLOAF:

1½ pounds ground turkey

1½ pounds ground beef

1 shallot, minced

1 cup shredded carrots, plus 1 pound carrots cut into 2-inch pieces

2 eggs

2 tablespoons Worcestershire sauce

5 ounces croutons, smashed to a coarse crumb

1 pound new potatoes

FOR THE GLAZE:

½ cup ketchup

1 tablespoon Worcestershire sauce

2 tablespoons honey

1. Preheat the oven to 350°F.
2. To make the meatloaf: Combine ground turkey, ground beef, shallot, shredded carrots, eggs, and Worcestershire sauce in a medium bowl until well mixed. Add the smashed croutons and continue to mix until just combined. Turn out meat mixture into a large roasting pan and begin to sculpt . . . *me*! Don't forget eye sockets, nose, and a mouth. Use two potatoes for my eyes and sliced carrots for lips. Add the rest of the potatoes and carrots to the pan around your sculpture for roasting.
3. To make the glaze: Combine all the glaze ingredients in a small bowl, and stir until well blended. Spoon about half the glaze over the face loaf, letting it drip over the sides and onto the veggies. Reserve the rest of the glaze. Bake for 45 minutes to an hour, until cooked through.
4. Heat the remaining glaze gently in a small saucepan, and serve with the meatloaf.

TIP:

I'M THE TYPE WHO LIKES TO DIG MY BARE MITTS INTO A BOWL FULL OF RAW MEAT, BUT FEEL FREE TO USE A STAND MIXER TO MAKE A FASTER, EASIER (BUT SLIGHTLY LESS CATHARTIC) MEAT MIXTURE.

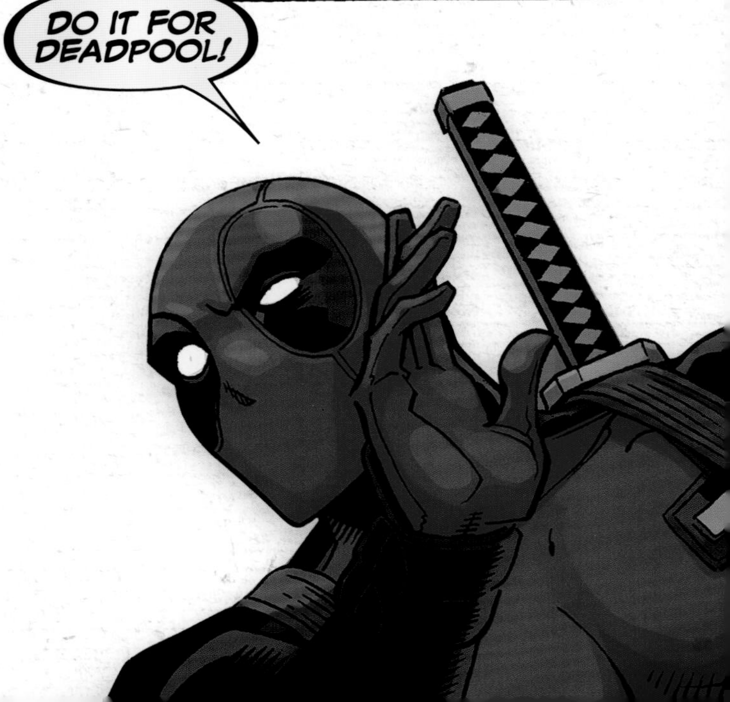
DO IT FOR DEADPOOL!

THIGH POUCHES

You can never have enough pouches. They're great for holding just about anything you could possibly need on a mission. Ammunition, thermal detonators, yogurt-covered raisins, more ammunition, lockpicks, throwing stars, even smaller pouches—the list is practically endless. There's nothing quite as exciting as opening a pouch to discover what surprises are stored inside. That's why I've started incorporating pouches into my meals. When basic dumplings and "piroshki" aren't enough, I go all in, pounding some chicken thighs nice and thin and wrapping them around a delectable filling. Sometimes, I make a bunch of these and then put them in my actual thigh pouches so I can enjoy them on the go. Now that's staying on theme!

1 to 2 tablespoons olive oil, for pan

4 tablespoons (½ stick) salted butter, divided

½ pound fresh cremini mushrooms, finely chopped

1 teaspoon salt

3 cloves garlic, minced

1 tablespoon fresh thyme leaves, chopped, plus more for garnish

4 tablespoons marsala or sweet vermouth, divided

Fresh black pepper

6 boneless, skinless chicken thighs

¼ cup heavy cream

1. Heat an oven-safe sauté pan on medium high. Coat the surface of the pan with oil, and add 2 tablespoons of butter. When the butter begins to foam, add the mushrooms and salt. Cook, stirring occasionally, until the mushrooms are reduced by half, tender, and have released their juices. Add the garlic and thyme, and cook for 2 minutes. Add 2 tablespoons of the marsala, and pepper to taste, and cook 2 minutes more. Remove the mushrooms from the pan, and set aside.

2. Preheat the oven to 350°F. Paillard the chicken thighs between 2 pieces of parchment paper until about ½ inch thick (see page 63). Be careful not to tear the meat. Spread about 2 tablespoons of filling across one of the thighs, leaving a ¼-inch border around the edges. Starting at the smaller end, roll up the meat around the filling, tucking in the edges and any loose pieces. Secure with a toothpick, making sure it goes through every layer in the roll. Repeat with remaining thighs until all the thigh pouches are complete.

3. Reheat the same sauté pan on medium high, and coat with olive oil. Melt the remaining 2 tablespoons of butter in the pan. When the butter begins to foam, place all the chicken thighs in the pan, seam side up. Brown 3 to 5 minutes, then turn them over and remove from heat.

4. Cover the pan with an oven-safe lid or foil, and bake in the oven for 7 minutes. Remove cover, and bake 5 minutes more. Remove the chicken from the pan to a plate, and set aside to rest.

5. Return the pan to the stove on medium heat. Add ¼ cup of water and the remaining marsala, and deglaze the pan, scraping up any brown bits from the bottom. Bring the liquid to a simmer. Stir in the cream, and cook 2 to 4 minutes, until sauce just begins to thicken. Remove the toothpicks, return chicken to the pan and spoon sauce over the pieces. Serve with a sprinkle of fresh thyme, if desired.

CABLE'S CUISINE: BEEF STEW

YIELD: 6 SERVINGS

Cable here again. It shouldn't come as a surprise, but Wade's short attention span seems to have gotten the best of him, and he took a random mission halfway through writing this book. He called me and asked me to cover for him by providing another of my go-to recipes. I'll be honest, the original MRE version of this particular dish wasn't ever what I'd call a crowd-pleaser. The flavor wasn't necessarily a problem, but the fact that it had to be warmed up in the pockets of my fatigues often made me wonder if the future was really worth fighting for. Thankfully, this era's easy access to fresh ingredients and proper cooking equipment has allowed me to discover what a proper beef stew should taste like. And it's not nearly as bad as I anticipated. Now this meal warms me up instead of the other way around.

2 pounds stew beef, cut into bite-size pieces

Salt and fresh black pepper

4 tablespoons all-purpose flour

1 to 2 tablespoons oil, for pan

2 tablespoons salted butter

1 onion, diced

½ tablespoon dried oregano

1 teaspoon paprika

6 cups vegetable broth

6 medium carrots, cut into bite-size pieces

1 pound new potatoes, left whole if small or cut in half

2½ cups (16 ounces) frozen peas

1. Spread out beef on a baking sheet or cutting board in a single layer, and season well with salt and pepper to taste. Scatter the flour over the beef. Set aside.

2. Heat a large Dutch oven on medium, coat the bottom with oil, and add butter. When the butter begins to foam, add the onion, and sauté until translucent and soft, about 5 minutes. Add oregano and paprika, and cook 1 minute more. Add beef, and brown on all sides (but do not let the beef cook through), 3 to 5 minutes.

3. Add about 2 cups of the broth and use it to deglaze the pan, scraping up the brown bits from the bottom. Add the remaining 4 cups of broth, reduce the heat to low, and simmer for 1 hour.

4. After an hour, add the carrots and the potatoes, and continue simmering until vegetables are tender, about 45 minutes. Add the peas, and bring to a boil for a few minutes, until they are cooked through. Serve hot.

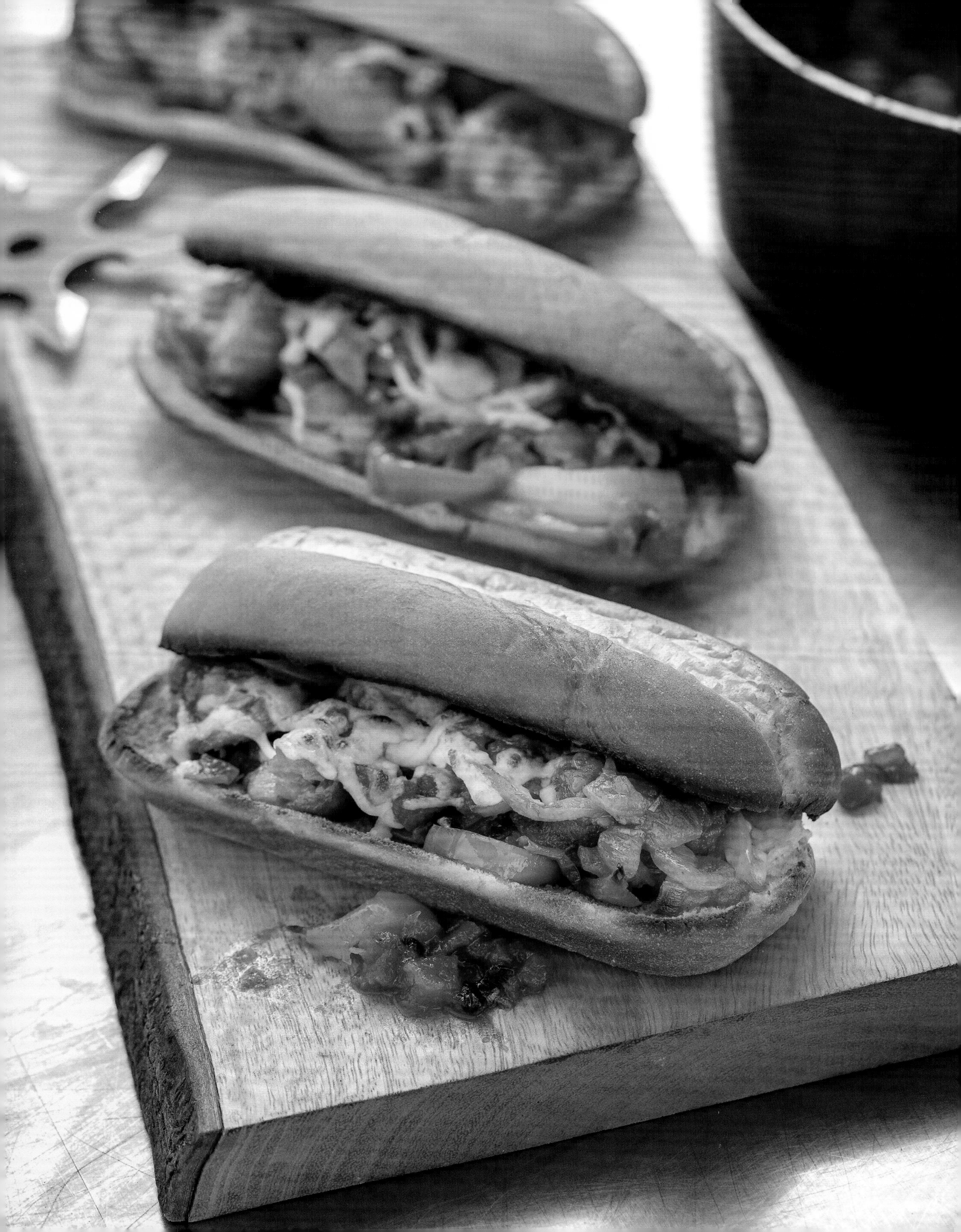

AWESOME SAUSAGE

I'm back! By now it should be clear that I find a significant amount of joy in cooking. But sometimes, all the detailed steps involved in creating a quality meal can be pretty daunting, especially when I've just gotten back from a long day of murder and mayhem. Sometimes the maximum effort I'm capable of is throwing all my ingredients into one big pan and letting it all cook together. Well, good news. For those of you who want all the flavor with only half the hassle, this killer combo of sausage, peppers, and onions gets the job done. There's still some slicing and dicing involved, but we all know that's the fun part anyway. Then it's just a matter of serving it up on a couple of hoagies and enjoying the awesomeness.

1 medium red onion, peeled, halved, and thinly sliced

2 tablespoons olive oil, divided

Salt and fresh black pepper

2 tablespoons light brown sugar

1 medium orange or yellow bell pepper, stemmed, seeded, and thinly sliced

1 medium red bell pepper, stemmed, seeded, and thinly sliced

4 to 6 links (12 ounces) Italian sausage

One 14-ounce can diced tomatoes

1 teaspoon fresh thyme leaves

½ teaspoon finely chopped fresh rosemary leaves

1 clove garlic, minced

4 hoagie rolls

2 cups (8 ounces) shredded mozzarella (optional)

1. Preheat the oven to 425°F, and line a baking sheet with parchment paper.

2. In a medium bowl, toss the onions with 1 tablespoon oil, plus salt and pepper to taste. Spread the onions in an even layer on baking sheet and roast for 7 minutes. Remove pan from oven, push onions to one side, and toss with the brown sugar.

3. In the same bowl, toss the bell peppers with the remaining 1 tablespoon of olive oil, and more salt and pepper. Place peppers in the center of the baking sheet, and place the sausages evenly spaced next to the peppers. Roast until the onions are caramelized and tender, the peppers are soft and charred in spots, and the sausages are cooked through, about 25 minutes. Turn sausages halfway through cooking time.

4. While vegetables and sausages are roasting, prepare tomato sauce. In a medium saucepan on medium heat, bring tomatoes, herbs, and garlic to a simmer. Salt and pepper to taste. Reduce heat, and stir occasionally. Once the sauce has thickened, remove from heat and set aside.

5. Once the sausages have cooked through, remove the pan from the oven, and cut the sausages into bite-size pieces. Add sausages, peppers, and onions to the tomato sauce, and mix together. Remove parchment from baking sheet and discard. Place hoagie buns on baking sheet and toast in the oven for 2 to 3 minutes. Fill the buns with sausage mix, top with mozzarella, if desired, and put back in the oven until cheese melts, about 2 to 3 minutes. Serve immediately.

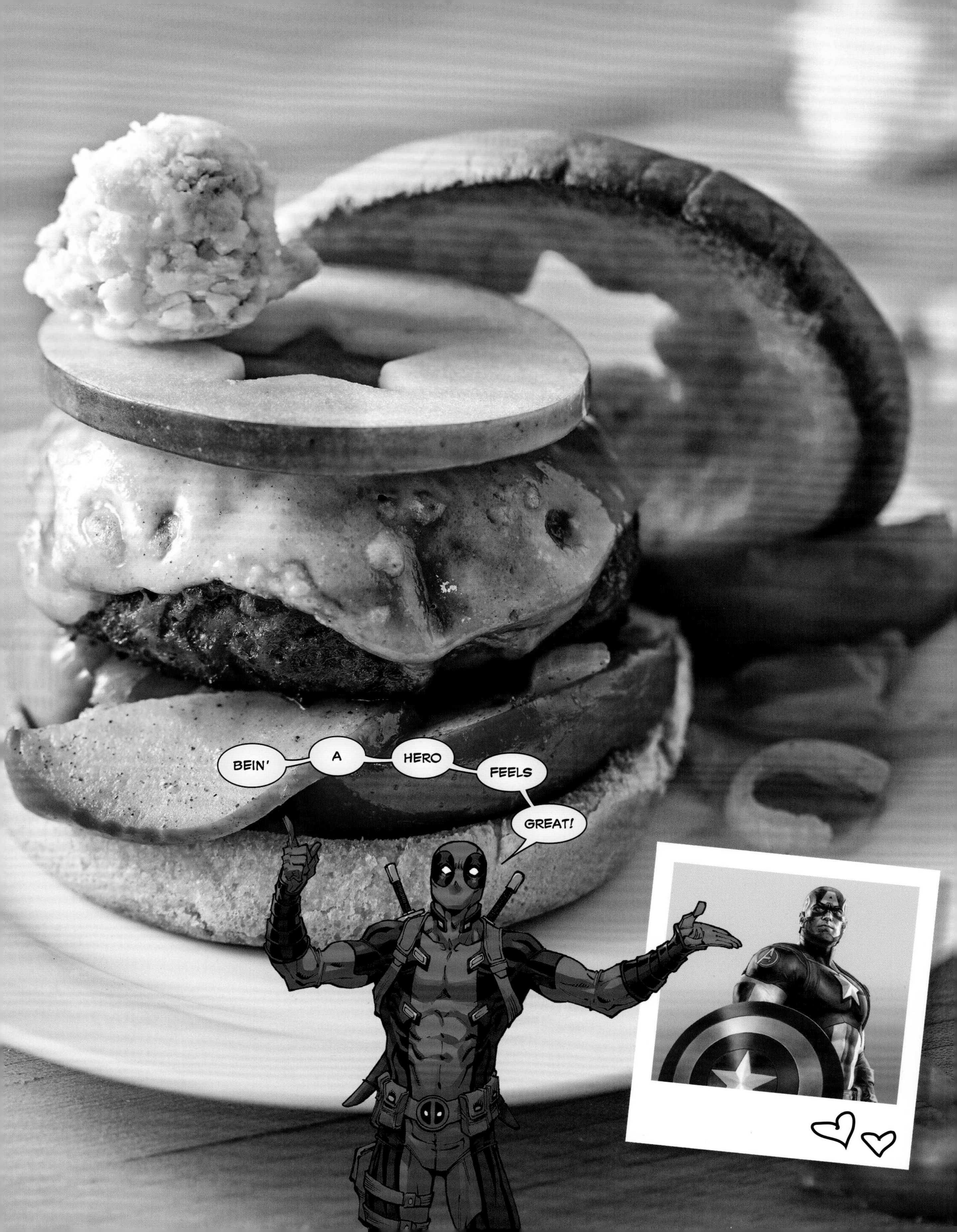
BEIN' A HERO FEELS GREAT!

ALL-AMERICAN BURGER

There are few people in this world who make me stand up and salute like the legendary Super-Soldier known as Captain America. Cap and I have teamed up on a few occasions, and while the big guy might not always approve of my methods, I think he appreciates my gumption. (Old people love gumption.) As a tribute to Mr. Red, White, and Blue Genes himself, I whipped up this special sandwich. The pork-and-beef patty is part hamburger and part hotdog, because I couldn't decide which one was more American. And since there's nothing more patriotic than apple pie, I threw some of those flavors into the mix as well!

FOR THE APPLE PIE FILLING:

2 tablespoons oil

2 tablespoons salted butter

1 onion, halved and sliced

2 apples, skin on, cored and thinly sliced

¼ cup packed light brown sugar

½ teaspoon ground cinnamon

FOR THE PATTIES:

1 pound ground pork

1 pound ground beef

1 tablespoon apple cider vinegar

Salt and fresh black pepper

6 slices white cheddar

FOR ASSEMBLY:

1 apple, skin on, cored and thinly sliced

1 tablespoon apple cider vinegar

6 buns

Butter, for buns

1¼ cup (5 ounces) crumbled blue cheese, divided

SPECIAL SUPPLIES:

Apple corer

1-inch cookie scoop

1½-inch star cookie cutter

Pastry brush

1. To make the apple pie filling: In a large sauté pan, heat oil and butter on medium heat, add onions, and cook about 5 minutes, until onions begin to soften. Add apples, brown sugar, and cinnamon, and cook 5 to 10 minutes more, until apples are tender but not soggy. Remove from heat, and set aside.

2. To make the patties: In a large bowl, combine pork, beef, vinegar, and salt and pepper to taste. Form meat mixture into 6 equal patties, and grill or fry as desired, melting a slice of cheddar on each patty toward the end of cooking.

3. To assemble: While the patties are cooking, preheat the oven to 375°F.

4. In a small bowl, toss the apple slices with the vinegar, and set aside.

5. Take the bottom of each bun, and press the center of the bread with your fingers, making a "dish" of each one. If desired, use the cookie cutter to cut a small star in the top of each bun and each round apple slice (see page 62). Spread butter on both sides of each bun, and toast in the oven for 5 to 7 minutes, until crisp and golden.

6. Fill each bottom bun "dish" with a generous scoop of apple filling. Place a burger patty on the bottom half of each bun, topped with an apple slice and a small scoop of blue cheese. Finish with top bun "shield."

MAKING THE ALL-AMERICAN BURGER

1.

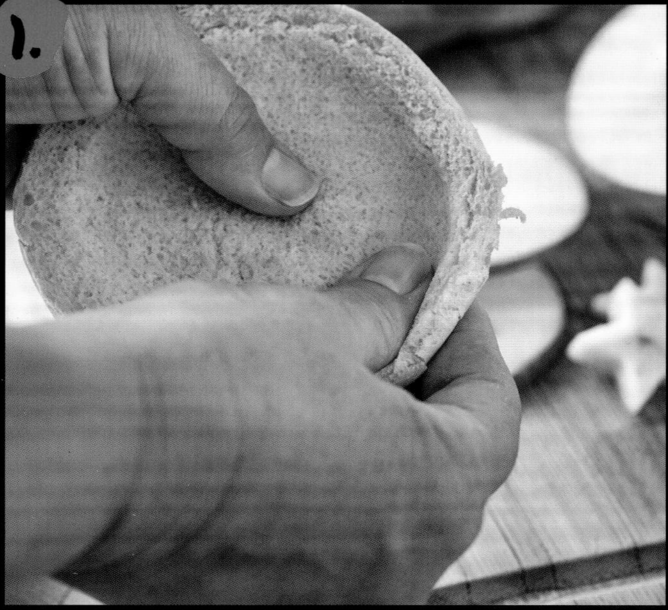

2.

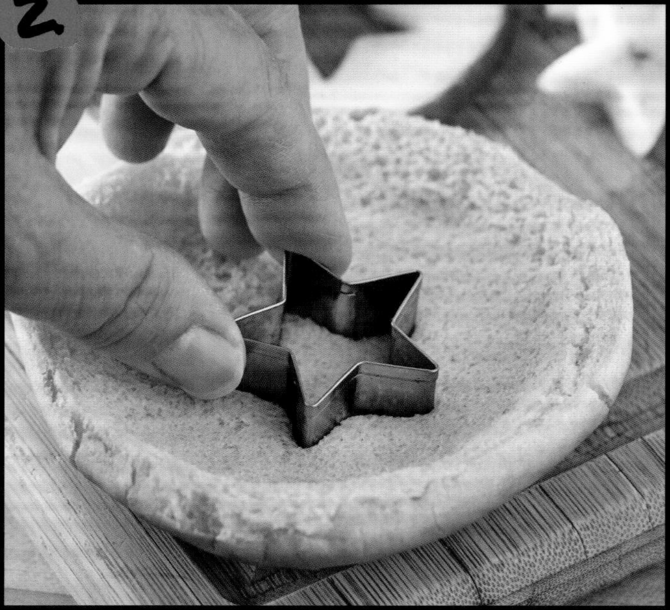

3.

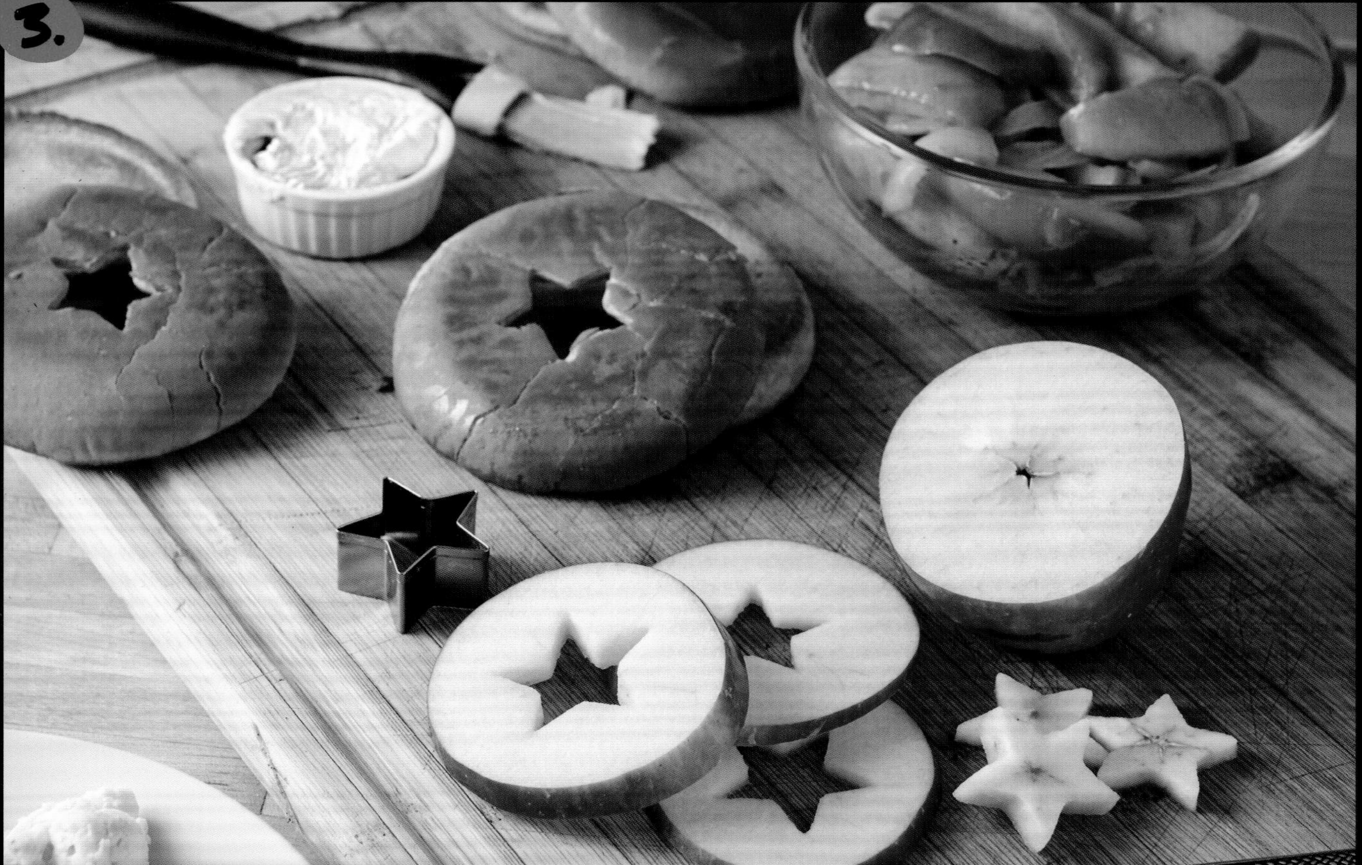

JUST THE TIPS:
TENDERIZING MEAT

As much as I love chomping into a thick slab of meat, some recipes require a bit more tenderness. Here's how to achieve a proper thinness for your protein, with the added bonus of releasing some serious aggression along the way:

1. Hit meat with hammer. Done.

2. Just kidding. (Sorta.) For a perfect *paillard*, place the chicken breast between two layers of parchment paper. Even my healing factor ain't a fan of salmonella.

3. Pound your meat with the flat side of a chef's mallet until it's nice and thin.

4. Don't have a mallet? Wait, who doesn't have a mallet?! I have, like, twelve! I guess you can always use the side of an unopened can of food instead. Just wrap that in plastic too, unless you want it to get all sticky. (You know, from the meat pounding.)

5. If you do have mallet, remember, the spiky side is only for puncturing holes into the meat for marinating. And also for fighting Hydra.

6. Now remove the parchment paper and—voilà!—meat so thin you could read a comic book through it. (But would you really want to?)

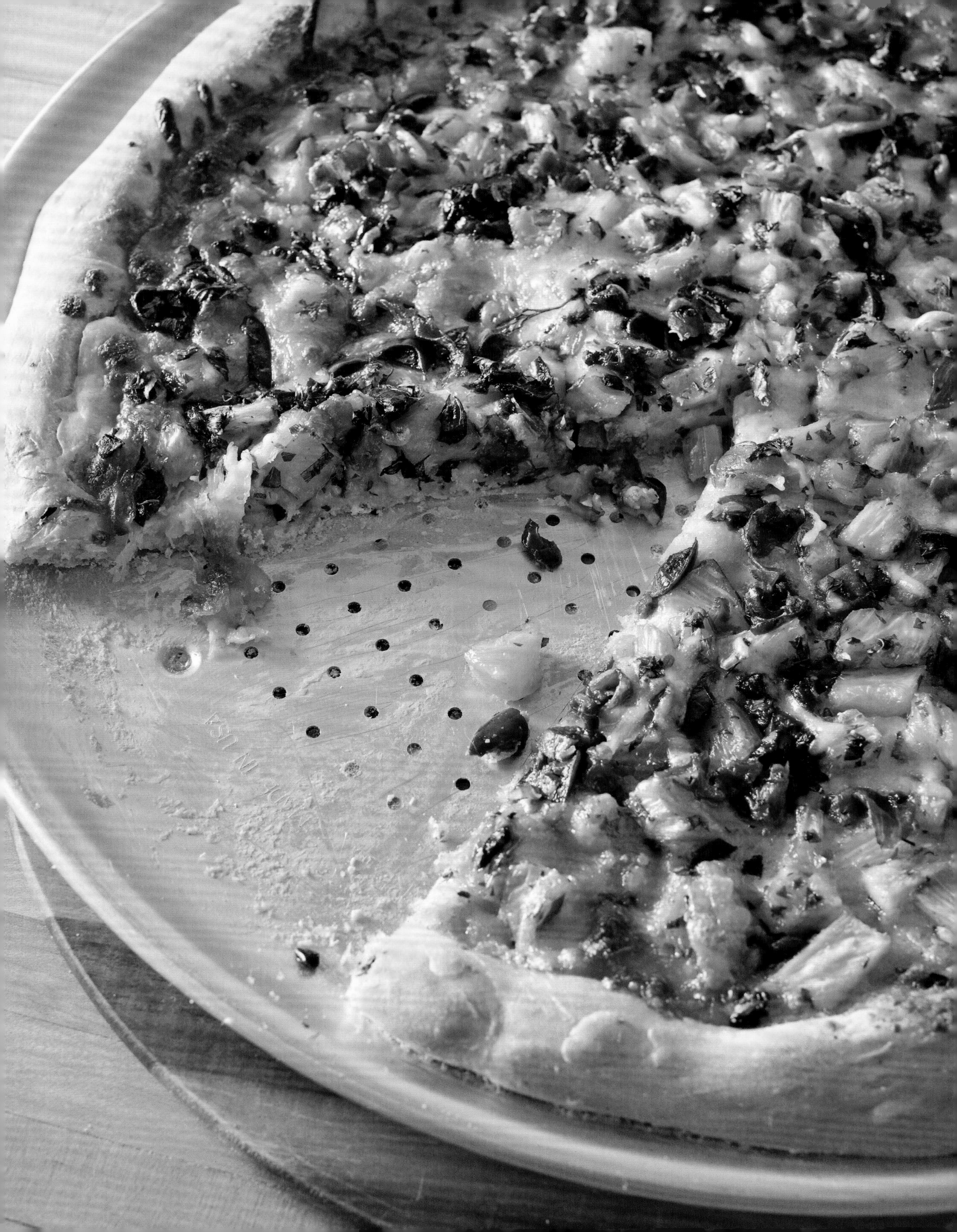

It's Not Delivery, It's Deadpool

YIELD: TWO 12-INCH PIZZA PIES

Being a mercenary isn't always glamorous work, but it has given me the opportunity to travel the world. If I've learned one thing on my adventures, it's that good pizza is hard to find. Sure, everyone claims they make the perfect pie, but if you're eating one outside Italy or New York City, you're basically just eating hot discs of mediocrity. Or, if you're in Chicago, three-inch-thick slices of sausage cake. For those of us tired of being disappointed by delivery, here's a homemade pizza designed to please. Top it with whatever you want, but I prefer mine with pineapple and olives. That might not appeal to everyone, but I promise it's infinitely better than whatever they're trying to pass off as pizza in Cleveland these days.

FOR THE DOUGH:

1⅓ cup warm water, around 100°F

1 tablespoon sugar

1 package (2¼ teaspoons) active dry yeast

3 tablespoons olive oil, plus more for bowl

3½ cups all-purpose flour, plus more for work surface

1 tablespoon salt

FOR THE TOPPINGS:

1 cup kalamata olives, pitted, drained, and roughly chopped

½ fresh pineapple, drained and roughly chopped into chunks (about 2 cups)

1 tablespoon olive oil, plus more for crust

1 tablespoon balsamic vinegar

Pinch dried rosemary, ground between fingers or smashed with a knife

1 cup loosely packed fresh parsley leaves, minced

Fresh black pepper

1¾ cups (6 ounces) shredded mozzarella

3 ounces prosciutto, cut into ribbons

FOR THE SAUCE:

½ cup heavy cream

1 cup finely grated Parmesan

1. To make the crust: In a small bowl, mix the water with the sugar and sprinkle with the yeast. Set aside until the yeast is foamy, about 5 minutes. Stir in the olive oil.

2. In the bowl of a stand mixer fitted with a dough hook, mix the flour and salt. Add the yeast mixture, and stir on low until the dough begins to pull away from the bowl. Tip the dough onto a floured surface, and knead by hand (you can also use the dough hook in the mixer on low) for about 10 minutes, until the dough is elastic. Transfer dough into a large oiled bowl, turn the dough in the bowl to coat with olive oil, cover with plastic wrap, and leave in a warm place to rise until double in size, about 1½ hours.

3. Punch down the dough, divide it in half, roll it into 2 balls, and let rest 10 to 15 minutes. On a lightly floured surface, roll or stretch into pizza rounds and place on parchment paper. Preheat the oven to 425°F.

4. To make the pizza topping: In a large bowl, combine all topping ingredients, except mozzarella and prosciutto. Set aside. In a small bowl, make a slurry by mixing the heavy cream and the Parmesan. Set aside.

5. To assemble: Brush pizza dough lightly with olive oil, spread evenly with half the sauce, and sprinkle with half the mozzarella and half the pineapple-olive mixture. Top with half the prosciutto ribbons. Repeat with the second pizza crust, using the remaining toppings. Bake for 10 to 12 minutes, until crust is golden brown and cheese is bubbly. Serve hot.

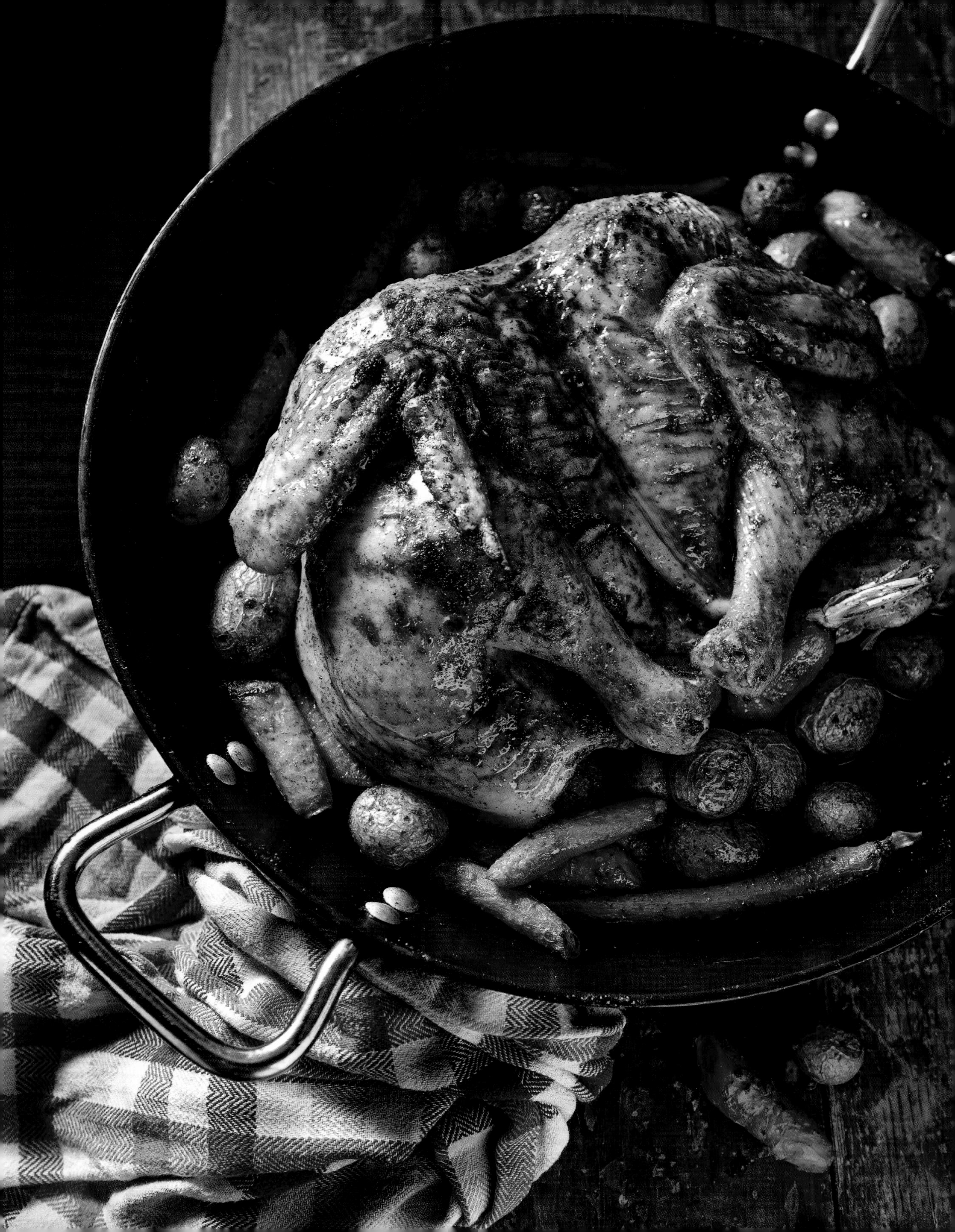

Spatchcocked Chicken

Yield: 4 servings

Little known fact: "SPATCHCOCK!" is the exact sound made when you run a super-villain through with your ninja sword at extremely high velocity. (I've got recordings if you don't believe me.) I'm pretty sure that's not even remotely close to how this crispy-skinned chicken got its ridiculous name, yet somehow it's still oddly appropriate. Why? Because this one takes some legit skills with a blade to properly prepare. Lucky for you, we've devoted two whole pages to helping you figure out how to carve that carcass without massacring the meat. Some folks might call this particular technique "butterflying" your bird, but life doesn't give you very many opportunities to say "*spatchcock!*" so you'd be a fool to pass this one up.

3- to 4-pound whole chicken, spatchcocked (see page 68)

½ tablespoon ground cumin

½ tablespoon chili powder

1 teaspoon fresh black pepper

½ teaspoon cayenne pepper

½ teaspoon allspice

4 tablespoons (½ stick) salted butter, softened

2 pounds new potatoes (optional)

4 to 5 large carrots (optional)

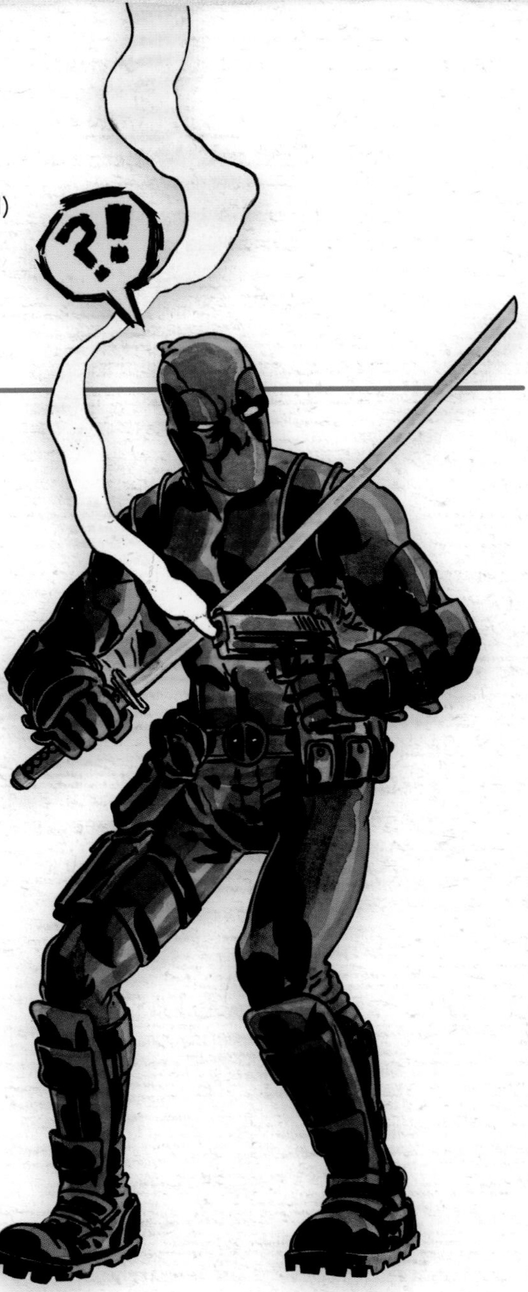
?!

1. Preheat the oven to 450°F. Select a roasting pan large enough to hold the chicken and vegetables, if using.
2. In a small bowl, blend all the spices into the softened butter.
3. Place your chicken in the roasting pan, and gently use your fingers to loosen the skin from the breast meat. Rub spice butter between the skin and the breast meat. Once the breast meat is coated, rub the rest of the spice butter on the outside of the entire chicken. Position the roasting pan in the oven with the legs of the bird facing the back of the oven. Roast for 10 minutes, remove pan from oven, and reduce heat to 400°F.
4. Add vegetables, if using, tucking them around the bird. Return pan to the oven and roast for another 20 to 30 minutes or until the internal temperature reaches 155°F in the thickest part of the thigh (temperature will continue to rise during resting). Remove from the oven, tent with foil, and let rest another 15 minutes, or until internal temperature is 165°F, before carving.

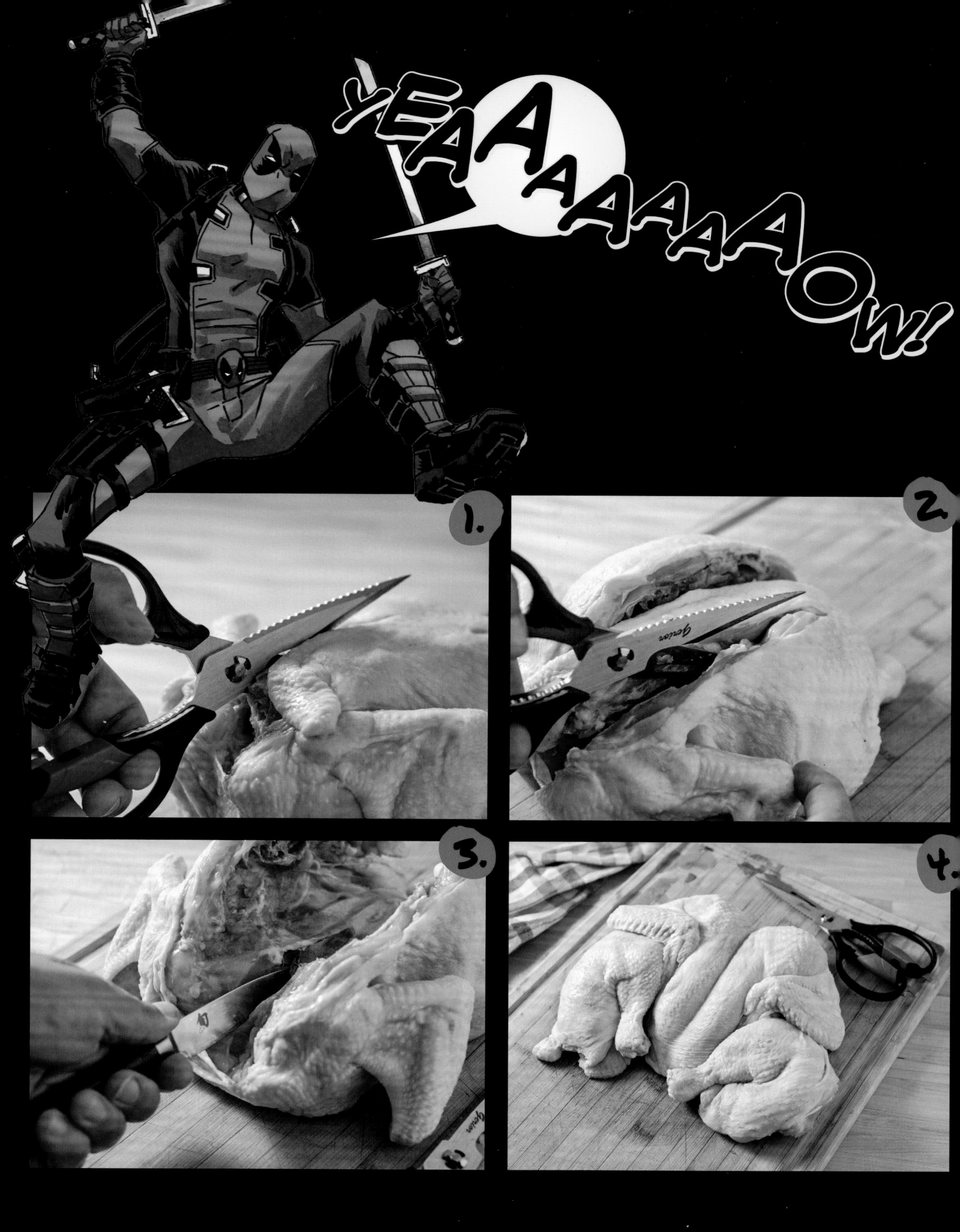
YEAAAAAAAAOW!
1.
2.
3.
4.

Just the Tips:
Spatchcocking a Chicken

I told you we were gonna spatchcock, kids, and you didn't believe me, did you? Well, guess what? Here it is . . . the moment you've been waiting for. No, not the end of this book, smartass. It's spatchcockin' time!

1. First, lay the bird breast side down on the table with its legs facing away from you. Then, apologize for the terrible things you're about to do to it.

2. Use kitchen shears to cut along each side of the backbone. Remove the backbone and save it for stock or to use as a tiny xylophone for your action figures.

3. Now, stick your fingers right in that empty chest cavity and find the area of cartilage directly above the breastbone. But be respectful. She's a lady.

4. Using a paring knife, cut into the cartilage about a quarter-inch, so the breastbone is exposed. (Anyone else feeling a bit squeamish?)

5. Pop that breastbone right through the hole—gross, but hilarious!—and lay that bird out nice and flat.

6. If you want to make it even flatter and slightly more ridiculous, flip the bird over and tuck its wing tips into its tiny little armpits. (I'm not kidding.)

7. Congratulations! You've spatchcocked, baby!

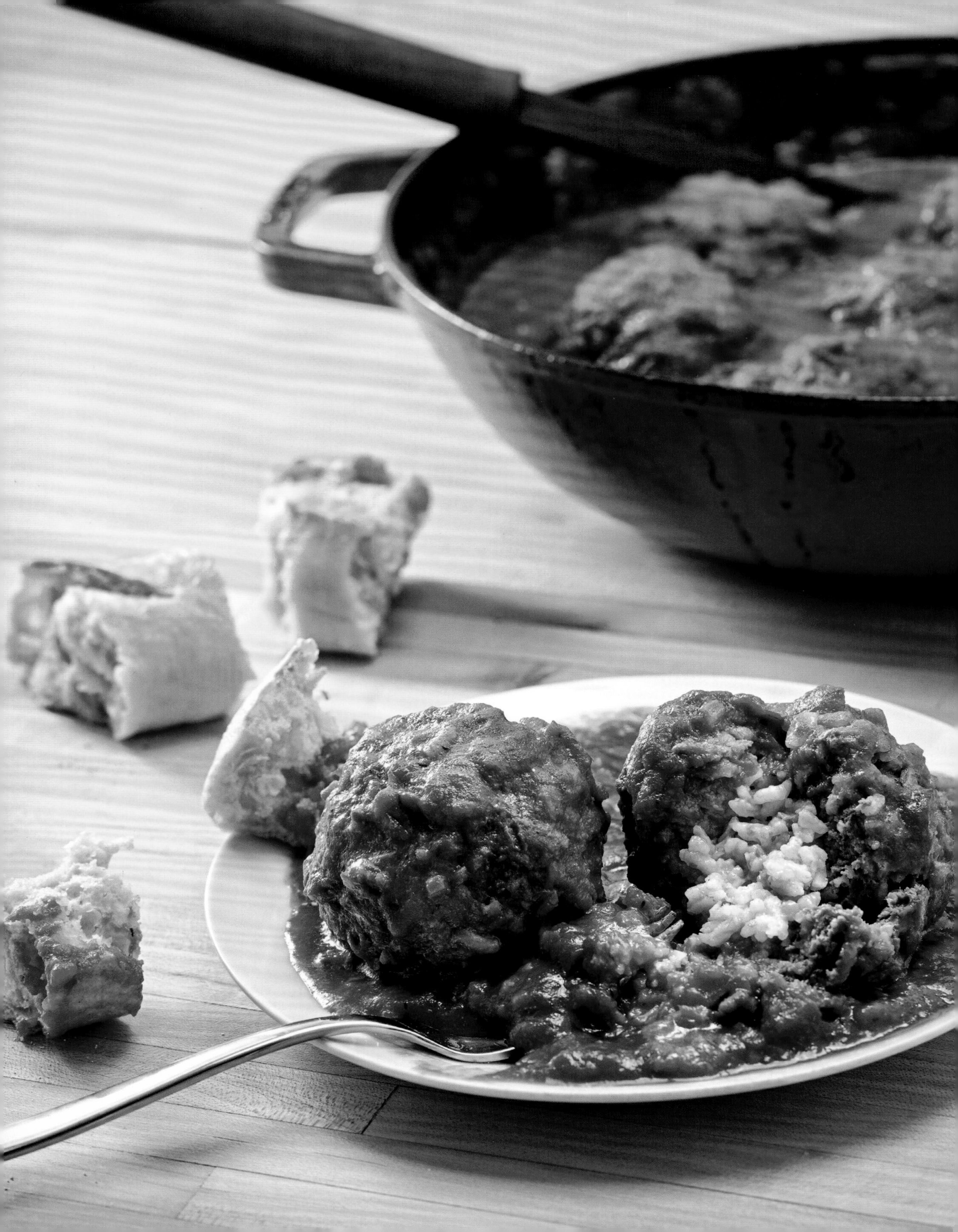

Bozhe Meat

YIELD: TEN 6-OUNCE MEATBALLS

I've said it before and I'll say it again: Piotr Nikolaievitch Rasputin is one handsome hunk of meat. Did you know that the first time Colossus manifested his metallic mutant muscles, he stopped a tractor with his bare hands? True story. The guy even has a move called the "fastball special" where he hurls Wolverine through the air at their enemies. Wolverine! Sure, Logan may look small, but his bones are covered in Adamantium alloy, which means he weighs more than the Blob! But does Pete seem to notice? I think *nyet!* One bite of these meaty balls and you'll be yelling "*Bozhe Moi!*," which I've always assumed is Russian for "Beef Man!" (I should probably look that up someday.)

FOR THE SAUCE:

1 to 2 tablespoons oil, for pan

1 small onion, diced

1 large carrot, grated

One 28-ounce can crushed tomatoes

One 30-ounce can tomato puree or sauce

2 tablespoons maple syrup or light brown sugar

1 teaspoon dried thyme

2 dried bay leaves

Pinch red pepper flakes

Salt and fresh black pepper

FOR THE MEATBALLS:

2 pounds lean ground beef

2 cups cooked basmati or jasmine rice, cooled

2 teaspoons salt

1 shallot, minced

2 cloves garlic, minced

1 large egg

FOR THE FILLING:

1 cup cooked basmati or jasmine rice

⅓ cup milk

2 tablespoons salted butter, melted and cooled

½ teaspoon salt

Pinch ground cloves

Fresh parsley, for garnish

Crusty bread or cooked rice, for serving

SPECIAL SUPPLIES:

2½-inch cookie scoop

1. To make the sauce: Heat the oil in a large Dutch oven on medium heat, and add the onions. Cook, stirring frequently, until well caramelized, 10 to 15 minutes. Add the grated carrot, and cook 3 to 5 minutes more. Add the remaining ingredients, and bring everything to a low boil. Reduce heat to low, and let sauce simmer, partially covered, while preparing meatballs.
2. To make the meatballs: In a large bowl, combine the beef, rice, salt, shallot, and garlic. Add the egg, and mix until it just comes together, being careful not to overwork the meat.
3. To make the filling: In a medium bowl, combine the rice, milk, butter, salt, and clove.
4. Use a 2½-inch cookie scoop to create a ball of the meat mixture. Make a large indentation in the ball, and add 2 tablespoons of the rice filling. Smooth the meat over the rice and gently shape into a ball. Set aside, and repeat. When all the balls have been filled and formed, gently lower them into the sauce with a spoon or ladle, doing your best not to crowd them. Bring sauce back up to a simmer, and cook 25 to 35 minutes, until the balls are cooked through.
5. Plate the meatballs with generous helpings of sauce and sprinkle with chopped fresh parsley. Serve with crusty bread or more rice to sop up sauce.

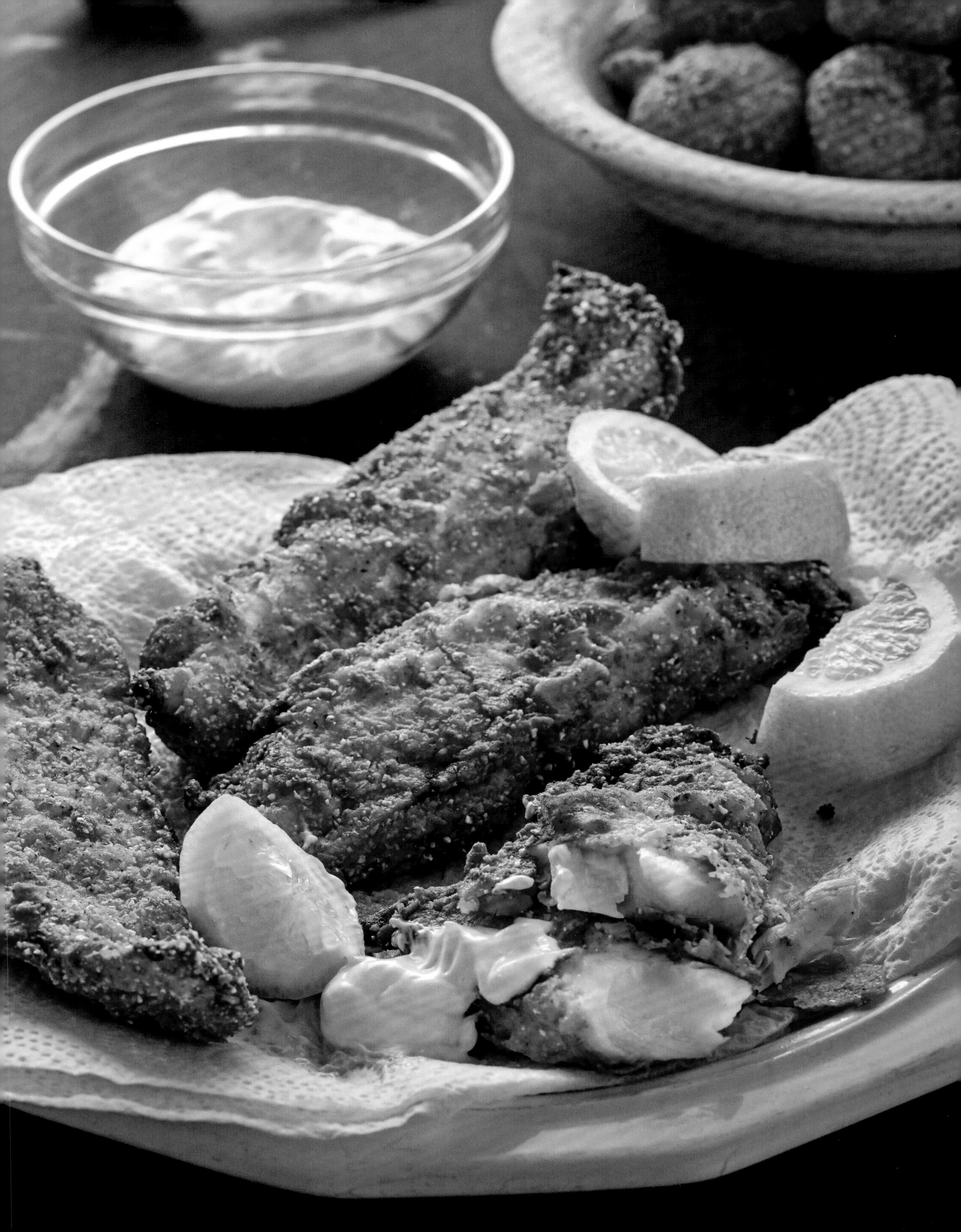

NOT THE ONLY FISH IN THE SEA

YIELD: 4 SERVINGS

I've had a lot of romances over the years. Vanessa. Siryn. Outlaw. Shiklah. Your mom. I even had a thing for Death herself for a while. And even though I'm back to being a bachelor these days, I still pay tribute to my lady loves every now and then by cooking up their favorite meal, lighting some candles, and dressing a mannequin in some of their spare clothes I never bothered to return. Back in that hot minute I was attempting to woo Rogue, I tried to impress her by whipping up some authentic down-home Southern vittles, like this here catfish dish. Our fling was short-lived, but thanks to this recipe, the memory lives on. (Which, when it comes to Rogue, is pretty rare.)

FOR THE MARINADE:

2 cups buttermilk

2 teaspoons Old Bay or other seafood seasoning

½ teaspoon cayenne pepper

2 pounds catfish or tilapia fillets, halved

FOR THE DREDGE:

1½ cups all-purpose flour

1 cup yellow cornmeal

¾ teaspoon fresh black pepper

¾ teaspoon paprika

¾ teaspoon cayenne pepper

1½ teaspoons Old Bay or other seafood seasoning

FOR FRYING:

About 2 quarts oil, such as peanut or canola, for frying

Salt and fresh black pepper

Lemon wedges, for serving

Tartar sauce, for serving

Look at Them Puppies! (page 25), for serving

1. To make the marinade: Combine the ingredients in a container that can hold the fillets, submerge them, cover, and marinate for half an hour to 1 hour.
2. To make the dredge: While the fish is marinating, combine the dredge ingredients in a shallow container.
3. To fry: Set up your fry station (page 91), and bring oil to 365°F. Remove each piece of fish from the marinade, letting the excess liquid drip off, and place in the dredge, turning to make sure each side is well coated. Fry each piece in oil until the crust is a deep golden brown and the fish is flaky but moist. Remove to a paper-towel-covered plate to drain. Salt and pepper each side to taste.
4. Serve with wedges of lemon, tartar sauce, and Look at Them Puppies!

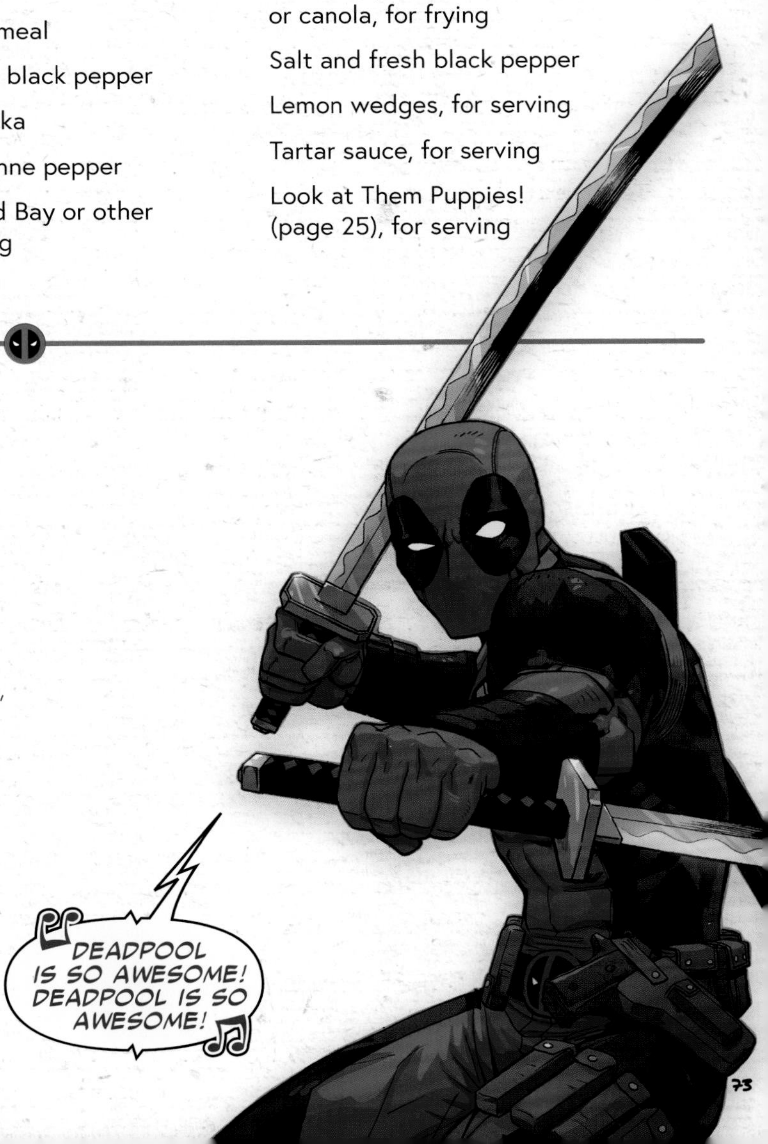
DEADPOOL IS SO AWESOME! DEADPOOL IS SO AWESOME!

READY OR NAUT

Ever since he got his hands on the Crimson Gem of Cyttorak and gained the power of the Juggernaut, Cain Marko has been eager to remind anyone who will listen that nothing can stop him. Well, if that were the case, he would have trampled me under his ridiculously large metal boots a long time ago. Turns out there are a lot of things that can stop the Juggernaut, the easiest of which is cooking him up a good meal. After all, a fella that big isn't fueled on demonic energy alone. When I'm entertaining someone with an appetite as huge as Juggy's, this classic coffee-rubbed tri-tip never fails. It satisfies even the biggest eater and gives them an extra burst of energy that will make them feel unstoppable without all the hassle of becoming the earthly avatar of some ancient demon-god.

2 to 3 teaspoons kosher salt

2 to 3 tablespoons unsweetened cocoa powder

2- to 3-pound tri-tip, trimmed

4 garlic cloves, smashed and peeled

1 cup strong brewed coffee, room temperature

¼ cup balsamic vinegar

¼ cup brown sugar

¼ cup olive oil

1 teaspoon fresh coarsely ground black pepper

1. Mix the salt and cocoa powder together in a small bowl. Rub the mixture over the surface of the meat, and set the meat aside.

2. Mix all the other ingredients together to make the marinade, and pour it into a large resealable plastic bag or container that can be flipped without leaking. Add the meat, making sure it gets thoroughly coated in marinade.

3. Refrigerate for at least 4 hours and as many as 8. Flip marinade container halfway through, or, if using a bag, reposition and massage.

4. Heat grill to 350°F. Cook tri-tip, rotating the meat so it gets brown on all sides, for 30 minutes or until internal temperature reaches 140°F (medium rare). Remove meat to serving dish, cover with foil, and let rest 15 minutes before carving.

5. Prefer not to grill? Brown the tri-tip on all sides in an oven-safe sauté pan, then transfer to a 350°F oven. Cook for 20 to 30 minutes, until internal temperature reaches 140°F.

> **TIP:**
> MAKE SURE THE MEAT IS PROPERLY TRIMMED BEFORE IT HITS THE GRILL. JUGGY MAY BE HUGE, BUT HE'S GOT, LIKE, ZERO EXCESS FAT. YOUR MEAT SHOULD FOLLOW SUIT.

Casserole, Agent of Tuna

I've taken out hordes of henchmen over the years, but every once in a while, a potential nameless target ends up becoming a dear and trusted friend instead. Bob, Agent of Hydra, was just another cog in the terrorist machine until I tortured him into switching sides and becoming my loyal companion. He may not have had super-powers, adequate combat training, or even an ounce of courage, but he sure had heart. (And plenty of other organs that my enemies could shoot at while I tried to get my job done.) He also had a wife who was one hell of a cook. I probably would have ditched Bob a lot sooner if he wasn't constantly trying to win my affection with casseroles like these. To be honest, I haven't called Bob in a while . . . but I've still got his wife on speed dial.

Vegetable oil, for casserole dish and pan

1 pound pasta, such as bow-tie, elbow, or penne

3 to 5 center stalks celery, leaves included, chopped

1 shallot, minced

1 teaspoon salt

One 24-ounce can tuna, packed in water, drained

½ cup chopped fresh parsley, divided

½ cup (1 stick, or 8 tablespoons) salted butter, divided

6 tablespoons all-purpose flour

3 cups milk

½ teaspoon paprika

1¼ cup (8 ounces) frozen peas

1 sleeve saltine crackers, smashed to a coarse crumb

1. Preheat the oven to 375°F. Grease a 3-quart casserole dish with oil.

2. Cook the pasta according to package directions. Drain and set aside, reserving ½ cup of the pasta water.

3. Heat a large sauté pan on medium, and add oil to coat. Add celery, shallot, and salt. Sauté until transparent and soft. Add tuna, ¼ cup of the parsley, and the reserved pasta water, and continue to cook until liquid is absorbed. Remove the pan from heat, and set aside.

4. In a large saucepan on medium heat, combine 4 tablespoons of the butter with the flour, stirring constantly until a smooth paste has formed. Slowly whisk in milk, add paprika, and continue to cook until sauce has thickened. Turn off heat, and stir in peas.

5. In a large bowl or the pasta pot, combine pasta, tuna mixture, and sauce. In a small sauté pan, melt the remaining 4 tablespoons of butter and toss with saltine crumbs and the remaining ¼ cup of parsley. Turn casserole mixture into the casserole dish, and top with cracker mixture.

6. Bake until topping is golden and casserole is bubbly, about 30 minutes.

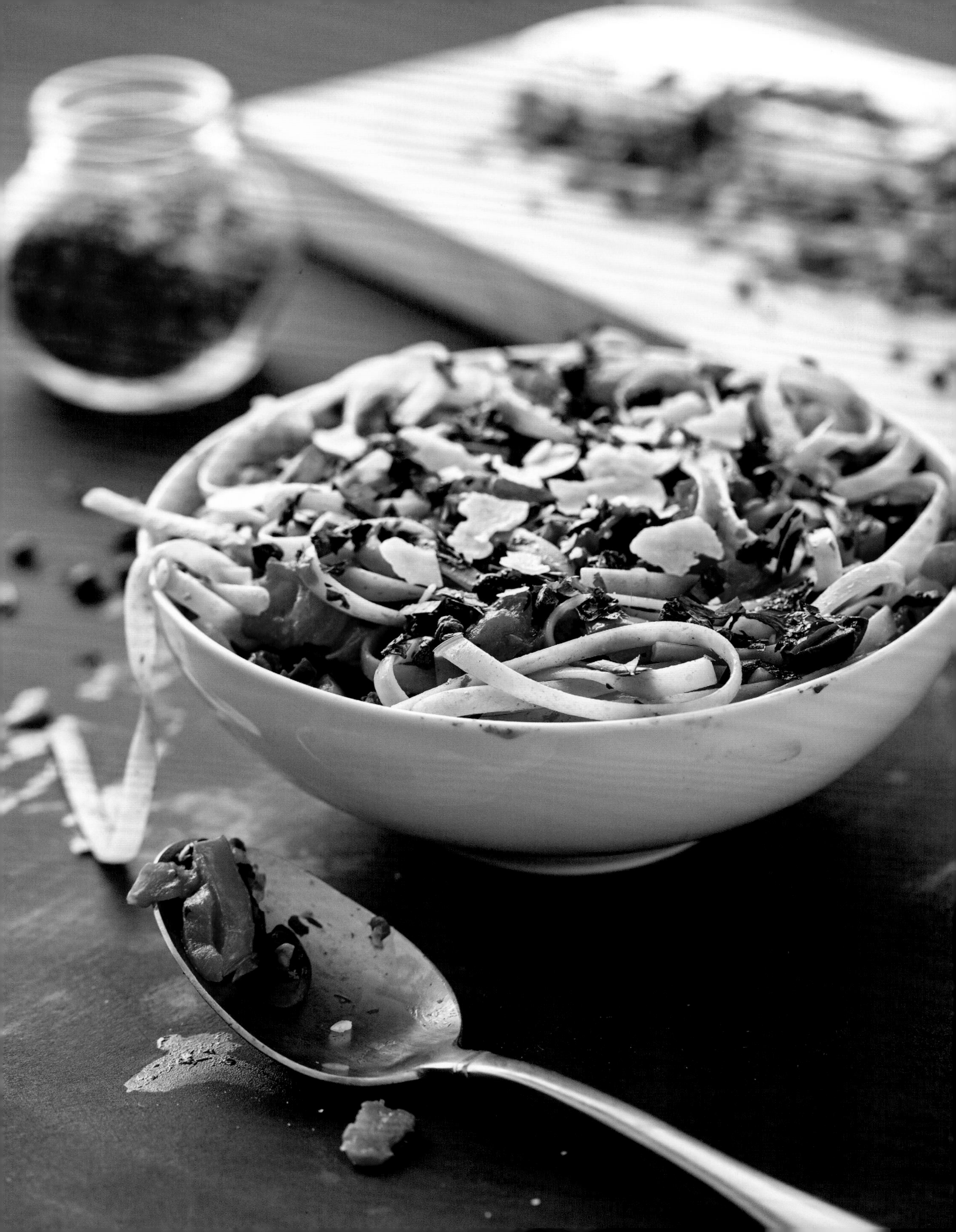

Shiklah's Special Sauce

Yield: 6 servings

So I got married once. It started out as your typical "boy meets Queen of the Undead" type of romance, but it eventually turned into a real nightmare. Who would have expected? Turns out the former Mrs. Deadpool, a succubus named Shiklah, never really believed in the sanctity of matrimony. (Particularly ours.) And while we may have had some fun ruling the monster underworld side-by-side, we just weren't meant to be. Now, when I catch myself reminiscing about all the glorious crimson carnage Shiklah and I used to create together, I just whip up a pan of this puttanesca sauce and try to find some "better" in all of the "worse."

2 pounds Roma tomatoes, diced

4 to 6 cloves garlic, chopped

1 teaspoon sea salt

¼ teaspoon red pepper flakes

3 tablespoons olive oil, divided

¼ cup capers

1 cup loosely packed fresh parsley leaves, roughly chopped

1 cup kalamata olives, pitted and roughly chopped

2 to 3 anchovy fillets, roughly chopped

1 pound dried pasta

Parmesan (optional)

1. Preheat the oven to 375°F.
2. On a large rimmed baking sheet, toss the tomatoes, garlic, salt, red pepper flakes, and 2 tablespoons of olive oil. Spread the mixture out in a single layer, and roast for 20 minutes, then remove from the oven.
3. Raise the oven temperature to 400°F. On a separate rimmed baking sheet, toss the capers, half the parsley, and the remaining tablespoon of olive oil. Toss the olives and anchovies with the tomato mixture on the first baking sheet, then put both sheets in the oven to roast for 10 minutes.
4. Cook the pasta according to package directions, and reserve a ladleful of pasta water.
5. In a large serving bowl, combine tomato mixture, pasta, reserved pasta water, and remaining parsley. Divide into bowls, and top with the fried caper and parsley mixture. Serve with Parmesan, if desired.

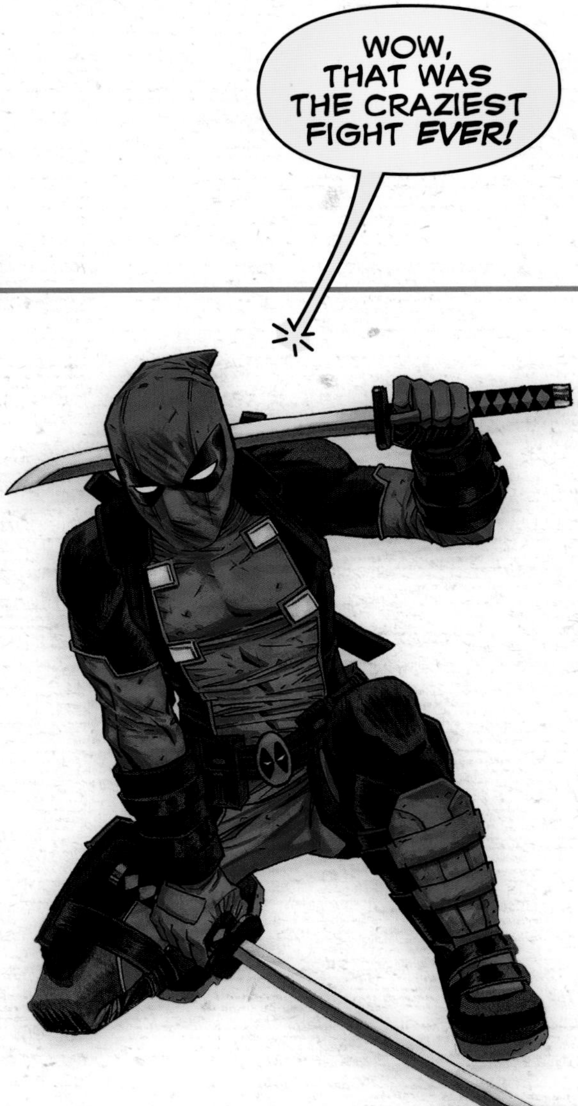
WOW, THAT WAS THE CRAZIEST FIGHT EVER!

HOW'S IT STILL SO CHILI?

YIELD: 20 SERVINGS

Humans have made a lot of revolutionary advances over the years, but they still base their February weather forecast on whether or not a random rodent happens to be scared of its own shadow. Stuff like that almost makes me agree with Magneto. Maybe mankind's time as the dominant species is behind us after all. I mean, I'm no fancy groundhog meteorologist, but even I can tell you with pretty reliable accuracy that February is going to be damn cold, shadow or not. To get me through those bitter winter days, I like to cook up a nice big pot of this white bean chili. With a mix of green chiles and jalapeños, it's got just enough heat to keep my insides nice and toasty until the platypus sees its reflection and summer finally arrives. Or whatever.

4 tablespoons (½ stick) salted butter

1 white onion, diced

5 cups vegetable stock

1 teaspoon ground cumin

1 teaspoon white pepper

2 dried bay leaves

1 pound dried northern beans, soaked according to package directions

Two 15-ounce cans cannellini beans with liquid

One 7-ounce can diced mild green chiles

One 4-ounce can diced jalapeños

Shredded Monterey Jack, for garnish (optional)

Fresh cilantro, for garnish (optional)

Muffin to See Here (page 107), for serving

1. Melt the butter in a large soup pot on medium heat. Add the onion, and sauté until translucent. Add the stock, spices, beans, and chiles. Bring to a boil, then reduce heat to low, and cook 1½ to 2 hours, until beans are tender.
2. Serve topped with shredded Monterey Jack and cilantro sprigs, if you like. Serve with Muffin to See Here.

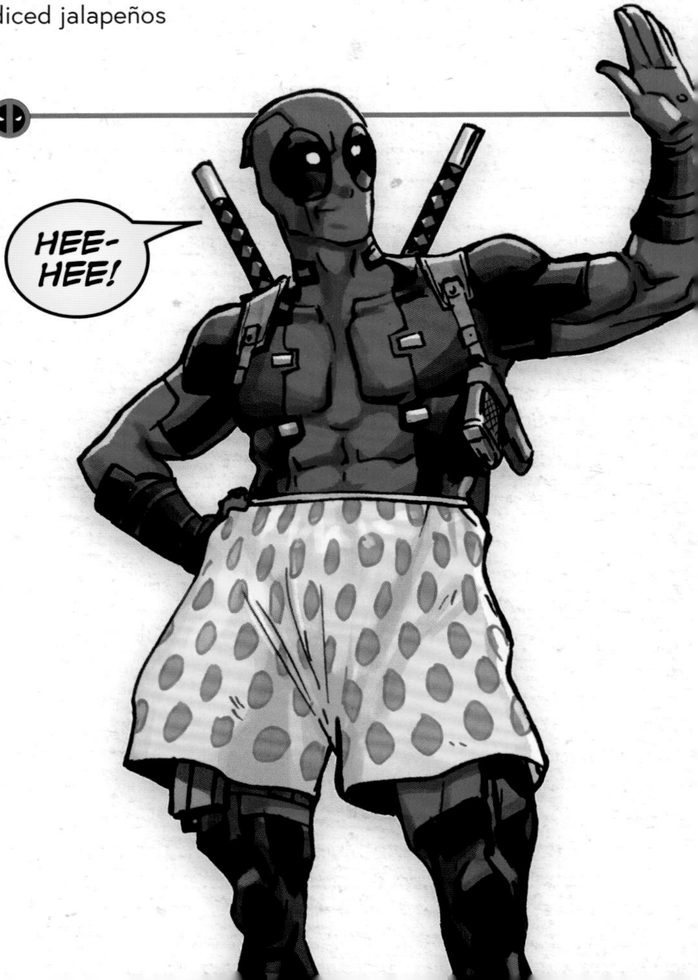
HEE-HEE!

TIP:

THE JALAPEÑOS IN THIS DISH ARE SPICY ENOUGH ON THEIR OWN, SO UNLESS YOU WANT YOUR TONGUE TO SPONTANEOUSLY COMBUST, BE SURE TO USE ONLY MILD CHILES.

JUST THE TIPS:
ORDERING TAKEOUT

Sometimes even the best chef botches a meal. Make sure you have a solid backup plan so you don't have to suffer your way through the charred remains of your horrendous failure:

• Stock a drawer full of menus from local eateries. Preferably ones that deliver.

• Call said eateries and order an item of food off the menu. Any item will do! Except Combo #27. (Really, has anyone ever ordered that?!)

• Wait with a sense of relief as the food is prepared somewhere other than in your nightmare of a kitchen.

• When someone arrives at the door, open it. If it isn't the person with the food, punch them in the face because your hunger has driven you into a blind rage.

• Accept the food from the delivery person and give them the required amount of money. And don't forget to tip! (I'm a mercenary, not a monster!)

• Drown your sorrows in a sea of calories as you try forgetting this whole experience ever happened.

• Try again tomorrow.

WHAT THE PEOPLE REALLY WANT

We've made our way through the meat of the book now (see what I did there?), so this seems like the perfect time to put our knives down and sort through some of our initial reader reactions. Go ahead and reach into Postman Wade's mailbag so we can all get a good feel for what my adoring public thinks about my culinary craftsmanship.

> DEAR DEADPOOL,
>
> YOUR COOKBOOK IS LOTS OF FUN. BUT YOUR FANS ARE DYING TO KNOW: WHERE ARE THE CHIMICHANGAS? I THOUGHT YOU LOVED THOSE THINGS! LET'S GET COOKING!
>
> YOUR DEVOTED FAN,
>
> STEVE

Well, Steve, I understand how you might think this book would have been filled with nothing but chimichanga recipes, based on my undying obsession with that word and, on occasion, the tasty treat to which it is attached. But I really saw this project as a chance for me to step outside my comfort zone and move beyond what most people would immediately expect from me. For once, I'd like the opportunity for some personal growth that isn't a tumor on my face, you know what I'm saying? Next!

First, who names their kid Gordon anymore? Second, as I mentioned above, there is far more to life than crispy tortillas jam-packed with mouth-watering fillings. Hard to believe, I know. Now, let's see what else we've got in here . . .

Another request for chimichangas . . . a death threat regarding the absence of chimichangas . . . an overdue gas bill . . . another chimi lover . . . someone wants the recipe for "chipachangos," whatever the hell those are . . . chimis again . . . a letter from someone named Jimmy Chongaz.

Okay, you know what? Fine. You want this monkey to dance? I'll dance. That'll teach me for trying to expand my horizons. Deadpool's not technically a mutant anyway, right? So why should he be able to evolve? Here you go, you unimaginative jerks. Chimichangas galore! Are you happy now?! Well, you should be . . . because, I gotta admit, these things are freakin' delicious. (Why was I angry again?)

'Sup 'Pool?!

Where my chimis at, bro??!!!?!?

Gordon

DEADPOOL'S
CHIMICHANGAS

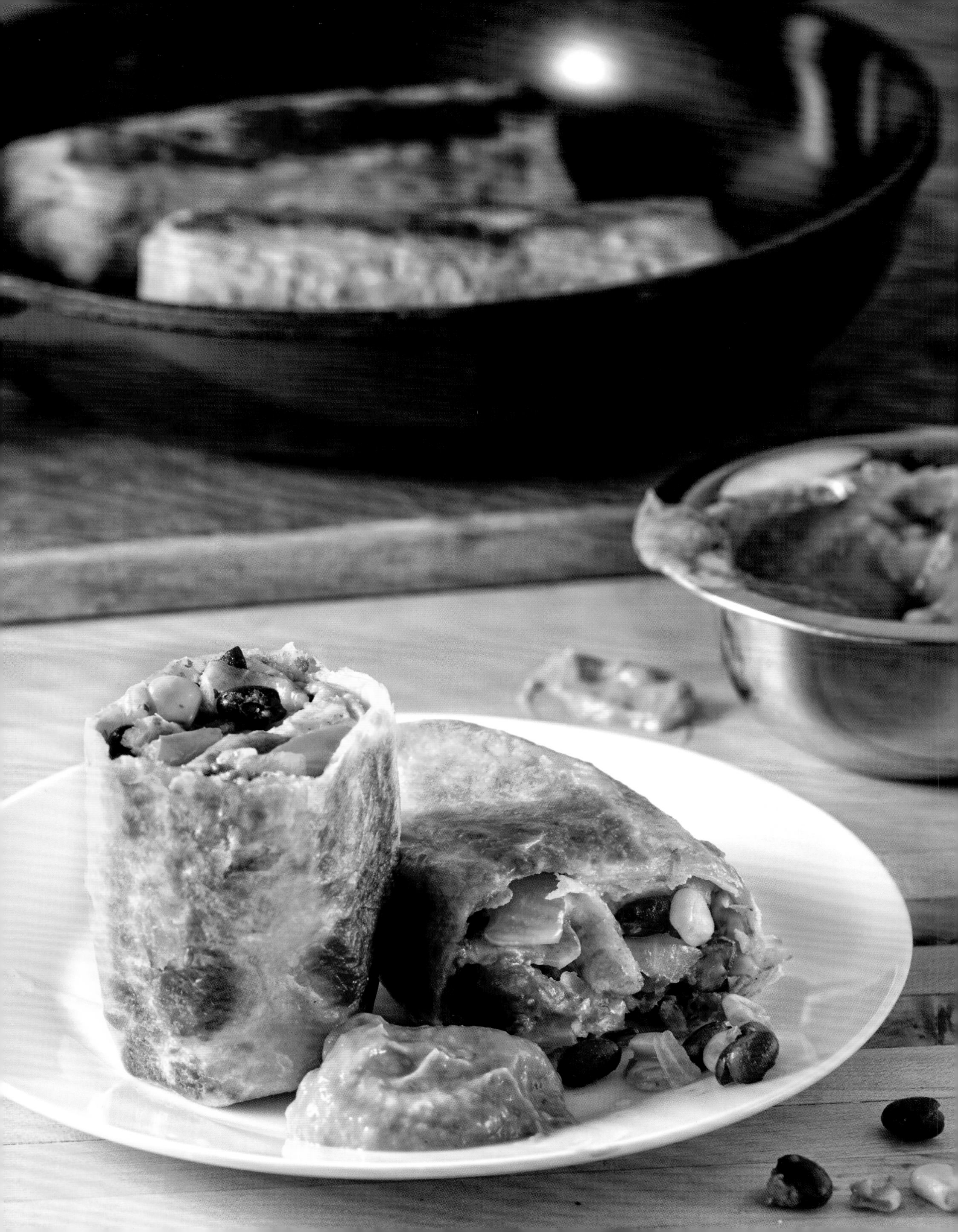

YA BASIC CHIMI

YIELD: 6 CHIMICHANGAS

What is a chimichanga anyway, you might ask? Well, it's basically the happiest accident in culinary history. It's said that long ago, some lady accidentally dropped a burrito into the deep fryer and decided to serve it to her customers anyway. The results were unexpectedly delicious, and a new legend was born! Don't know if that's even remotely true, but I've always had a bit of a soft spot for mistakes that happen to become world famous. Chimis can be filled with just about anything, like this classic chicken, cheese, and bean combo. It may not be all that creative as chimis go, but I guarantee it'll please any merc, no matter the size of their mouth!

2 quarts oil, such as peanut or canola, for frying

½ pound cooked chicken, shredded (can be pre-cooked)

One 4-ounce can diced green chiles

One 15-ounce can pinto beans, drained and rinsed

½ teaspoon chili powder

Juice of half a lime

Salt and fresh black pepper

Six 10-inch flour tortillas

1 cup shredded cheddar

Krakoan Salsa (page 40), DP Dip (page 42), or Nacho Average Cheese Sauce (page 44), for serving

SPECIAL SUPPLIES:

Toothpicks

> **TIP:**
>
> DID YOU GET OVEREXCITED ABOUT SPATCHCOCKING AND CUT UP A FEW TOO MANY CHICKENS? THEN USE YOUR LEFTOVER SPATCHCOCKED CHICKEN (PAGE 67) TO KICK THIS RECIPE UP A NOTCH!

1. Preheat the oven to 250°F. Set up your fry station (see page 91), and begin heating oil to 365°F.
2. In a large sauté pan or microwave-safe bowl, combine the chicken, green chiles, beans, chili powder, lime juice, and salt and pepper to taste, and warm through.
3. Assemble each chimi (see page 84). Start with a layer of chicken mixture on each tortilla then add a layer of shredded cheddar. Roll chimi, and secure seam with toothpicks. Fry chimis one at a time in the oil, turning with tongs, until all sides are golden brown. Drain on a wire rack or paper towel before transferring to a baking sheet. Keep warm in the oven until serving.
4. Serve with Krakoan Salsa, DP Dip, or Nacho Average Cheese Sauce.

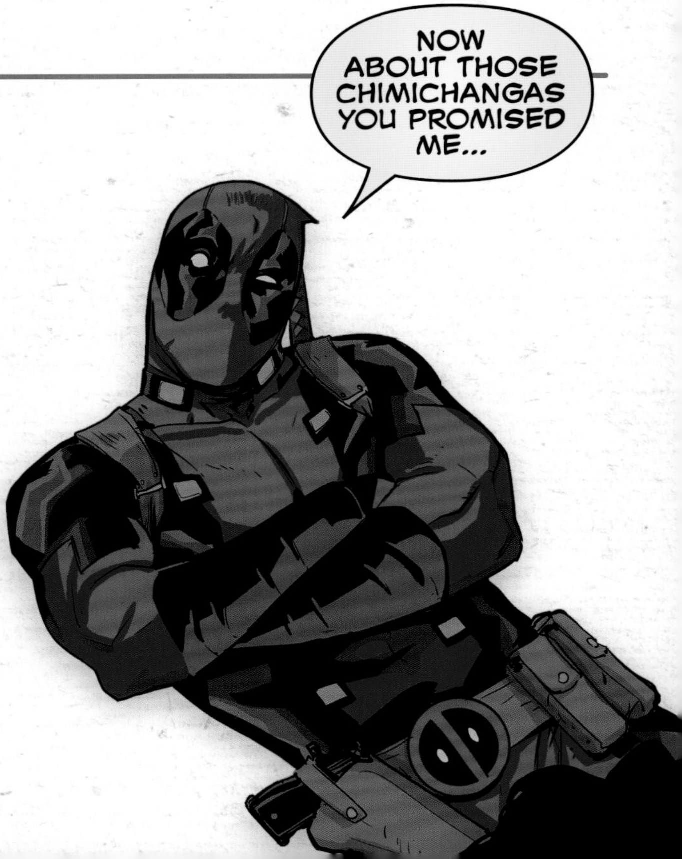
NOW ABOUT THOSE CHIMICHANGAS YOU PROMISED ME...

ROLLING A CHIMI

There's nothing worse than being seconds away from having a fresh chimi on your plate, only to watch in horror as it spills its guts into the frying oil. With this proper rolling technique, you'll be able to prevent such world-shattering disasters:

1. Wrap your tortillas in a damp dishcloth and warm them up in the microwave, two or three at a time, so they get nice and supple. Have your preferred chimi fillings nearby and ready to go. (Remember when we talked about mise en place? Yeah, well, this is a great place to put that concept to use!)

2. Lay out a warmed tortilla and spoon a long line of filling across the center bottom third, parallel to you (crosswise). Leave about an inch or so of empty space on each side. Don't get greedy.

3. Fold in the sides (they should not overlap), mushing them down against the filling a bit so they stay neatly in place. (Ooh! This is like food origami!)

4. Hold the sides in place as you fold up the bottom so it overlaps the sides, but doesn't reach the top edge. Try to eliminate any air pockets. It should look like you've got a tiny purse full of all the yum.

5. Roll the shaft of your chimi over the top of the open flap, sealing the contents inside as tightly as possible. There will be no escape!

6. If any of the rounded edges of the tortilla are sticking out all crazy-like, tuck 'em under the open seam and pin the whole thing shut with a couple of toothpicks. Then it's off to the deep fryer for all the crisp and none of the mess!

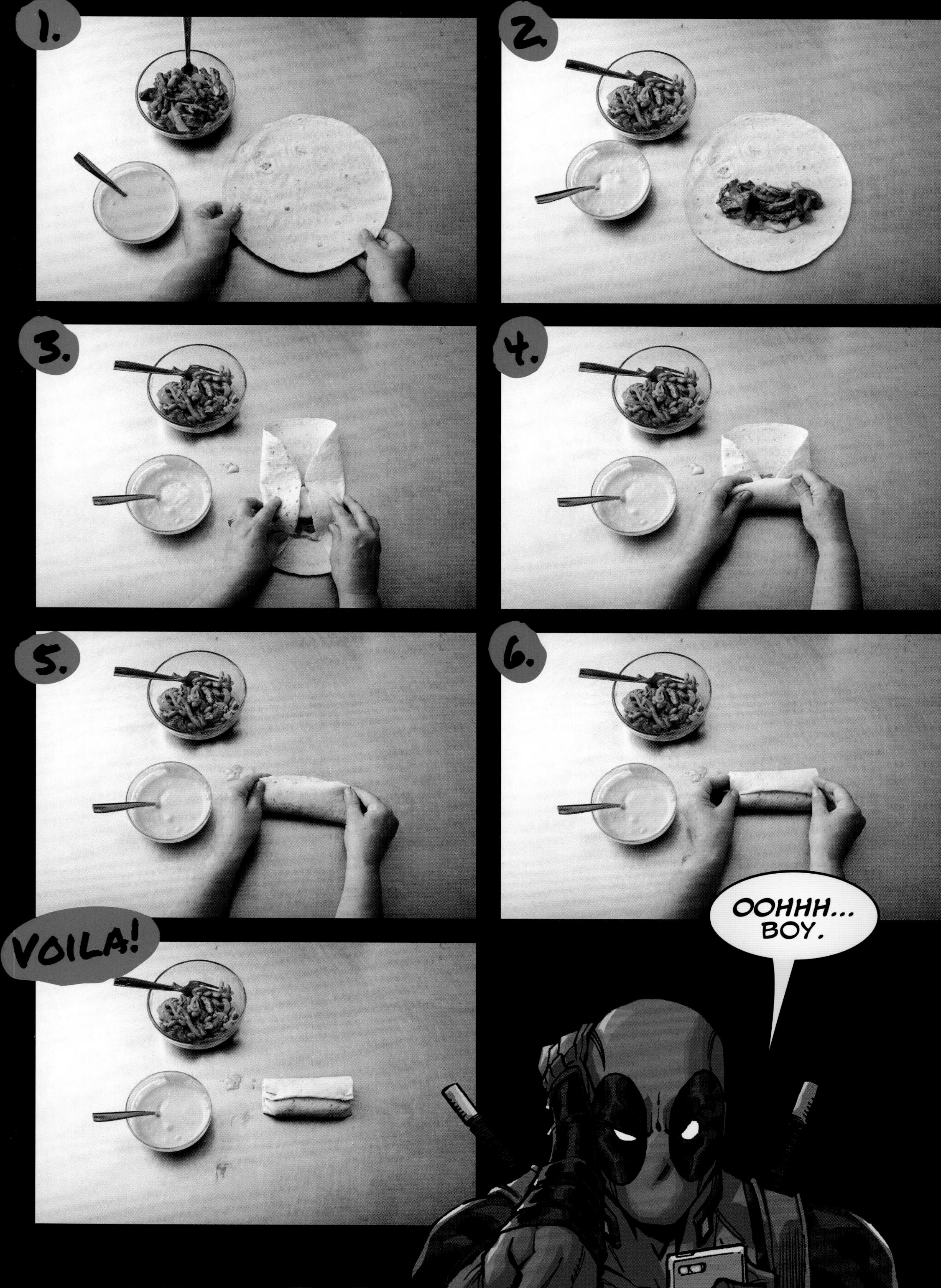
1.
2.
3.
4.
5.
6.
VOILA!
OOHHH...
BOY.

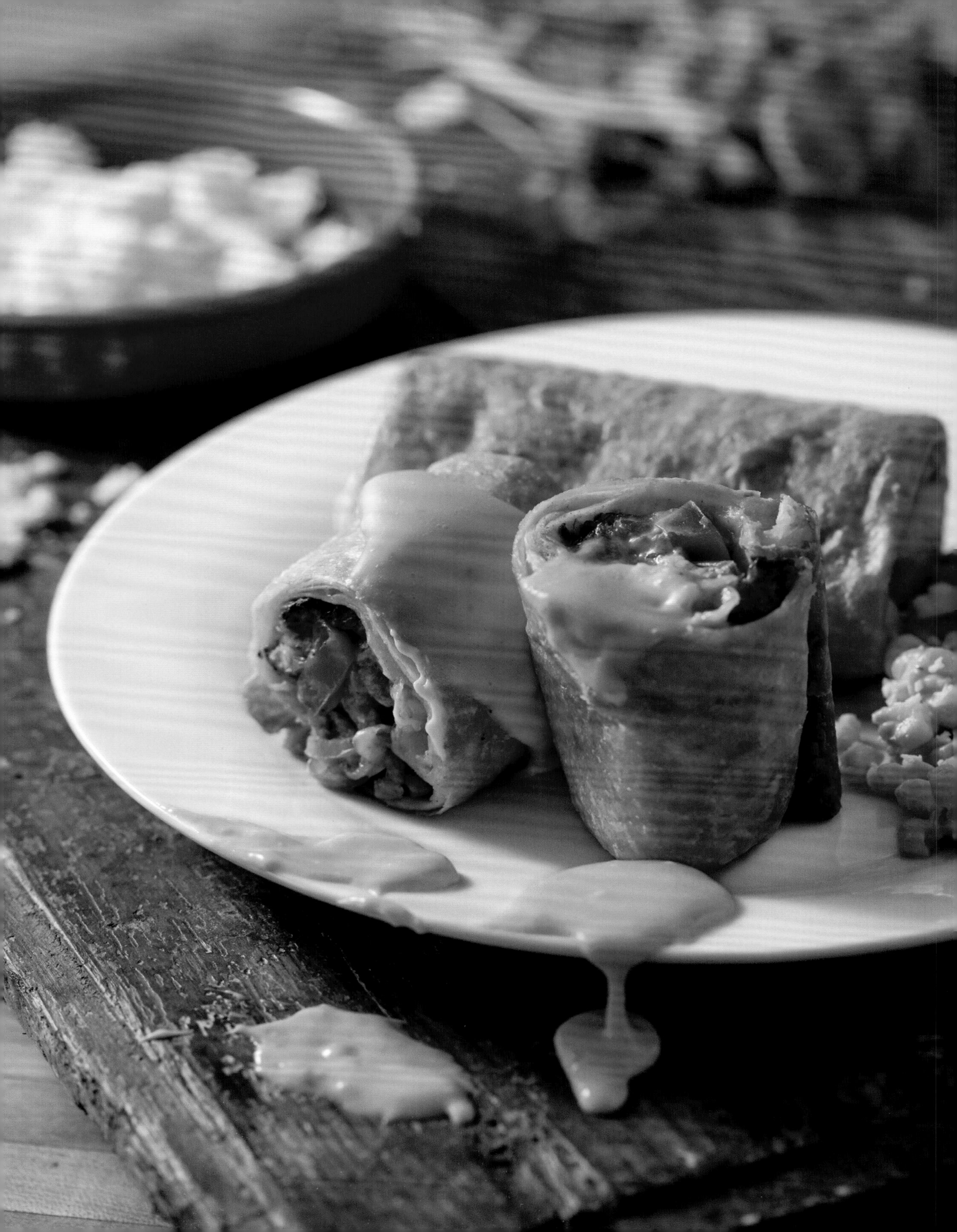

STEAK FAJITA CHIMI

YIELD: 6 CHIMICHANGAS

Got a fat paycheck from your latest successful hit job? Well, there's no better way to celebrate than with the king of all chimichangas: the steak fajita chimi! This one is stuffed to the point of bursting with strips of sizzling steak, onions, and peppers—not to mention loads of cheese! It's a good thing we've devoted some space to proper chimichanga construction techniques (see page 84), or this baby would probably split open at the seams the second you dunked it into the deep fryer. Of course, even if it does, I wouldn't blame you if you just scooped the crispy goodness out of the oil and ate it anyway. It's not like I haven't done it before—who am I to judge?

FOR THE STEAK:

1 tablespoon kosher salt

1 tablespoon chili powder

1 teaspoon fresh black pepper

½ teaspoon cayenne pepper

1½ pounds flat iron steak, flank steak, or skirt steak

FOR THE VEGETABLES:

1 teaspoon salt

½ teaspoon ground cumin

½ teaspoon chili powder

1 red bell pepper, cut into strips

1 yellow pepper, cut into strips

1 yellow onion, halved and thinly sliced

3 tablespoons oil

One 15-ounce can pinto beans, drained and rinsed

1 cup Nacho Average Cheese Sauce (page 44), plus more for serving

Six 10-inch flour tortillas

Krakoan Salsa (page 40), for serving

1. Preheat the oven to 375°F.

2. To make the steak: Combine the spices in a small bowl, and rub mixture over the meat. Set aside. Set up your fry station (see page 91) and begin heating oil to 365°F.

3. To make the vegetables: Combine the salt and spices in a small bowl, and toss the vegetables with the spices and oil. Place them in a single layer on a large roasting pan. Roast for 15 minutes, until vegetables are soft and begin to brown.

4. Remove the pan from the oven, and push the vegetables to the sides, creating a space in the middle for the steak. Add the steak and return to the oven for 7 to 10 minutes. Flip the steak, and cook 7 to 10 minutes more.

5. Remove from the oven, tent with foil, and let rest for 10 minutes. Slice meat into thin strips going across the grain, and toss with the vegetables and pinto beans.

6. Assemble each chimi (see page 84). Start with a layer of fajita mixture, then add a layer of Nacho Average Cheese Sauce. Roll chimi and secure seam with toothpicks.

7. Fry the chimis in the oil one at a time, turning with tongs, until all sides are golden brown. Drain on a wire rack or paper towel briefly before transferring to a baking sheet in the oven to keep warm until serving.

8. Serve with more Nacho Average Cheese Sauce and Krakoan Salsa.

Crab Rangoon Chimi

Yield: About 6 Chimichangas

Okay, this might not seem like a traditional chimichanga in any sense, but I've never been a traditional guy, so I don't see the problem. Think of this one as Mex-Asian fusion or, more accurately, what would happen if your favorite Mexican and Chinese takeout joints had a steamy rendezvous behind the kitchen and got their secret sauces all mixed up. Oh! And speaking of secret sauces, remember that creamy DP Dip (page 42) I taught you how to make way back in the first section of the book? Well, it's the perfect condiment to accompany this cuisine-combining concoction. One bite and I promise you'll be thanking me . . . but you won't know whether to say *gracias* or *xièxiè*.

About 2 quarts oil, such as peanut or canola, for frying

1 shallot, minced

1 jalapeño, seeded and minced

1 teaspoon ground coriander

Juice of 1 to 2 lemons, depending on juiciness and desired tartness, divided

1 cup (8 ounces) cream cheese, softened

Salt and fresh black pepper

12 ounces canned crab meat

4 scallions, white and light green parts only, chopped

1 cup chopped celery

Six 8-inch flour tortillas

DP Dip (page 42), for serving

1. Preheat the oven to 250°F. Set up fry station (page 91), and begin heating oil to 365°F.
2. In a small bowl, mix the shallot, jalapeño, coriander, and half the lemon juice into the cream cheese. Blend thoroughly, add salt and pepper to taste, and set aside.
3. In a separate bowl, mix the remaining lemon juice into the crab, and set aside. In a third small bowl, combine the scallions and celery, and set aside.
4. Assemble each chimi. Spread ⅙ of the cream cheese mixture across the center of the bottom third of a tortilla, top with ⅙ of the crab, and ⅙ of the scallion and celery mixture. Roll (page 84), and secure seam with toothpicks. Repeat until all the chimis are assembled.
5. Fry each chimi in the oil, turning with tongs until all sides are golden brown. Place on a baking sheet, and keep warm in the oven until ready to serve.
6. Serve with DP Dip, and enjoy.

PASS THE CHIMIS

What's the best way to whet one's appetite for a never-ending feast of chimichangas? Why, with a tray full of smaller chimichangas, of course! These bite-sized beauties are an ideal appetizer for any fiesta. Of course, just because they're an adorably tiny variation of the classic chimi doesn't mean they have to be used strictly as a starter. Maybe you have a smaller appetite than the average chimi-chomping individual. Or maybe you occasionally like to pretend that you're a giant and that these are normal-sized chimis you're devouring by the handful. Whatever the case, these mini chimis (or "chiminis," as I call 'em) are always a good choice!

1 to 2 tablespoons oil, for pan

1 small yellow onion, diced

9 ounces fresh pork chorizo, removed from casing

1 pound lean ground beef

One 7-ounce can chipotle peppers in adobo sauce

1 package spring roll wrappers

2 cups shredded Monterey Jack

About 2 quarts oil, such as peanut or canola, for frying

1. Heat a sauté pan or skillet on medium, and add oil to coat the pan. Add the diced onion, and sauté until translucent. Add the chorizo, and stir constantly until cooked through, 3 to 5 minutes. Add the ground beef, and cook until brown, 3 to 5 minutes more. Pour extra grease into a heat-proof jar or bowl, and discard when cool.

2. Pour the peppers into a small bowl. Fill the can with water, swish it around to get all the sauce from the sides of the can, and add liquid to the pan with the meat. Dice 2 to 4 peppers, depending on desired spice level, and add to the meat. Reserve remaining peppers for future use. Continue to cook the mixture until the liquid is absorbed, about 10 minutes. Refrigerate the mixture, for at least 30 minutes, until easy to handle and firm.

3. Set up your wrapping station with a cutting board, spring roll wrappers, small dishes of water, filling, and cheese.

4. Set up your frying station, and begin heating oil to 365°F.

5. To assemble your chiminis: Position a spring roll wrapper on cutting board in front of you with a short side facing you. Use a spoon to drop 2 tablespoons of filling toward the bottom end of the wrapper, leaving enough room below and to the sides of the filling to make your folds. Add a generous sprinkle of cheese on top of the filling. Using your fingertips, wet the edges of the wrapper. Roll your chimi (page 84), and seal the top edge with a bit more water if necessary. Repeat with the remaining wrappers until all the chimis are ready.

6. Fry the chimis in small batches until golden brown, turning in the oil until all sides are brown. Drain on a wire rack or a paper-towel-lined baking sheet. Serve hot.

Breakfast Chimi

YIELD: 6 CHIMICHANGAS

If you're the kind of person who mistakenly believes that chimichangas are only appropriate for two meals a day, let me set you straight. Chimis are a 'round-the-clock cuisine. But for those of you who enjoy starting the day with some slightly more traditional foodstuffs, let me introduce you to my friend, the breakfast chimi. It's got all the things you love waking up to, like scrambled eggs and meat products that, for some reason, have been deemed appropriate specifically for consumption during the early hours of the day. This one's so good that you'll soon find it entering your chimi rotation at all hours of the day.

½ pound pork sausage, casing removed

½ onion, diced

½ red bell pepper, diced

One 10-ounce can black beans, drained and rinsed

½ cup frozen corn

Salt and fresh black pepper

Six 10-inch flour tortillas

2 to 3 tablespoons salted butter, melted

2 cups shredded cheddar

4 to 5 eggs, soft scrambled

2 avocados, peeled, pitted, and sliced

Krakoan Salsa (page 40), DP Dip (page 42), or Nacho Average Cheese Sauce (page 44), for serving

1. Preheat the oven to 250°F.
2. In a large sauté pan on medium heat, crumble and brown the sausage until cooked through. Add the onion and bell pepper, and continue to cook until soft, 5 to 7 minutes. Add the black beans, corn, and salt and pepper to taste, and cook until everything is warmed through, 2 to 3 minutes more. Cover to keep warm, and set aside.
3. To assemble chimis: Brush one side of a tortilla with butter. Add meat-and-bean filling to the center of the tortilla, and top with a small handful of cheddar, egg, and a few slices of avocado. Brush with more melted butter to help seal, and roll (page 84). Once rolled, brush the outside with butter. Repeat until filling is gone.
4. Heat a clean sauté pan on medium high. Starting with seam side down, pan fry each chimi until all the side are crisp and golden brown, approximately 4 to 5 minutes per side. Transfer to a baking sheet, and keep warm in the oven until ready to serve.
5. Serve with Krakoan Salsa, DP Dip, or Nacho Average Cheese Sauce.

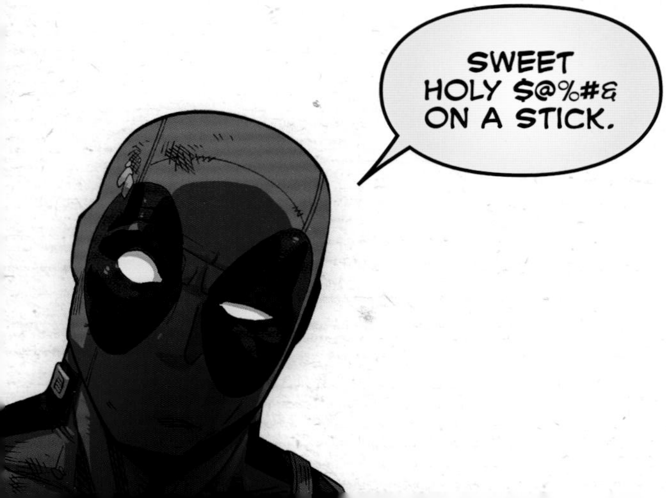
SWEET HOLY $@%#& ON A STICK.

JUST THE TIPS:
FRYING SAFETY

You may have noticed that I make a lot of jokes. But frying safety isn't one of them. If you're making something that requires deep frying, like my glorious chimis, here are some important tips to prevent you from setting your house (and yourself) on fire:

1. If you don't have a dedicated deep fryer, use a Dutch oven or a high-walled sauté pan. I may be shallow, but my frying pans aren't!

2. Never have too much oil in the pan! You don't want hot oil spilling out as soon as you put the food in.

3. Only use a suitable cooking oil, like canola, peanut, or vegetable oil. Motor oil is a big no-no.

4. Always keep track of the oil temperature with a thermometer. 350°F to 375°F should do the trick.

5. Never put too much food in the pan at the same time! One chimi at a time, kids!

6. Never put wet food in the pan unless you want to get showered in searing hot droplets of liquid pain!

7. Always have a lid nearby to cover the pan in case it starts to spill over or catch fire. And a properly rated fire extinguisher probably wouldn't hurt to have on hand either.

8. Never leave the pan unattended, not even for a second. We all know you have nothing better to do anyway.

9. Never let children near your pan. Or your chimis. Those are for Daddy.

10. Never, ever put your face, hand, or any other body part in the hot oil, or you'll end up with skin that permanently looks like mine. Believe me, not even a healing factor will fix you up from burns like that. So be careful!

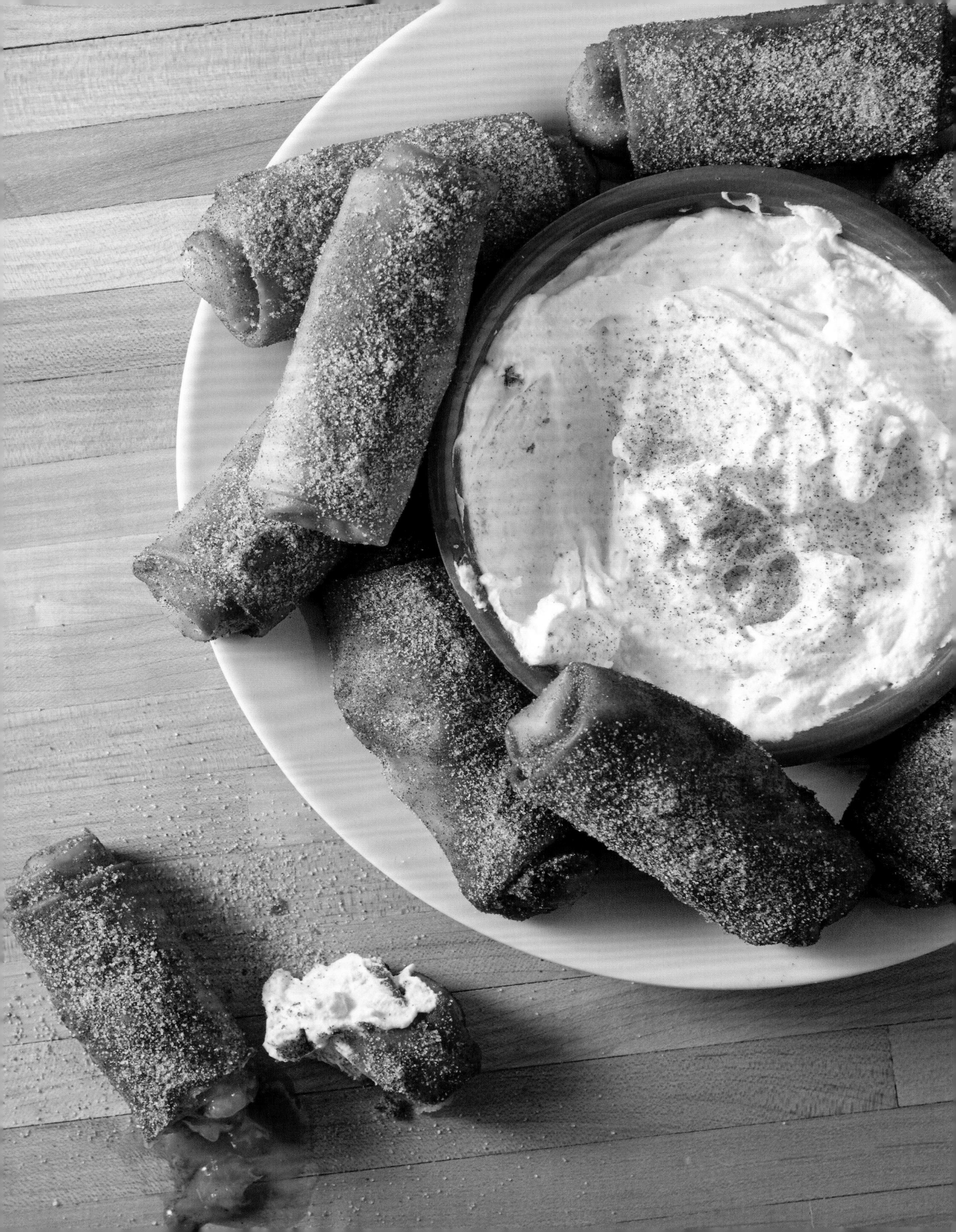

Dessert Chimi

Oh man! You ate all the chimis! Now what?! Dessert, of course! If you're looking for a wider variety of confectionary creations, you're welcome to skip ahead a few pages to the final chapter of the book. But if you're one of those dear readers who demanded chimichangas, then do me a favor and stick around so we can see this theme through to the bitter end. Well, actually, this end is as sweet as they come, with bananas and caramel bundled up inside a warm, flaky, sugar-coated tortilla. Skip the meat and beans and hand me a plate full of these bad boys!

FOR THE CHIMIS:

4 bananas, just ripe

Zest of 1 lime

¼ cup fresh lime juice

½ cup (1 stick, or 8 tablespoons) salted butter, divided

½ cup light brown sugar

½ package spring roll wrappers

FOR THE CINNAMON SUGAR:

¼ cup sugar

2 teaspoons ground cinnamon

FOR THE WHIPPED CREAM:

½ cup heavy cream

1½ teaspoons ground cinnamon

2 tablespoons sugar

1. To make the chimis: Peel and cut each banana in half lengthwise, then slice into 1-inch pieces, and place in a medium bowl. Toss the bananas in the lime zest and juice, and set aside.

2. In a nonstick skillet, melt 6 tablespoons of the butter completely, then remove from heat, and evenly sprinkle the brown sugar over the bottom of the pan. Add banana lime mixture in a single layer over the sugar. Return to heat and cook, shaking pan occasionally, for 10 to 15 minutes or until all the sugar is dissolved and a thick syrup has formed. Remove from heat, and cool until filling can be handled, about 20 minutes.

3. Preheat the oven to 375°F, and line a baking sheet with a silicone mat or parchment paper. Melt the remaining 2 tablespoons of butter in a small pan or in the microwave.

4. Position a spring roll wrapper on a cutting board in front of you with a short side facing you. Brush wrapper lightly with melted butter, then flip wrapper over, and drop about 2 tablespoons of filling onto it toward the bottom edge. (Make sure you leave enough room around the bottom and sides of the filling to fold in your edges.) Roll the chimi (page 84), and place it seam side down on a baking sheet. Repeat with remaining wrappers until filling is gone. Bake chimis in the oven for 15 to 20 minutes or until golden brown and crisp.

5. To make the cinnamon sugar: Combine sugar and cinnamon in a large shallow dish.

6. To make the whipped cream: Beat all ingredients together until soft peaks form. Refrigerate until ready to serve.

7. When chimis are just cool enough to handle, roll each one in cinnamon sugar. Serve warm with cinnamon whipped cream.

Taco Night

Let's face it—no matter how many tutorial pages we include about frying safety, some folks just aren't capable of crispifying their food without also ending up covered in burns so severe that they make my skin look as smooth as a newborn baby's behind. For those unfortunate few, I invented a special nonfried variation that allows for the same delicious fillings you can find inside a chimi, with only a fraction of the danger. I call this mysterious creation a "taco." And it is culinary perfection. Just to be extra nice, I've come up with a few extra filling options you can try, including mole chicken, carnitas, and—if you're feeling really fancy—ceviche, to give you a leg up on all your chimi-making rivals. With the right spread of fixings, you'll be able to throw a party so good your friends will never even realize the utter shame of your chimi-less existence.

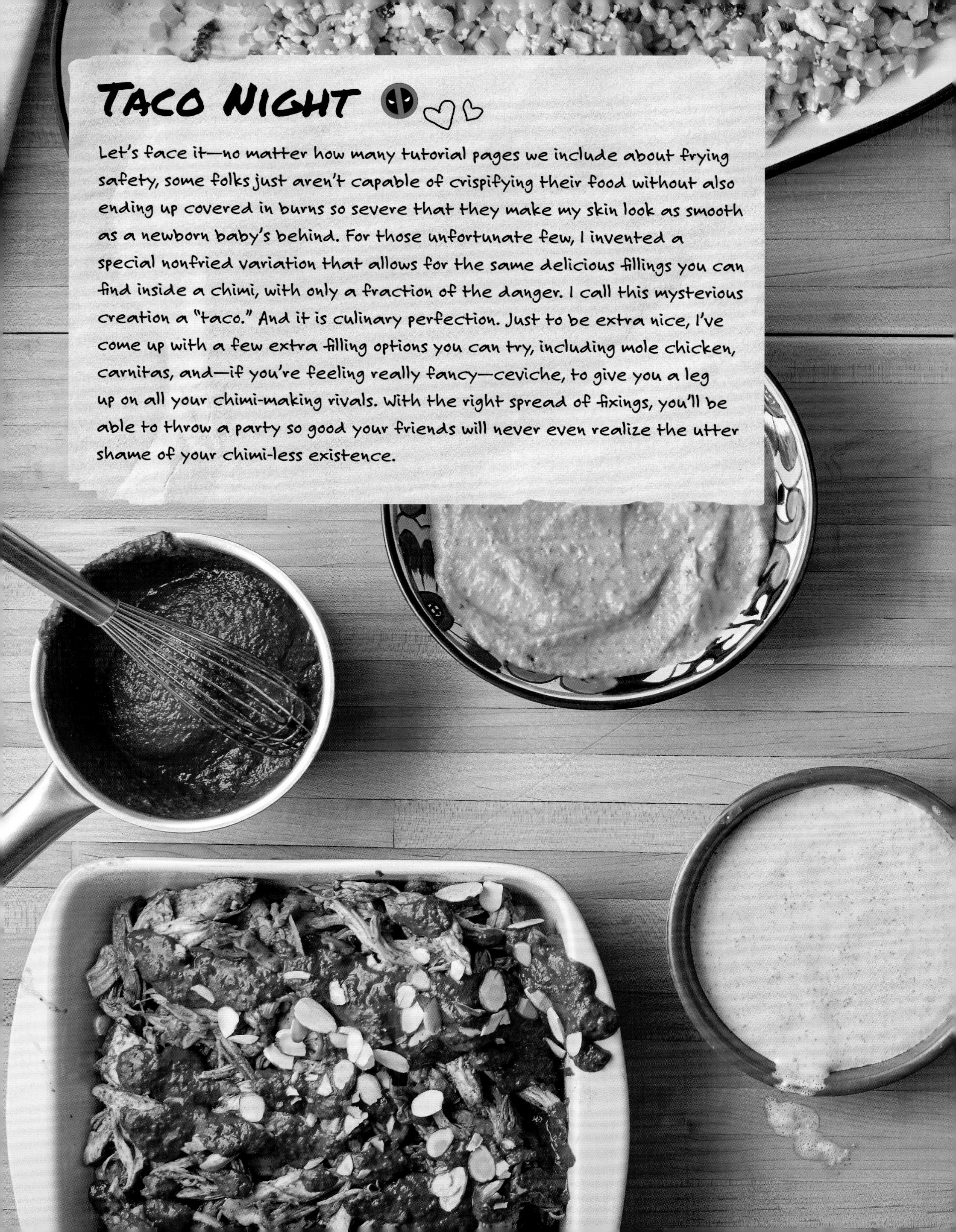

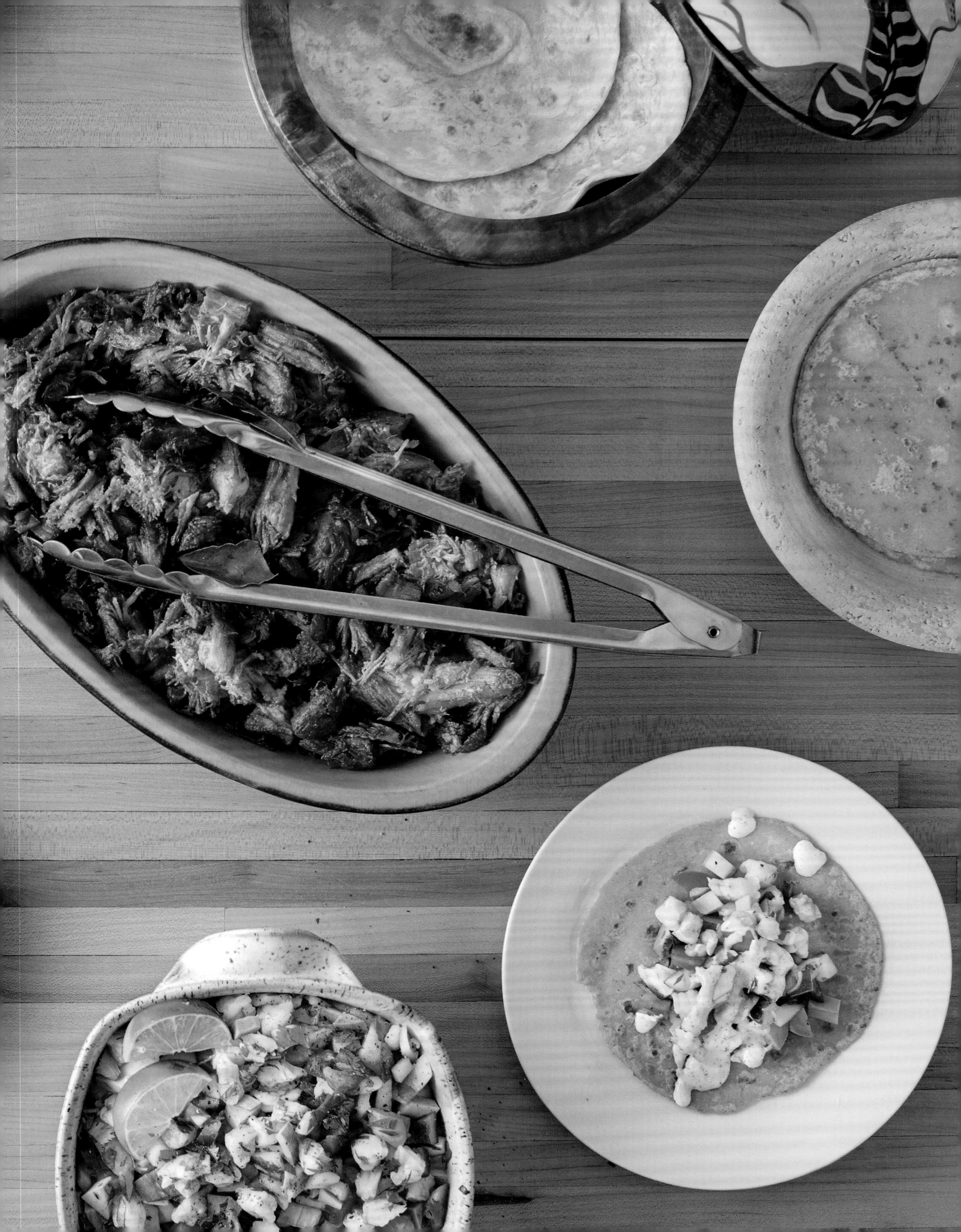

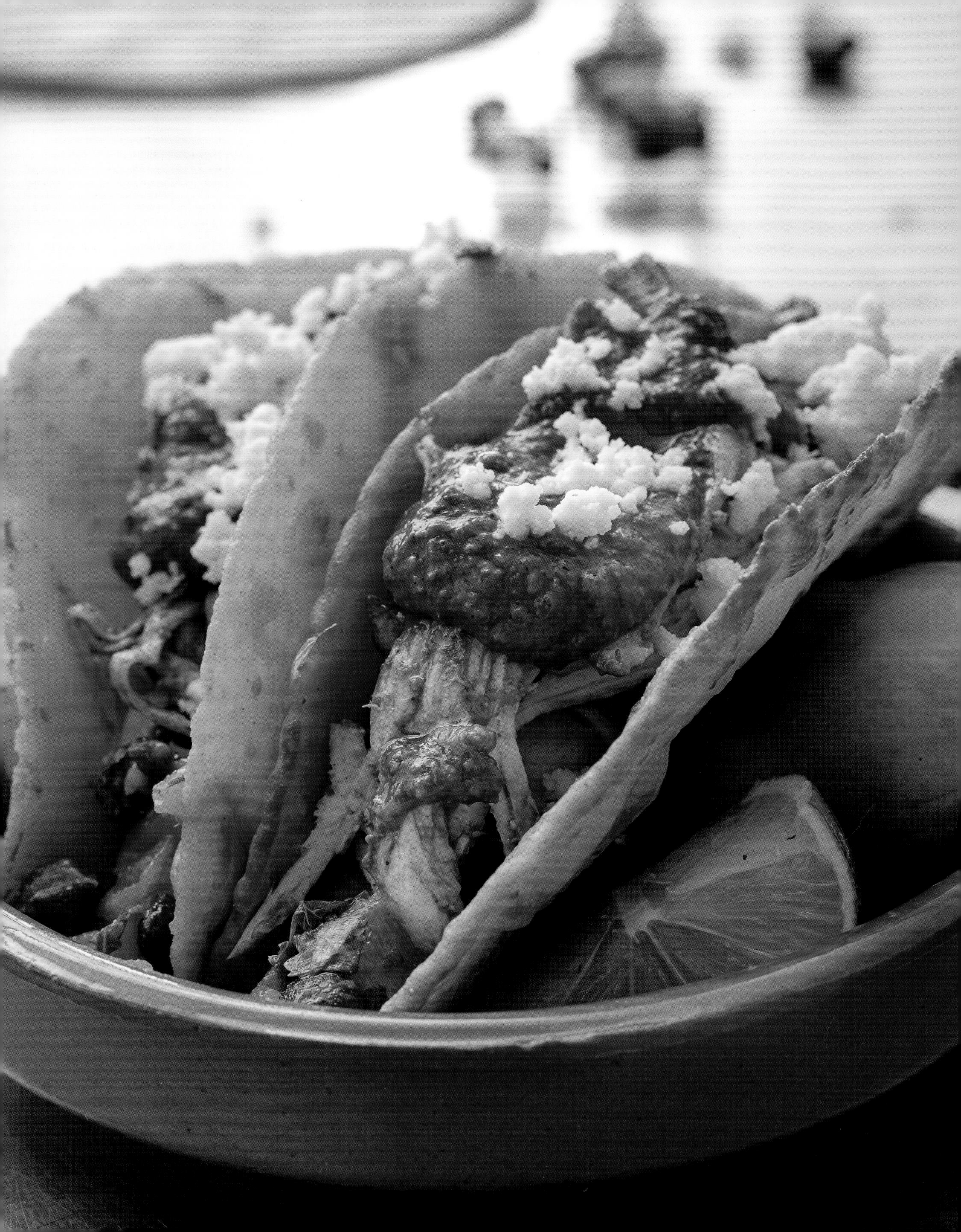

Mole Chicken

YIELD: 6 SERVINGS WITH EXTRA SAUCE

FOR THE SAUCE:

1 to 2 tablespoons oil, for pan

1 small yellow onion, diced

5 garlic cloves, minced

1 jalapeño, seeded and minced

¼ cup raisins

2 tablespoons chili powder

1 teaspoon ground cinnamon

1 teaspoon ground coriander

¼ cup bread crumbs

2½ cups vegetable broth

2 dried bay leaves

4 tablespoons unsweetened cocoa powder

2 tablespoons smooth almond butter

1 tablespoon ketchup

1 teaspoon salt

FOR THE CHICKEN:

1 to 2 tablespoons oil, for pan

1 to 1½ pounds boneless, skinless chicken breasts, thighs, or combination

TO SERVE:

Tortillas

Black Ops Salsa (page 41)

Street Corner Street Corn (page 37)

1. To make the sauce: Heat a large saucepan on medium, and coat with oil. Sauté the onions until translucent and starting to brown. Add the garlic, jalepeño, and raisins, and continue to sauté until vegetables are soft and fragrant. Add chili powder, cinnamon, coriander, and bread crumbs. Cook until mixture is fragrant and beginning to stick.
2. Slowly add the broth, and stir to deglaze the spices from the bottom of the pan. Add the bay leaves, and simmer 5 to 10 minutes. Remove the bay leaves and blend with an immersion blender until smooth. Add the bay leaves back in along with the cocoa powder, almond butter, ketchup, and salt. Simmer another 15 minutes.
3. To make the chicken: Preheat the oven to 350°F. Heat the oil in an oven-safe sauté pan or skillet on medium-high heat. Add the chicken in a single layer, and brown it on both sides. Remove pan from heat. Add ½ cup of sauce to the pan, and turn the chicken to coat.
4. Transfer pan to oven, and bake for 20 to 25 minutes, until the chicken is cooked through. Remove the chicken from the pan and shred it using a fork and a sharp knife, then return it to the pan and give it a quick stir to mix the chicken with the sauce. Return pan to the oven for 10 more minutes to let the sauce reduce.
5. Serve with the extra sauce for drizzling, tortillas, Black Ops Salsa and Street Corner Street Corn.

TIP:

DON'T OWN AN IMMERSION BLENDER? (OR DON'T EVEN KNOW WHAT ONE IS?) NO PROB. JUST LET THE MIXTURE COOL DOWN TO AROUND ROOM TEMPERATURE AND USE A STANDARD BLENDER. (YOU MIGHT HAVE TO WORK IN BATCHES, DEPENDING ON THE SIZE OF YOUR BLENDER.) ONCE EVERYTHING IS NICE AND SMOOTH, IT GOES RIGHT BACK INTO THE PAN, WHERE IT BELONGS.

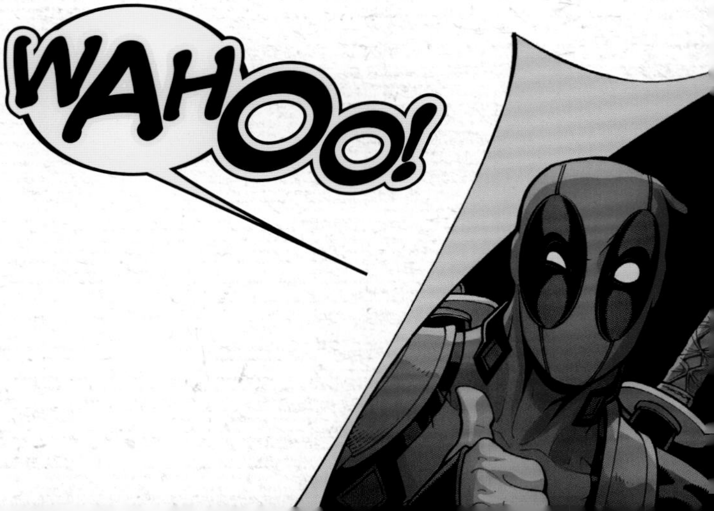
WAHOO!

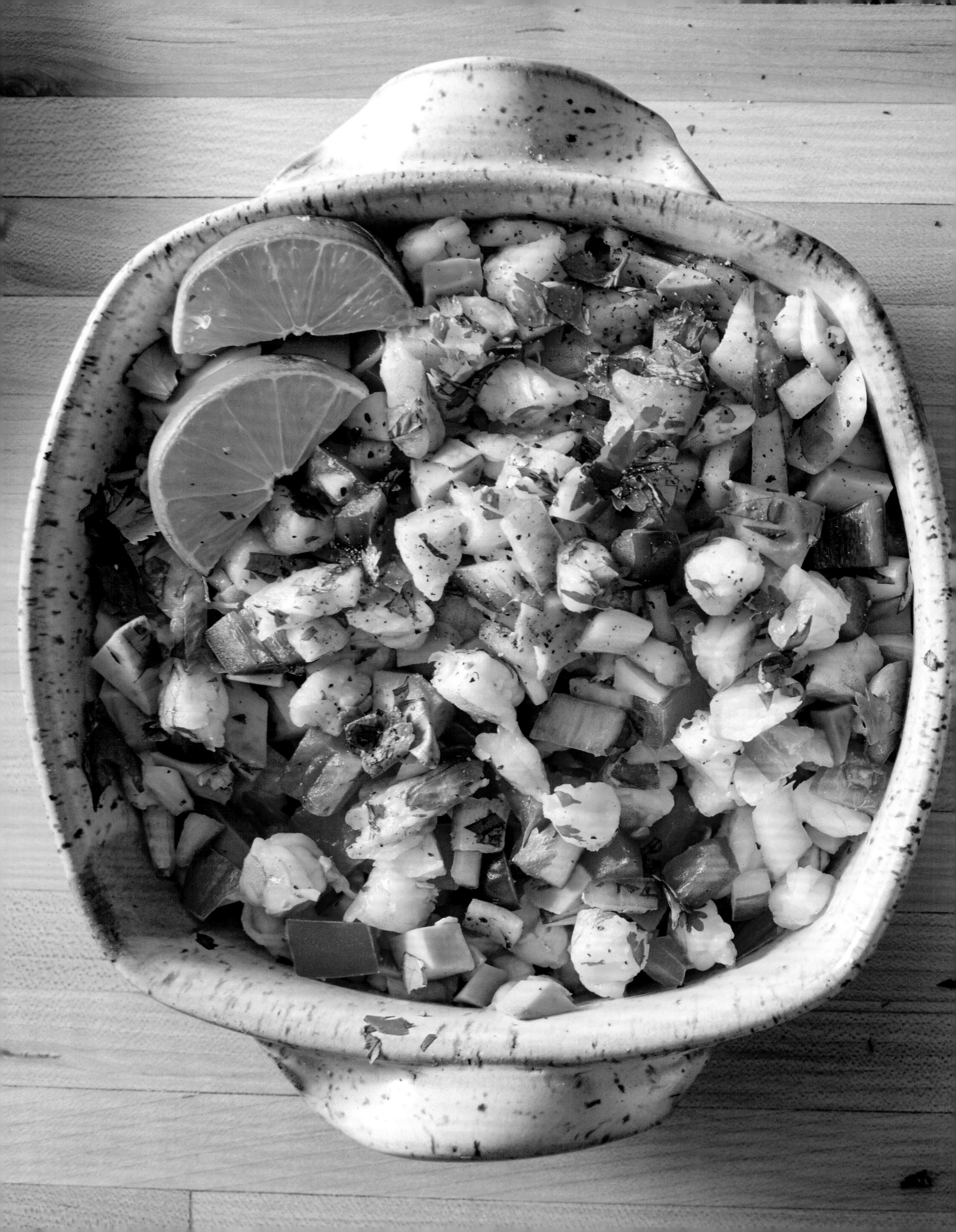

Shrimp Ceviche

¼ cup fresh lime juice

1 pound shrimp, peeled
and deveined, cooked and chopped

¼ cup fresh lemon juice

2 tablespoons olive oil

1 red onion, diced

2 Roma tomatoes, cored, seeded,
and diced

1 avocado, peeled, pitted, and diced

1 to 2 jalapeños or serrano chiles,
seeded and diced

½ cup loosely packed fresh cilantro
leaves, chopped

Salt and fresh black pepper

Limes, for garnish

Chips or fried corn tortillas, for serving

1. In a large serving bowl, combine the lime and lemon juice. Toss the shrimp in the juice. Cover, refrigerate, and marinate for 1 hour. After 1 hour, drain the shrimp, put them back in the bowl, and mix in the rest of the ingredients.

2. Give the ceviche an extra squeeze of fresh lime right before serving and garnish with lime wedges. Serve with chips or fried corn tortillas.

Carnitas

YIELD: 6 SERVINGS

4 to 6 pounds boneless pork shoulder,
trimmed and cut into 5-inch strips

2 tablespoons kosher salt

1 to 2 tablespoons oil, for pan

Water

2 teaspoons chili powder

2 teaspoons hot paprika

1 teaspoon ground coriander

1 cinnamon stick

2 dried bay leaves

TO SERVE:

Tortillas

Black Ops Salsa (page 41)

Street Corner Street Corn (page 37)

DP Dip (page 42)

1. Preheat the oven to 350°F. Rub the pork strips with salt, and set aside.

2. Heat a stovetop-friendly roasting pan on medium high (you may need to straddle two burners). Coat the pan with oil, and add pork strips, working in small batches if necessary. Brown strips on all sides. Each piece of pork should have a deep golden brown crust. When all the pork is brown, remove from pan, and set aside.

3. Add 1 cup of water and all the spices to the pan, using the liquid to deglaze the pan of all the crispy brown bits. Return the pork to the pan, and add enough water until the pork is about two-thirds submerged.

4. Braise in the oven for 2½ hours. Check to see if the meat is pull-apart tender. If not, put it back in the oven for as long as another hour, checking regularly to assess the tenderness. Once the pork is completely tender, remove the pan from the oven and shred all of it. Return meat to the oven and roast for another 30 minutes to an hour, until it is deeply caramelized.

5. Serve with tortillas, Black Ops Salsa, Street Corner Street Corn, and DP Dip.

TIP:

THIS RECIPE COOKS WAY DOWN, SO DON'T GET STINGY ON THE MEAT. NO ONE LIKES A HALF-FILLED TACO.

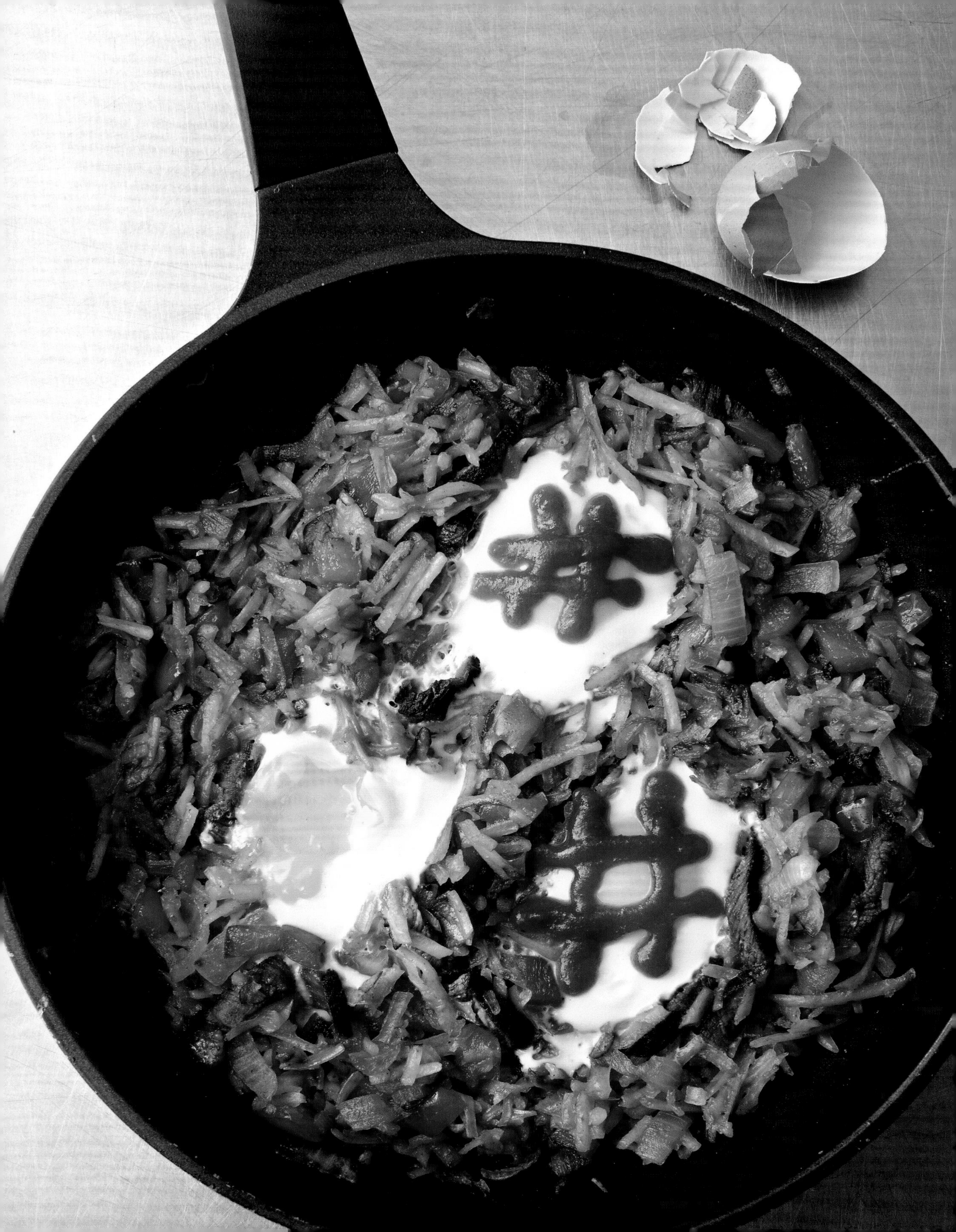

Waking Up with Wade

Good morning, sunshine! If you're anything like me, you've got a busy day ahead of you, saving the world from its own depravity. That kind of work takes skill, discipline, and a ridiculous amount of ammo. If you want to maintain peak performance for the duration of your mission, you need to make sure that more than just your arsenal is fully loaded. That's why I start every day the same way: with a well-balanced breakfast.

When I was a younger merc, I was fine grabbing a quick cup of coffee and a banana on my way out to assassinate the prime minister of Sokovia. But these days, I like to take my time and savor those quiet morning hours before everything starts blowing up around me. A little Wade time does me good and puts me in the right headspace for head shots.

LI'L OL' ME. THE **POOL** OF **DEAD**.

Also, huge news flash: I've just been informed that breakfast foods can now be enjoyed any time of the day. Domino introduced me to this thing called "brunch," where, unbelievably, you can have breakfast for lunch! Count me in! Hell, with breakfast bites this bombastic, I wouldn't blame you for whipping up "brinner" and a few "bridnight snacks" as well!

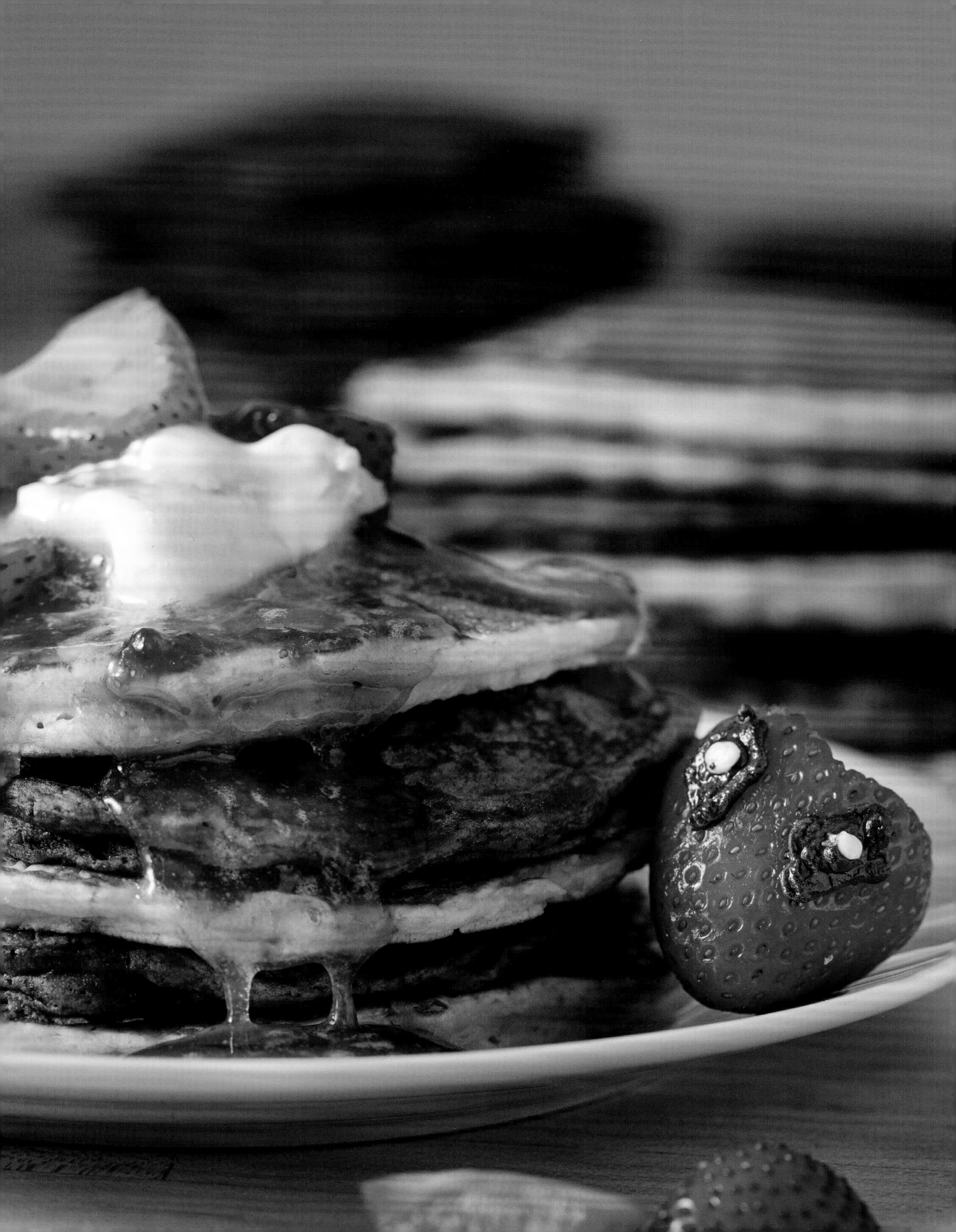

Smells Like Victory

Yield: Thirty 4-Inch Pancakes

Ask anyone who's ever gone on a mission with me, and they'll all have wildly different opinions about my methods, my general mental stability, and the long-term ramifications of my actions. But there's one thing I can assure you they'll all agree on: Deadpool sure loves him some pancakes! Once a job is completed and I've been fully debriefed (by which I mean I've taken my pants off), I like to invite over my colleagues-in-chaos for an all-you-can-eat flapjack fiesta. Because, let's be honest, nothing says "Congratulations on saving the city from subterranean monsters . . . again" quite like 372,844 pancakes.

WET INGREDIENTS FOR BOTH BATTERS:

4 eggs

2¾ cups milk

1 tablespoon vanilla

6 tablespoons (¾ stick) unsalted butter, melted

DRY INGREDIENTS FOR THE CHOCOLATE BATTER:

1½ cups all-purpose flour

4 tablespoons powdered sugar

1 tablespoon baking powder

¼ teaspoon salt

3 tablespoons unsweetened cocoa powder

DRY INGREDIENTS FOR THE MALTED MILK BATTER:

1½ cups all-purpose flour

3 tablespoons powdered sugar

1 tablespoon baking powder

¼ teaspoon salt

2 tablespoons malted milk powder

FOR THE STRAWBERRY SYRUP:

¼ cup strawberry jam, whisked into a thick syrup

½ cup maple syrup

2 tablespoons salted butter

1. Combine all the wet ingredients in a medium bowl, and whisk until smooth. Set aside.
2. In two separate bowls, mix the dry ingredients for each batter thoroughly. Add half the wet ingredients to each of the dry ingredient bowls, stirring each until they just come together, about 10 strokes. (Some lumps are okay.)
3. Heat a nonstick skillet or griddle on medium high. Pour about ¼ cup of batter onto the griddle and cook until bubbles form and pop. Flip pancake, and cook until the other side is golden, about 2 minutes total. Alternate between flavors, or marble together by using some of each batter and swirling with a spatula.
4. To make the strawberry syrup: Add all ingredients to a small saucepan on medium heat, and whisk until butter is melted and syrup is well combined. Serve immediately. Pancakes can be kept warm in a 250°F oven or served to order.

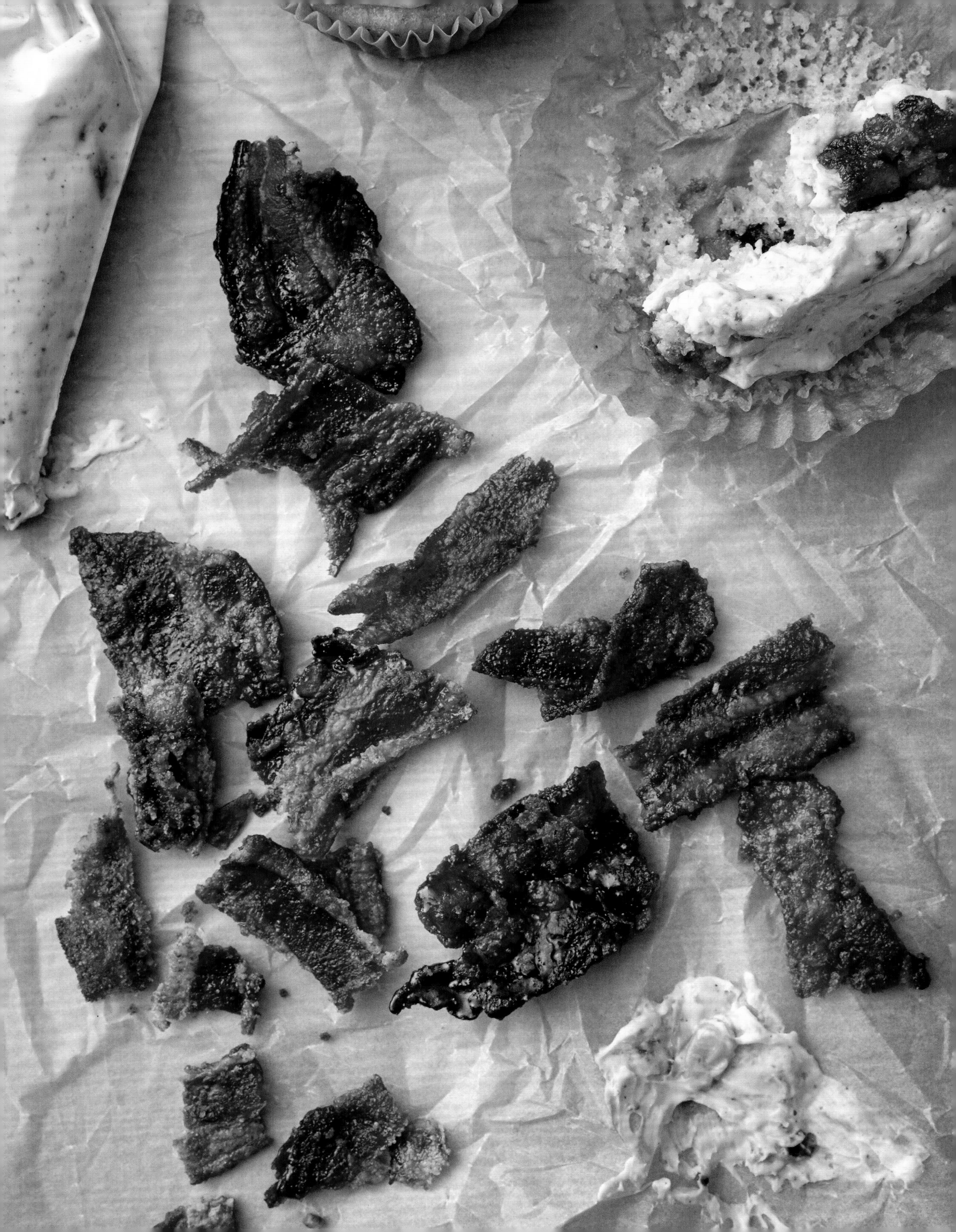

What's Shakin' Bacon?

YIELD: 1 POUND BACON

Nothing says breakfast in America like crispy strips of porcine belly fat. Back home in Canada, we've got bacon too, but it's basically just fancy ham. Talk about false advertising! Luckily, I live here now, 'cause you Yankees have the kind of bacon that I want to put in literally everything I eat, from salads and sandwiches to breakfast baked goods (check out Muffin to See Here, page 107). As if bacon wasn't already good enough on its own, your pal Wade has gone and found a way to make the stuff even more addictive! Just shake it in some brown sugar and spices and bake it to caramelized perfection, and you'll have a candied delight that's one of the few things worth waking up for in this nightmare of a world.

1¼ cups dark brown sugar

1 teaspoon cayenne pepper

1 teaspoon paprika

1 pound bacon, not thick cut

SPECIAL SUPPLIES:

2 wire racks fit into baking sheets

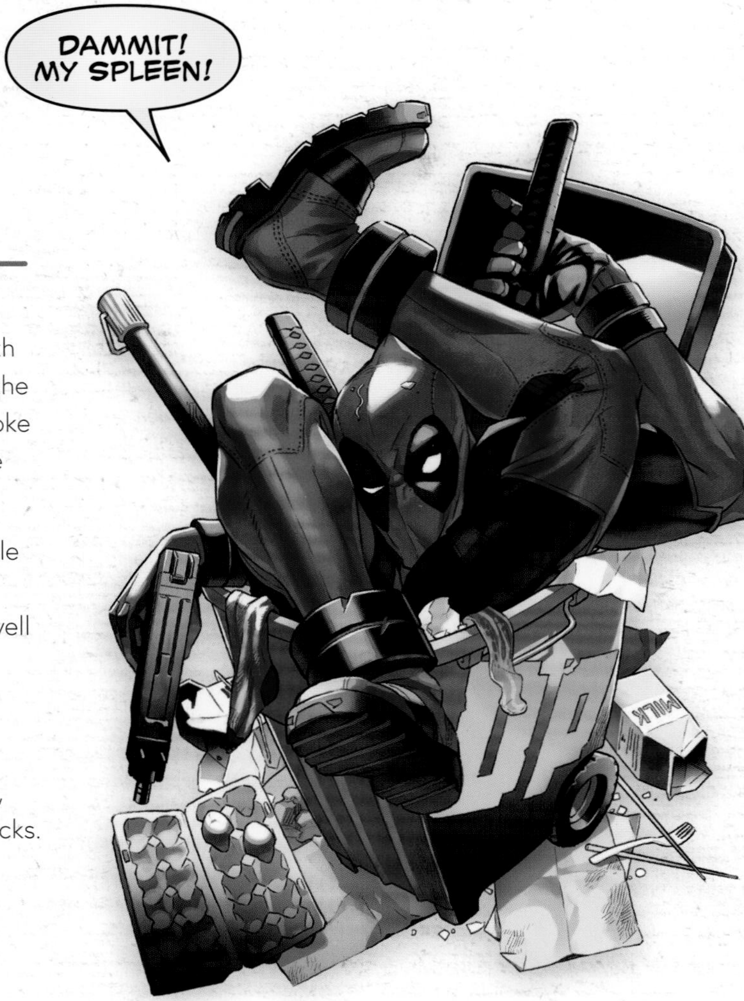
DAMMIT! MY SPLEEN!
MILK

1. Preheat the oven to 375°F. Line 2 baking sheets with parchment, and place a wire rack into each. Cover the wire racks with another sheet of parchment, and poke holes in the parchment at 2-inch intervals to let the bacon fat drain onto the baking sheet below.
2. Mix the brown sugar and the spices in the resealable bag. Working with a few slices at a time, place the bacon in the bag, seal it, and shake until bacon is well coated. Lay each piece flat on the prepared sheet. Repeat until all the bacon is coated.
3. Cook in the oven until the bacon is crisp and the coating is shiny and sticky, about 20 to 25 minutes, rotating the sheets halfway through. Let cool on racks. Break up and store in an airtight container.

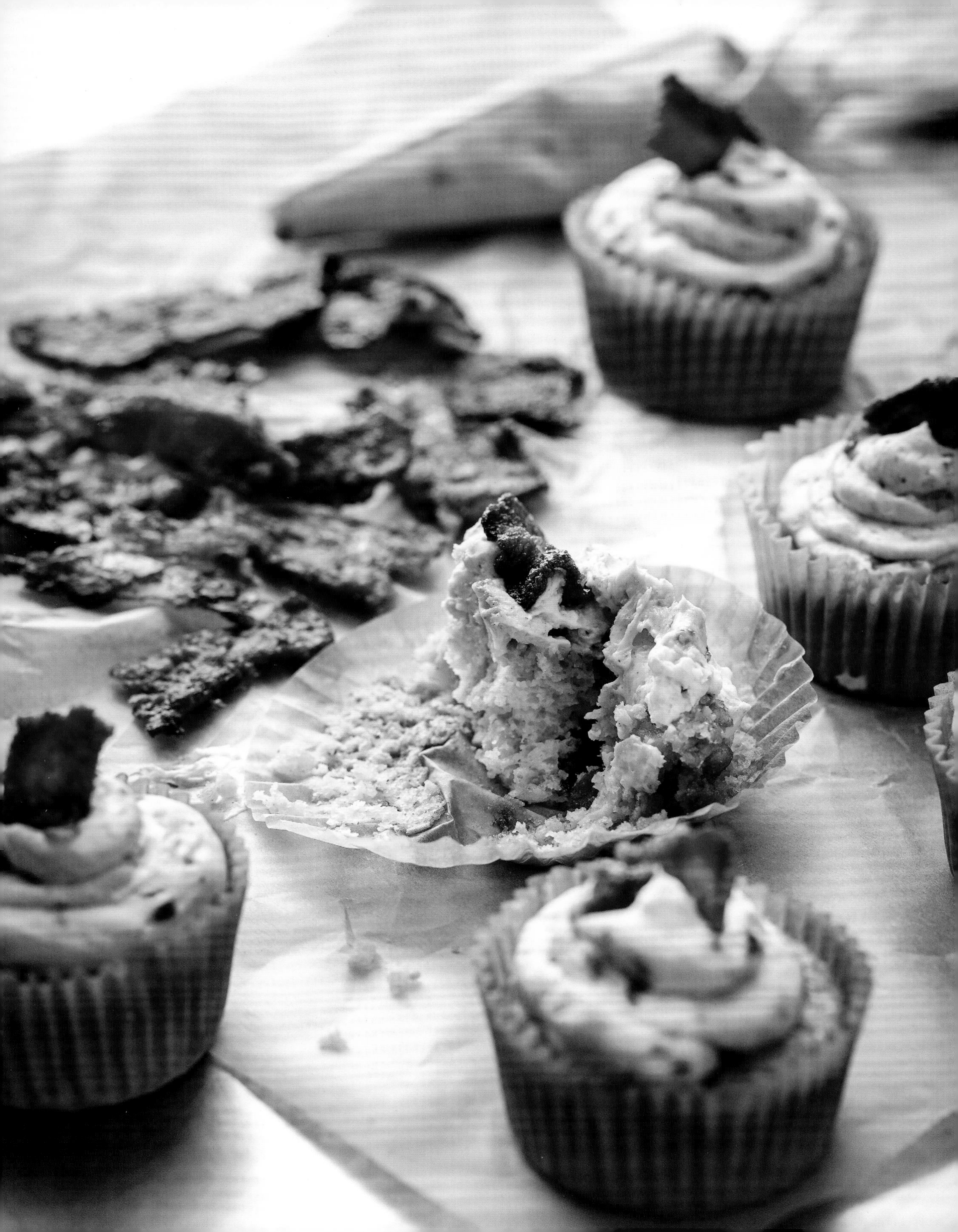

Muffin to See Here

We're conditioned to love our morning pastries loaded with more sugar than our pancreases can handle. Fortunately for those folks who have grown tired of going into diabetic shock before noon, there's a whole world of savory flavors out there just waiting to take a shot at your taste buds. I'll be honest—I discovered this recipe by accident one time when I was low on funds and had nothing in my pantry but a bag of flour and a can of creamed corn. But the results were surprisingly tasty and a hell of a lot more nutritious than my usual box of quadruple-fudge donuts. Since your sweet tooth deserves a little reward for letting the rest of your mouth eat healthier, go ahead and mix in some of my special candied bacon (see What's Shakin' Bacon?, page 105). I won't tell.

FOR THE MUFFINS:

1½ cups milk

1 tablespoon apple cider vinegar

1 cup all-purpose flour

1 cup yellow cornmeal

2 tablespoons sugar

½ teaspoon baking soda

2 teaspoons baking powder

½ teaspoon salt

2 eggs

4 tablespoons (½ stick) salted butter, melted

One 15-ounce can creamed corn, divided

6 pieces (ha! like you didn't eat it all already) What's Shakin' Bacon? (page 105), broken into small pieces

FOR THE FROSTING:

1 cup (8 ounces) cream cheese, softened

½ cup (1 stick) salted butter, softened

½ cup reserved creamed corn

½ teaspoon paprika

2 to 3 pieces What's Shakin' Bacon? (page 105), broken into small pieces

SPECIAL SUPPLIES:

Parchment cupcake liners

Pastry bag

Pastry tips

1. Preheat the oven to 375°F. Prepare a muffin pan by lining the cups with parchment liners.

2. To make the muffins: Combine milk and apple cider vinegar in a small bowl, and let stand 10 minutes. Combine all dry ingredients in a separate bowl. Whisk eggs into the milk mixture, then add wet ingredients to dry ingredients. Stir to combine. Add butter, and mix until well combined. Add the creamed corn, reserving ½ cup for the frosting, and the bacon bits, and stir. Pour batter into the muffin tins, filling each cup about three-quarters full. Bake for 20 to 25 minutes, until cake tester or toothpick inserted into the center comes out clean.

3. To make the frosting: Combine the slightly softened cream cheese and butter in a medium bowl, and beat with a hand mixer until fluffy. Add reserved ½ cup creamed corn and the paprika, and blend until mixture comes together. Use a spatula to fold in bacon bits. Refrigerate frosting until muffins are cool.

4. To frost the muffins: Using a pastry bag with a large tip, pipe a small dollop of frosting on each muffin. Top with a piece of the candied bacon.

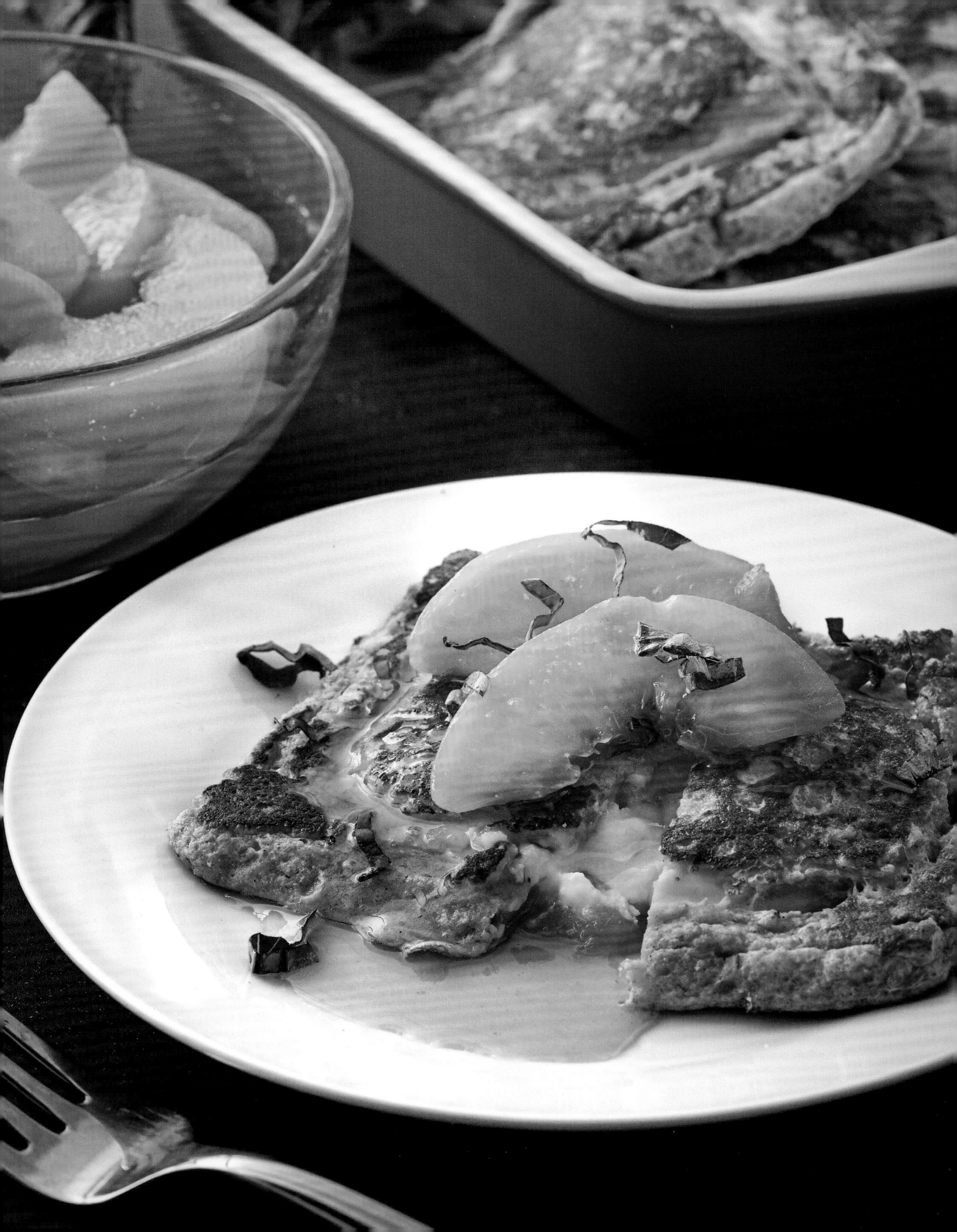

Oh, Stuff It

I've been fortunate enough to travel the globe through my life as an international man of misery, so I can say with great confidence that the French have a natural way to make just about anything normal seem fancy. When we North American types want breakfast bread, we just pop a couple of slices into the toaster and wait until it's so burned that we have to scrape the char off with a knife. But the French take toast to the next level, dipping each slice in an eggy mixture and frying it to golden perfection. You can even stuff your morning masterpiece full of delicious surprises, like the ones in this recipe here, as a way to add a little extra ooh to your *la la!*

FOR THE PEACHES AND SYRUP:

One 10-ounce package frozen peach slices

½ cup sugar

¼ cup fresh lemon juice (Meyer is best)

1 stalk fresh basil or ½ teaspoon dried

¼ teaspoon ground ginger

FOR THE RICOTTA FILLING:

1 cup (8 ounces) ricotta cheese

2 tablespoons powdered sugar

FOR THE CUSTARD:

⅔ cup half-and-half

4 eggs

1 tablespoon powdered sugar

1 teaspoon vanilla paste or vanilla extract

FOR THE FRENCH TOAST POCKETS:

12 pieces white or wheat sandwich bread

4 tablespoons (½ stick) unsalted butter, softened

1. Preheat the oven to 350°F, and line a baking sheet with a silicone baking mat or parchment paper.

2. To make the peaches and syrup: In a small saucepan, combine the peaches, sugar, lemon juice, basil (if using fresh, drop the stalk in whole), and ground ginger. Bring to a boil, then reduce heat, and simmer until syrup thickens, about 10 minutes. Remove from heat. Using a slotted spoon, remove the peach slices (and basil stalk if using) from the syrup and set aside. Reserve syrup in saucepan.

3. To make the ricotta filling: Whisk together the ricotta and powdered sugar in a small bowl.

4. To make the custard: Whisk together the custard ingredients in a shallow dish that's big enough to hold a bread slice.

5. To make the French toast pockets: Place the baking sheet in the oven. Working in pairs, trim the crust of the bread slices, making them as square as possible, and set aside. (Reserve the crust for future uses, such as bread crumbs.)

6. Working with one pair of bread slices at a time, use your fingers to press a circular "dish" into each piece, about the size of a golf ball, being careful not to tear through.

7. Put a spoonful of the ricotta mixture and several of the peach slices into the center of one "dish" and top with the matching piece of bread. With your three middle fingers press "pleats" around all four sides, closing the pocket. Repeat with remaining bread pairs.

8. Heat a nonstick skillet or griddle on medium, brush with softened butter before cooking each pocket. One at a time, dip each pocket gently into the custard mixture, coating both sides, and place on the griddle. Do not let the pocket soak in the custard or it will begin to fall apart. Brown the pocket on both sides and then, using a clean, dry spatula, remove from griddle onto baking sheet in the oven. Bake for 8 to 12 minutes or until the egg is cooked and the bread is golden and puffed. Repeat with remaining French toast pockets.

9. To serve, gently reheat the peach syrup on the stove. Place each pocket on a plate, drizzle with peach syrup, and garnish with any reserved peaches or some chopped fresh basil.

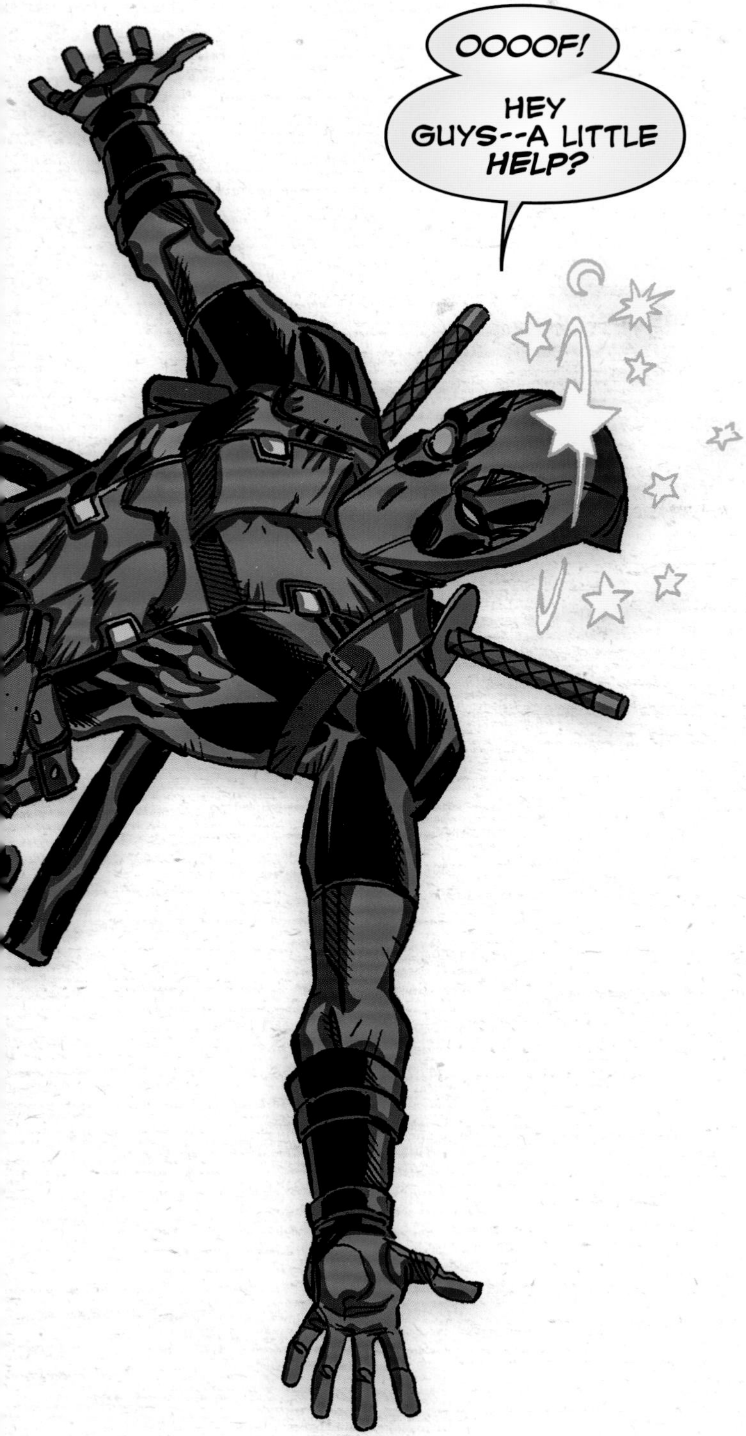
OOOOF!
HEY GUYS--A LITTLE HELP?

TIP:

YOU DON'T REALLY NEED FANCY TOOLS TO MAKE THIS RECIPE, BUT IF YOU HAPPEN TO HAVE A SLOTTED SPATULA, A FLAT SPATULA, A PASTRY BRUSH, AND A NONSTICK SKILLET OR GRIDDLE, IT CERTAINLY WOULDN'T HURT!

TIP:

WANT TO MAKE THINGS ALL PRETTY BY ADDING SOME PEACHES FOR GARNISH AS WELL AS STUFFING? THEN JUST DOUBLE THE INGREDIENTS LISTED UNDER "FOR THE PEACHES." EASY PEACHY!

Hashtag Hash

As much as I enjoy making fun of the younger generation for their complete lack of ambition and their horrible taste in music, they do occasionally win me over with their social media trends. I've been at the center of dozens of hilarious memes, and I've even live-streamed a few of my recent mercenary jobs. But what really turns me on is a newsfeed full of pictures of other people's food. If you're eating it, I want to see it. Preferably before it goes in your mouth. Of all the dishes I cook, this hearty hash is the one most worthy of internet fame! While it may look like it took all morning to cook, it is actually surprisingly easy to throw together if you've already got your tri-tip ready to go (Ready or Naut, page 74). I may not be a professional food stylist, but this breakfast is ready for its close-up!

2 tablespoons maple syrup

1 teaspoon instant coffee granules

1 to 2 tablespoons oil, for pan

1 small yellow onion, diced

1 small red bell pepper, diced

2 teaspoons salt

2 tablespoons salted butter

3 cups frozen hash browns

Leftover Ready or Naut (page 74, optional)

4 eggs

Fresh black pepper

1. In a small bowl, combine maple syrup and instant coffee. Set aside.

2. Heat a large nonstick skillet on medium, adding just enough oil to coat the bottom. Add the onion and pepper, and sauté until soft and starting to brown. Add salt, and sauté 3 minutes more. Add maple syrup mixture and butter, and sauté until the vegetables are well coated and butter is melted. Add the potatoes, and stir to combine.

3. Shake pan to create a flat layer of potatoes and veggies, and cook undisturbed for 5 minutes. Using a spatula, gently stir and flip the mixture. If using, add beef at this time, stirring gently to combine.

4. Shake pan again to flatten the hash back into a single layer, and use the spatula to create 4 wells in the mixture for each egg. Crack an egg into each well, and add salt and pepper to taste. Cover the pan with a lid, and continue to cook 8 to 10 minutes, until eggs are done.

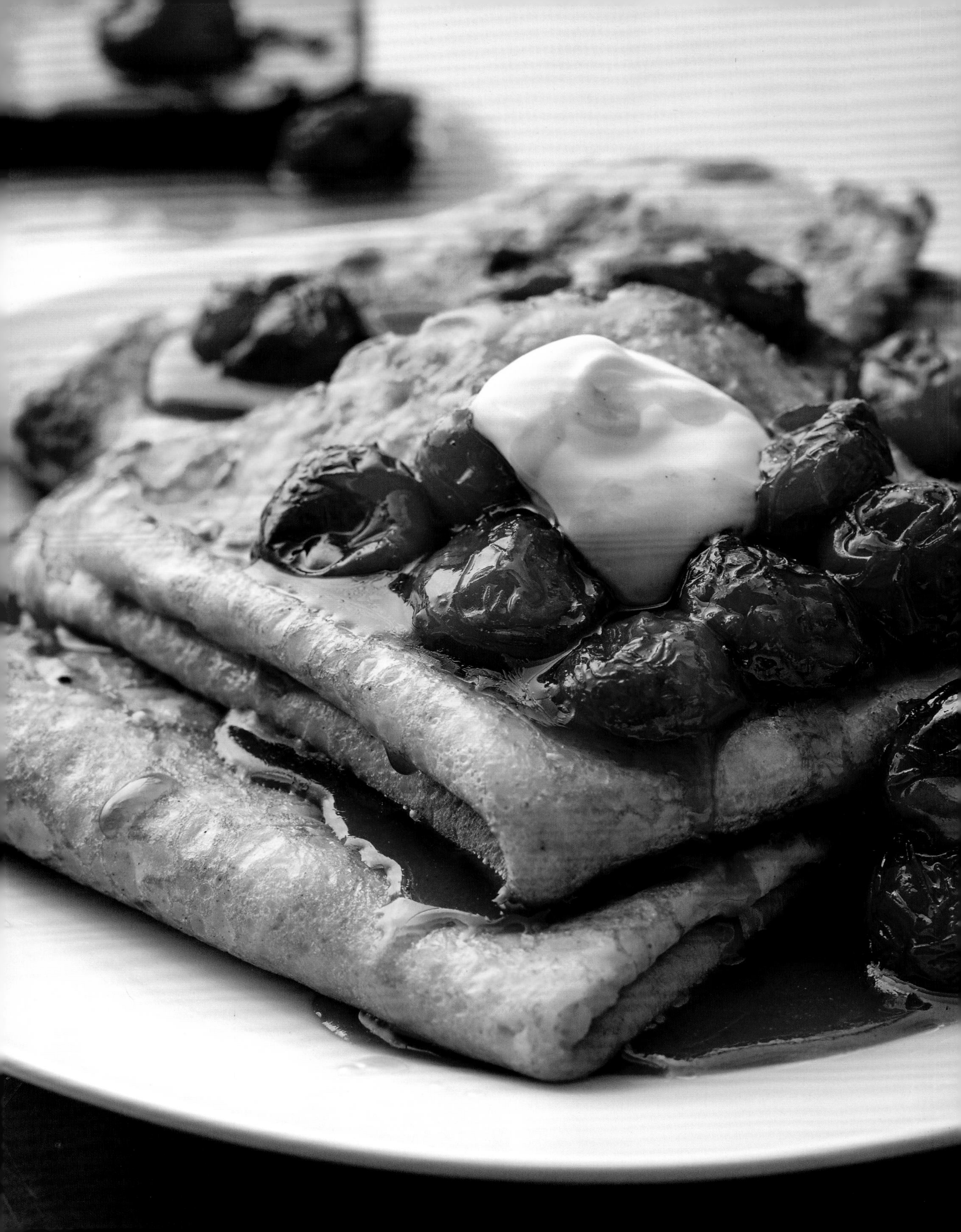

CREPES OF WRATH

Remember when I said that the French have a way of making everything fancy? Well, you should. It was literally in the intro for the recipe before this one. Wanna go back and check? I'll wait. Okay, now that we're all on the same page again—the crepe is basically the fancy French version of a pancake. But unlike the thick blobs of batter I like to toss on my griddle, crepes are so delicate and ultrathin that it takes a stack of about twenty-seven of them to equal one of my pancakes. Traditional crepes are usually topped with fruit and powdered sugar, but they can also be used like a tortilla to hold all sorts of breakfast-y fillings. Crepes are the perfect way to start off any day, but since they're so high class, I like to save them for special holidays, like Bastille Day. After all, like some famous French lady named Marionette said, "Let them eat pancake!"

FOR THE CREPE BATTER:

½ cup all-purpose flour

½ cup milk

¼ cup lukewarm water

2 eggs

2 tablespoons unsalted butter, melted, plus 2 tablespoons, melted, for pan

1½ tablespoons sugar

¼ teaspoon ground allspice

Pinch of salt

FOR THE ROASTED GRAPES:

2 pounds black or red seedless table grapes, rinsed and stemmed

2 tablespoons olive oil

1 tablespoon balsamic vinegar

Pinch of salt

2 to 3 grinds fresh black pepper

2 to 3 sprigs fresh thyme

2 tablespoons sugar

Crème fraîche or whipped cream, for serving (optional)

1. To make the crepe batter: Combine flour, milk, water, eggs, and 2 tablespoons melted butter in a blender, and blend until smooth. You can also use an immersion blender in a medium mixing bowl. Let batter stand for 30 minutes, or cover and refrigerate overnight.

2. To make the roasted grapes: Preheat the oven to 425°F. On a baking sheet, combine the grapes with oil, vinegar, salt, pepper, and thyme sprigs. Bake for 20 to 30 minutes, until caramelized and soft. Transfer to a heatproof bowl, sprinkle with sugar, and smash gently with a fork, until some but not all the grapes have split open. Cover with a lid or plastic wrap, and set aside.

3. To make the crepes: Heat an 8-inch nonstick skillet on medium. Use a pastry brush to lightly coat the pan with melted butter, gently stir the batter, and pour a scant ¼ cup onto the center of the pan. Gently roll the pan to coat the bottom with the batter, being careful to avoid rolling the batter up the sides. Cook crepe for about 2 minutes, then use a very thin spatula to lift the edge of the crepe and flip it over. Brush the cooked side with butter, and cook about 2 more minutes. Remove crepe to a plate and fold in fourths, making a shape like a piece of pie. Repeat until all batter is used.

4. Serve 2 or 3 crepes with a generous spoonful of grapes and their sauce. Dollop with crème fraîche or whipped cream, if desired.

AUNT MAY'S WHEAT CAKES

I team up with Spider-Man a lot, because frankly, the guy loves me. I always act like the feeling is mutual, but truthfully, I feel sorry for the kid. He's essentially me if I were significantly less hilarious and completely unable to do my job because of a crippling moral code. While Spidey may be a pale imitation of yours truly in most facets of his life, there's one area where he may have me beat. The guy makes a mean pancake. Or wheat cake, actually. Which I guess is a sort of healthier pancake that his sweet old aunt used to make him. Just like Spidey himself, these wheat cakes are as wholesome as they come. And to be honest, maybe that ain't such a bad thing now and then. Just don't tell him I said so.

1 cup buckwheat flour

1 cup sifted whole wheat flour

2 tablespoons baking powder

1 teaspoon baking soda

1 teaspoon salt

2 cups buttermilk

2 teaspoons molasses

2 eggs, yolks and whites separated

4 tablespoons (½ stick) salted butter, melted, plus softened butter for pan

Syrup of choice, for serving

1. Mix all dry ingredients together in a large bowl. In a separate bowl, mix buttermilk and molasses. Add egg yolks and melted butter to the flour mixture, along with buttermilk and molasses mixture, and stir to combine.

2. Whip egg whites just until stiff, then gently fold into batter with a spatula until blended.

3. Heat a nonstick skillet or griddle on medium. Brush the pan with softened butter, and pour a quarter cup of batter onto the center of the pan. Cook until bubbles form on top, 3 to 5 minutes. Flip once, and cook until bottom of pancake is golden brown, another 3 to 5 minutes. Serve with your favorite syrup.

Zen-Pool's Organic Bowl

A little ways back, the Red Skull stole Professor X's mutant brain and used its psychic powers to turn heroes into villains and vice versa. Trust me, it was just as confusing as it sounds. While everyone else was scrambling to find their true identity, I was perfectly content finding personal enlightenment and tending to my rock garden. Eventually, I realized that peace and serenity weren't really my style, but despite returning to my more violent tendencies, I haven't forgotten how good it feels to take the time to properly feed your body and soul now and then. My path to finding this recipe may have been unnecessarily complicated, but this simple, nutritious breakfast bowl packed with organic ingredients like coconut, chia seeds, oats, and fruit is one of the few things from that period of my life that still makes sense.

½ cup toasted old-fashioned or steel-cut oats

½ cup oat milk

1 tablespoon chia seeds

1 to 2 tablespoons honey, according to desired sweetness

¼ teaspoon ground cinnamon

TOPPINGS:

Raspberries

Unsweetened shredded coconut

Pecans

Coconut cream, optional

---

1. In a container that holds 2 cups and has a lid, mix all ingredients together until well combined. Toppings can be added now, or right before serving.

2. Refrigerate oat mixture overnight or at least 6 hours. Enjoy cold, or heat in the microwave for 1 minute, followed by 30-second intervals, until warm.

> **TIP:**
> NOT A FAN OF RASPBERRIES OR PECANS? FIRST OFF, YOU'RE WRONG. SECOND, YOU COULD SWAP IN BLUEBERRIES, PEACHES, DRIED CRANBERRIES, OR RAISINS, AND OTHER NUTS LIKE WALNUTS OR ALMONDS FOR ANY OF THE TOPPINGS . . . IF YOU JUST HAVE TO BE A REBEL.

> **TIP:**
> LOCAL HONEY WORKS BEST FOR THIS RECIPE, WHICH IS A RELIEF, BECAUSE I REALLY HATE TRAVELING THOUSANDS OF MILES JUST FOR HONEY.

The Healing Factor

Yield: 4 servings

Not everybody is lucky enough to have super-powers. Hell, even some of the people who do have super-powers aren't lucky enough to have decent ones. (Have you seen some of the lower-tier students at the X-Men school? Yeesh!) But when it comes to enhanced abilities, some say I hit the jackpot. My healing factor allows me to regenerate all my important bits if and when they get blown up or chopped off. But the very same power that has saved my life time and again was given to me through a series of Weapon X experiments so brutally painful that they left emotional scars a million times deeper than my physical ones. If I had known how to make a breakfast drink like this one, packed full of ingredients with natural healing properties like turmeric, ginger, and pepper, I probably would have just turned on the stove instead.

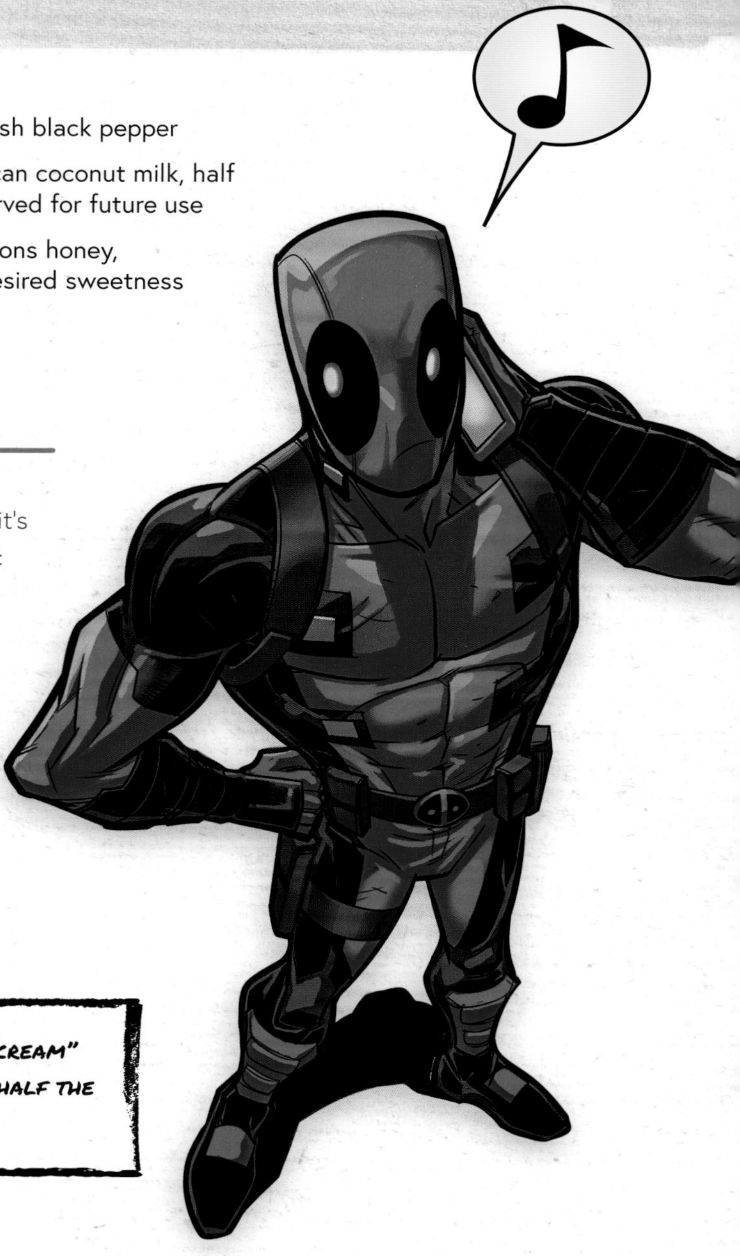

1 tablespoon ground turmeric

1 cinnamon stick or ½ teaspoon ground cinnamon

2 large thumbs fresh ginger (about 2 inches each), peeled and gently crushed

2 cups almond milk

¼ teaspoon fresh black pepper

One 13-ounce can coconut milk, half the cream reserved for future use

2 to 3 tablespoons honey, according to desired sweetness

1. Heat a dry medium saucepan on medium high. When it's hot to the touch, remove from stove and add turmeric and cinnamon. Stir spices in pan until fragrant.
2. Add ginger, black pepper, almond milk, and coconut milk, and return to the stove on medium heat. Bring mixture to a gentle simmer, then reduce heat to low, and let steep for 10 to 15 minutes. Add honey and stir to dissolve. Remove cinnamon stick and ginger pieces. Enjoy immediately, or refrigerate for up to 3 days.

TIP:

COCONUT MILK, UNLESS IT'S LOW FAT, HAS A LAYER OF "CREAM" AT THE TOP. THIS RECIPE CALLS FOR ALL THE MILK AND HALF THE CREAM. RESERVE THE SECOND HALF FOR FUTURE USE.

CHILLA-KILLERS

So you threw a fierce fiesta that raged into the wee hours of the night, but now you've suddenly woken up with a grumble in your tummy and an empty fridge? No worries. If you've still got chips and salsa left over from the previous evening's festivities, you're already well on your way to having yourself a killer breakfast. Chilaquiles are a traditional Mexican dish of fried tortillas simmered in salsa (or some other delicious sauce). Of course, using leftovers is the easy way out. If you really want to do things right, then you've gotta fry up your own tortillas and make a batch of sauce from scratch. Once the tortillas start to soften up in the sauce, top 'em with some cheese (and maybe an egg if you're feeling a little frisky), and you're ready to give your *dias* the most *buenos* start it's ever had!

Two 28-ounce cans whole tomatoes

3 cloves garlic, smashed and peeled

2 teaspoons salt, plus more for tortillas

1 serrano chile or jalapeño, stemmed

Sixteen 8-inch corn tortillas

1 quart oil, for frying

6 eggs, fried to order

Crumbled cotija cheese, for garnish (optional)

Sliced avocado, for garnish (optional)

---

1. Add the tomatoes, garlic, salt, and whole chile to a medium saucepan on high heat. Bring to a low boil, then reduce heat, and simmer until garlic and chile are very soft, about 30 minutes.

2. Use an immersion blender to blend the sauce until it's smooth. If you don't have an immersion blender, let sauce cool enough to safely blend in a countertop blender. (You may need to do this in batches.)

3. Cut the tortillas like a pie, into sixteenths. Prepare your frying station (page 91), and heat the oil to 365°F. Fry the tortillas in small batches. Remove and drain on paper towel, lightly salting while still hot.

4. To assemble: Heat ½ cup of sauce in a large sauté pan on medium. Add 2 handfuls of tortilla chips to the pan, and simmer until chips are tender but not soggy. Transfer chips to a plate, and top with a fried egg. Add avocado and cheese, if desired.

> **TIP:**
> WANT A SHORTCUT? YOU CAN USE STORE-BOUGHT CORN CHIPS! BUT BE CAREFUL: THEY WILL BECOME SOGGY MUCH FASTER THAN FRESHLY FRIED TORTILLAS.

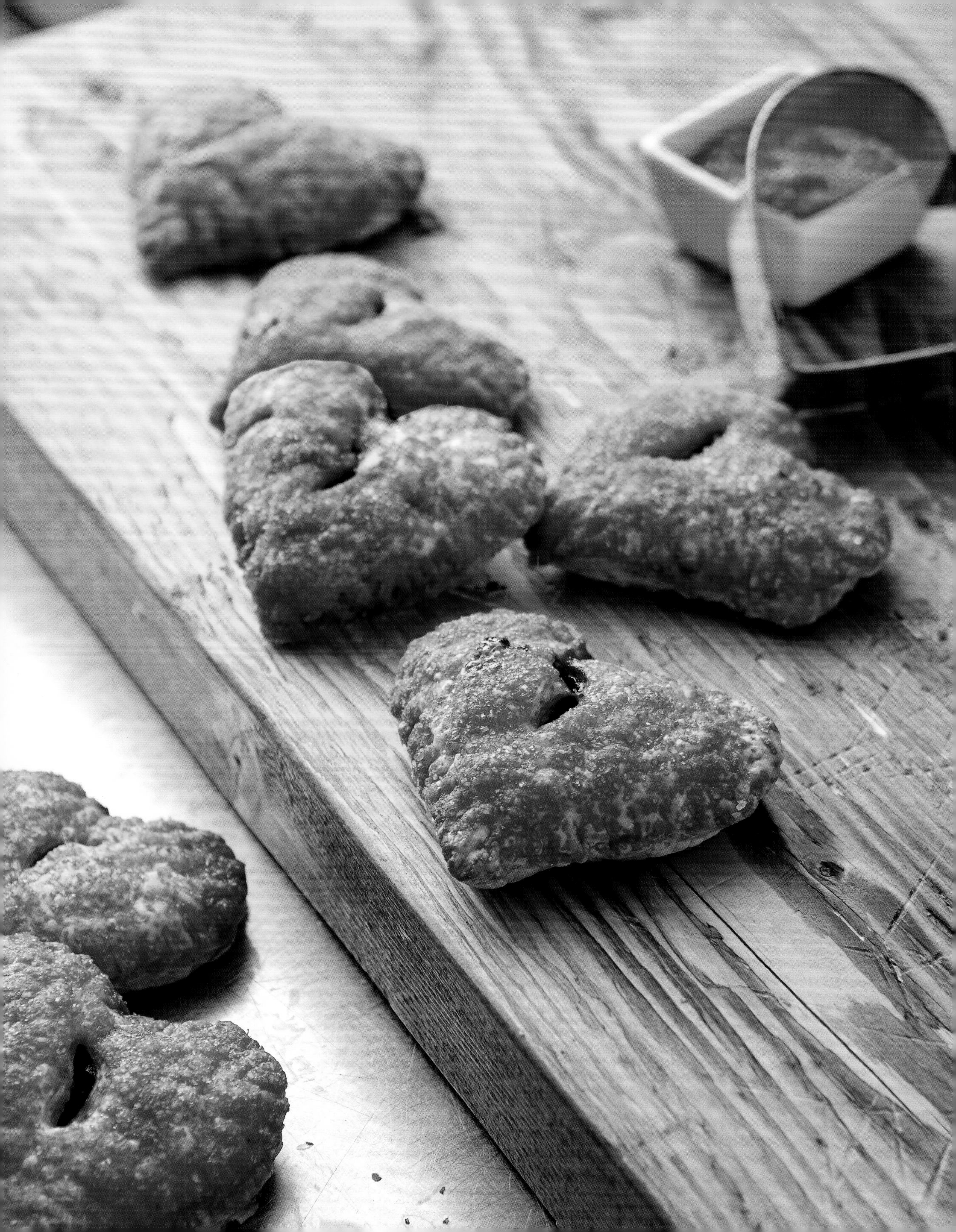

Sweetest Things

Did everybody clean their plates? Good job! Now you get to partake in my favorite part of any meal: dessert!

There's something about a sugary snack that sends me straight back to simpler times. I mean, I can barely remember anything about my childhood after all the crazy stuff the Weapon X program did to my brain, but every time I close my eyes and try to find my happy place, I can somehow smell a warm batch of cookies fresh out of the oven. So either I've got a deep subconscious connection with wholesome baked goods from my forgotten youth or I'm having a series of small strokes. (It's probably the latter. I've been hit in the head a lot over the years. And I've deserved it.)

But whether or not my sense memories are even remotely reliable, it doesn't change the fact that I get all gooey inside every time I see a pie cooling on the windowsill, a scoop of ice cream glistening in the hot summer sun, or a guy with his face covered in chocolate pudding. I'll be honest—there aren't many things in life better than getting paid to sow discord, but these sweet treats make the short list!

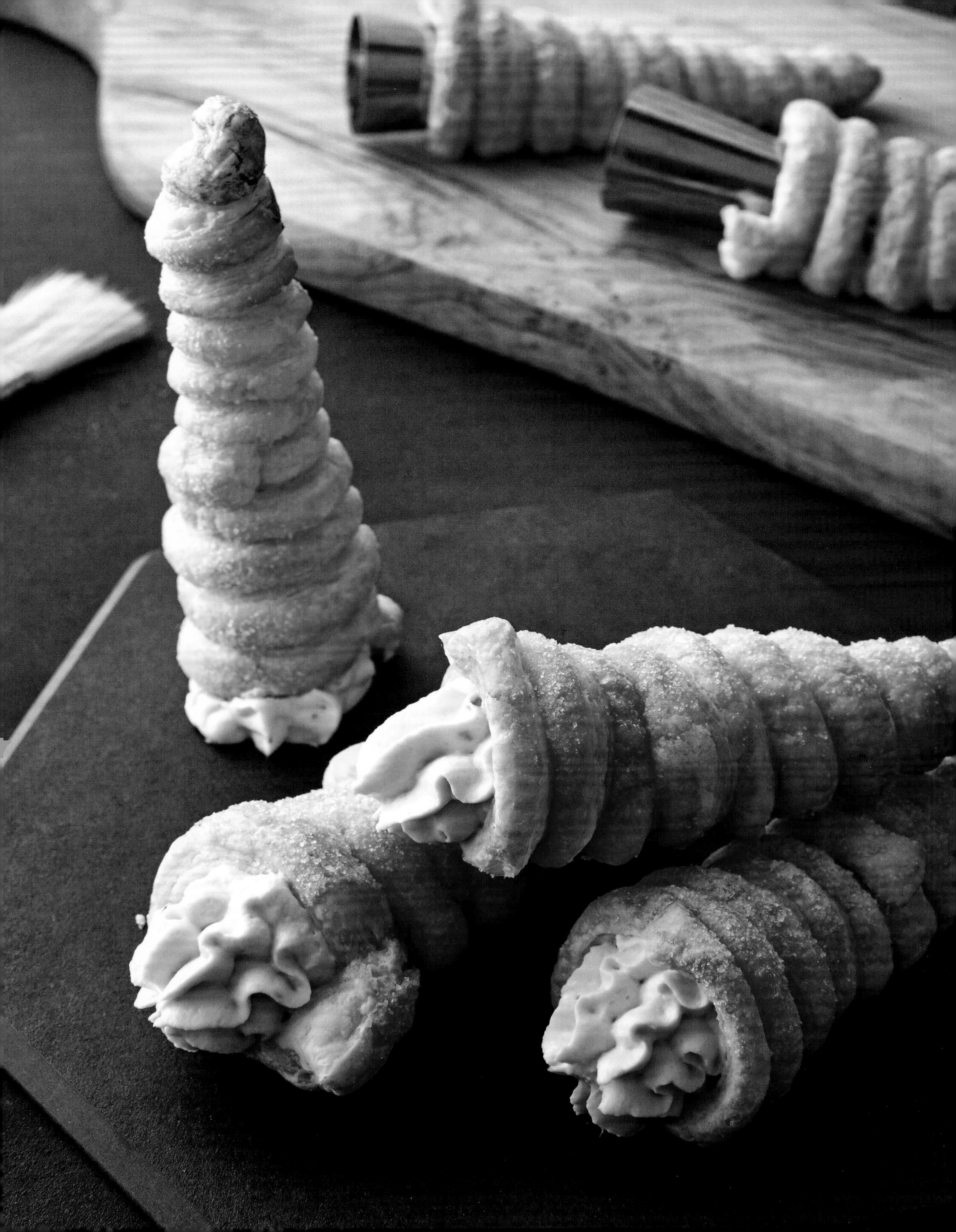

Unicorn Horns

As one of the world's most recognizable mercenaries, I find myself out there in the public eye more often than I'd like. Hardcore fans think they know everything about me, including my favorite catchphrases, my preferred brand of ammo, and my Wi-Fi password (it's W4D3RUL3S!). But even with every facet of my life under constant scrutiny, there are a few things I like to keep just for Wade. For instance, my inexplicable affection for unicorns and rainbows. Wait, you knew about that? There are T-shirts? Crap. Well, since I apparently can't have anything just for myself, I might as well share my secret recipe for my rainbow unicorn cream horns too. It's not exactly as joyous as I imagine riding a unicorn over a rainbow would be . . . but it's gotta be damn close.

3 tablespoons salted butter, softened, for brushing molds

2 cups heavy cream, plus ¼ cup more for color wash

2 tablespoons water

1 package frozen puff pastry, thawed according to package directions

Flour, for work surface

Granulated sugar, for sprinkling

1 cup (8 ounces) cream cheese, softened

½ cup strawberry jam, whisked

Food coloring in pink, purple, blue, green, and yellow

SPECIAL SUPPLIES:

Cream horn molds or sugar cones wrapped with foil inside and out

Pastry bag or resealable bag

1. Brush each mold with softened butter. Set molds on a cookie sheet lined with a silicone baking mat or parchment paper.

2. Prepare color washes by mixing ¼ cup of cream with the water. Divide cream wash into 5 small bowls, and add a few drops of food coloring to each.

3. Lay pastry on a lightly floured surface, and cut into ½-inch strips. A pizza cutter works well for this. Working with one strip at a time, wind strips of dough around the mold starting at the point and overlapping slightly until mold is mostly covered. This should take about 2 strips. When all molds are covered in pastry, create the rainbow. Using your pastry brush, brush each color wash onto the horn in 1- to 2-inch sections, thoroughly rinsing the brush between colors. When all horns are fully colored, freeze for 15 minutes.

4. Preheat the oven to 400°F. Remove horns from freezer, and sprinkle each with sugar. Bake for 10 to 15 minutes, until pastry is golden and crisp. If the colors begin to darken too much during baking, lightly cover with a sheet of foil. Remove from the oven when done, and let cool completely.

5. To prepare the filling: Mix the cream cheese and jam together until smooth. In a separate bowl, whip the cream until soft peaks form. Add the cream cheese mixture and continue to whip until filling is firm and well blended. When pastry horns are cool, use a pastry bag or a resealable bag with the corner snipped off to fill each horn completely with the filling. Serve immediately.

> **TIP:**
> THESE CAN BE STORED IN THE FRIDGE, BUT THEY LAST ONLY ABOUT 4 HOURS BEFORE THEY START TO GET SOGGY.

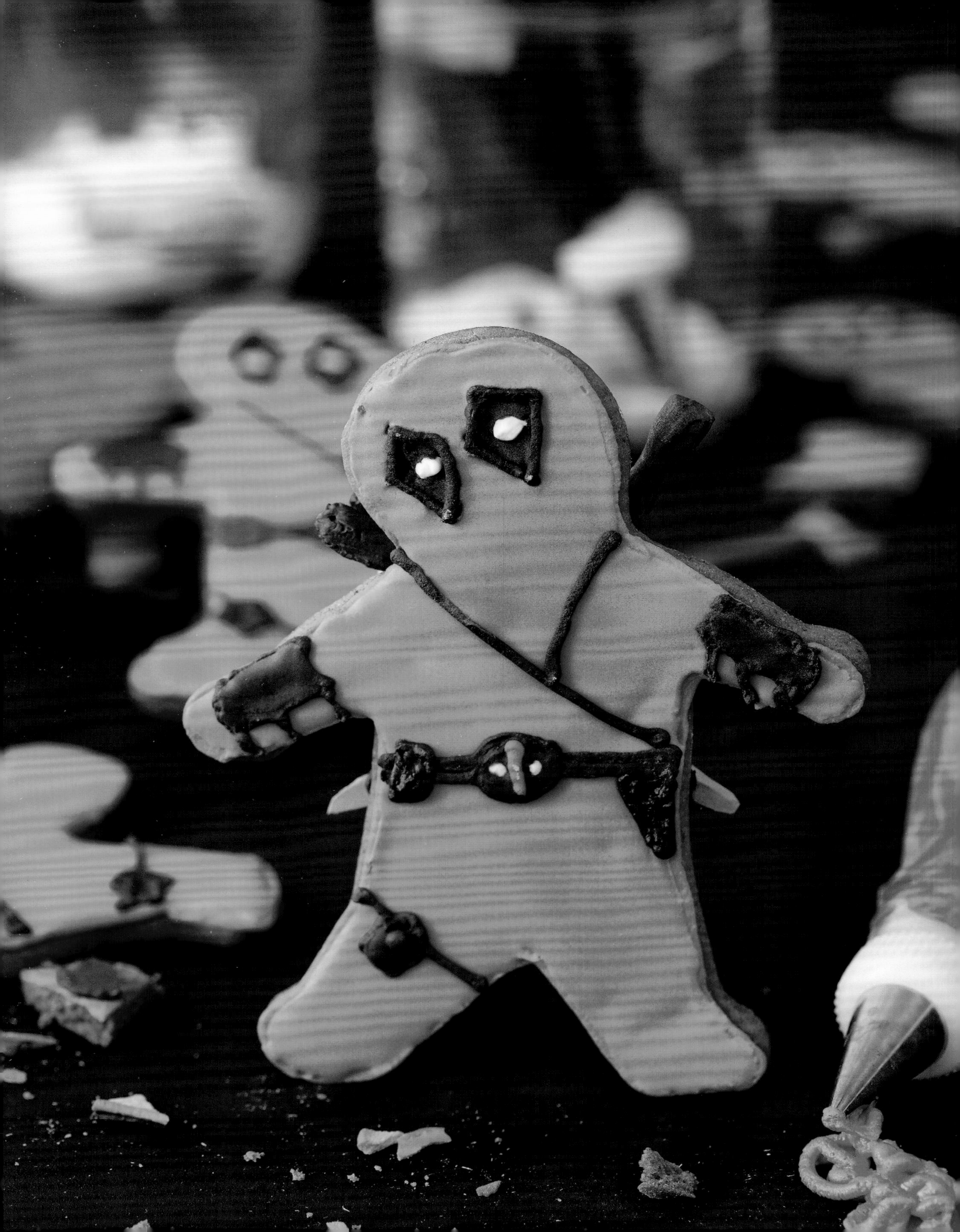

GingerPools

YIELD: APPROXIMATELY 30 MERCS FOR MONEY

Every once in a while, I reach a point where I've got more jobs coming in than I can handle. When the public demand for Deadpooling is higher than I'm able to satisfy on my own, I occasionally call in a bit of extra help from my fellow mercs. There was even a short span where I ran a whole team of Deadpools, called the Mercs for Money. To stay on brand, I made them all dress in color-coded versions of my costume. We were like a beautiful rainbow of pure destruction! But the operation didn't last long, and most of them won't return my calls anymore. Sometimes when I'm lonely, I bake up a batch of these cookies, decorate them to look like my former partners, and break their limbs off one by one. Makes me feel better every time.

FOR THE GINGERPOOLS DOUGH:

6 cups sifted all-purpose flour, plus more for work surface

1 teaspoon baking soda

½ teaspoon baking powder

1 cup (2 sticks) unsalted butter, room temperature

1 cup packed dark brown sugar

1 tablespoon ground ginger

1 teaspoon ground cardamom

4 teaspoons ground cinnamon

1½ teaspoons five-spice powder

1 teaspoon white pepper

1½ teaspoons kosher salt

2 large eggs

1 cup molasses

FOR THE ICING:

3 tablespoons meringue powder

4 cups powdered sugar, sifted

6 tablespoons water

Food coloring of choice

SPECIAL SUPPLIES:

Gingerbread man cookie cutter

Pastry bags or resealable bags

1. To make the GingerPools dough: In a large bowl, combine sifted flour, baking soda, and baking powder. Set aside. In the bowl of a stand mixer fitted with the paddle attachment, cream butter and brown sugar until light and fluffy. Mix in spices and salt. Add eggs and molasses, and mix well. With the machine on low speed, gradually add flour mixture, and beat until combined. Divide the dough into thirds, and wrap each piece of dough in parchment. Refrigerate for at least 1 hour.

2. Preheat the oven to 350°F. Line cookie sheets with silicone baking mats or parchment paper, and set aside.

3. On a lightly floured work surface, roll out dough to ¼ inch thick. Cut out GingerPools using a gingerbread man cutter. Transfer to baking sheets, and refrigerate at least 15 minutes before baking. This lets the dough keep its shape and prevents spreading. Bake for 9 to 12 minutes or until slightly brown and firm to the touch. Let cool completely before decorating.

4. To make the icing: Combine meringue powder, powdered sugar, and water in the bowl of a stand mixer, and beat at low speed for 7 to 10 minutes (or combine in a large bowl, and beat with a hand mixer at high speed for 10 to 12 minutes). Divide the icing among small bowls, and use food coloring to create desired hues. Transfer icing to a pastry bag or a resealable bag with the corner snipped off, and decorate as desired. Let cookies dry completely before serving, packaging, or storing, at least 3 hours.

> **TIP:**
> TUMMY TOO FULL AFTER ALL THE COOKIE CARNAGE? STORE THESE IN AN AIRTIGHT CONTAINER FOR UP TO A WEEK OR IN THE FREEZER FOR A MONTH!

CANNONBALLS

YIELD: 30 TO 35 BALLS

The X-Men and their spinoff squads have been fighting for a better world for decades. While most of their members have become hardened soldiers through their years on the front lines, there are a few who have managed to hold on to their innocent charm. One of those is my pal Sam Guthrie, aka Cannonball. If the phrase "aw shucks" suddenly came to life, it would look like a total badass compared to this hayseed. Cable tried to toughen Sam up during his X-Force days, but the kid somehow managed to keep his boyish charm intact through even the team's darkest hours. I named these little chocolate balls in his honor, not because their flavor is explosive like Sam's mutant power, but because they're just about as sweet as I can handle.

8 ounces semisweet chocolate, in bar form

¾ cup heavy cream

1 tablespoon vanilla extract

1½ cups gingersnap cookie crumbs

Silver coarse sparkling sugar

1. Break chocolate bars into small pieces, and place in a heatproof bowl. Pour cream in a separate microwave-safe bowl, and heat 1 minute at a time until scalding. Carefully pour cream over chocolate, and let stand for 3 minutes without stirring.

2. After 3 minutes, stir until chocolate is completely melted and smooth. Add the vanilla and cookie crumbs, and stir until well incorporated. Refrigerate 1 to 1½ hours, until mixture is firm.

3. Add the silver sparkling sugar to a medium bowl. Use a spoon to scoop up a small amount of chocolate mixture and roll into a 1-inch ball. Roll the ball in the sugar. Repeat until all the chocolate is used.

4. Let the balls set in the fridge at least 30 minutes, then bring them to room temperature before serving.

> **TIP:**
> STORE YOUR CANNONBALLS IN AN AIRTIGHT CONTAINER WITH PARCHMENT BETWEEN EACH LAYER. YOU CAN KEEP 'EM AT ROOM TEMPERATURE FOR THREE DAYS OR IN THE FRIDGE FOR TWO WEEKS.

CABLE'S CUISINE: RANGER PUDDING

Cable here. (Again.) No matter how Deadpool may try to glorify violence, it's important for any soldier to recognize this harsh reality: War isn't a game. When you're out there fighting for your very existence, there's rarely time to breathe, let alone to stop and make dessert. But even those of us on the front lines need a bit of comfort now and then, which has led to some creative options for satisfying our cravings. I bet you wouldn't believe that some random odds and ends from your breakfast rations—hot cocoa mix, sweetener packets, powdered creamer, and a touch of water— would combine to make a pudding that most soldiers would describe as "edible." This at-home version adds real milk and removes all chances of being shot at while preparing it. Enjoy.

FOR THE PUDDING BASE:

½ cup hot chocolate mix

2½ cups milk, whole or 2 percent

3 tablespoons cornstarch

OPTIONAL MIX-INS:

2 tablespoons malted milk powder

2 tablespoons powdered peanut butter

2 teaspoons instant coffee or espresso powder

Chocolate chips

Mini marshmallows

Toffee chips

Whipped cream, for serving

1. To make the pudding: Whisk together the base ingredients in a microwave-safe bowl or measuring cup until smooth. Add any desired powdered mix-in options—malted milk, powdered peanut butter, coffee—and whisk until combined. Cook in the microwave on full power, 2 minutes at a time, for a total of 10 minutes, whisking vigorously between cooking times and scraping down the sides of the bowl. Pudding will get thicker and thicker each time, but be careful: It will also get very hot.

2. Once the pudding has cooked the full 10 minutes, add any additional mix-ins you want. You can add one set of toppings to the whole batch or divide pudding between cups and customize them individually. Pudding can be served warm or chilled. To chill, place parchment directly on the surface of each pudding to prevent a skin from forming, then refrigerate for at least 2 hours. Serve with whipped cream, if desired.

> **TIP:**
> You might be tempted to use unsweetened cocoa powder instead of the hot chocolate mix. Don't do it! Trust me, the prepackaged, overly sweetened stuff is the only way to go!

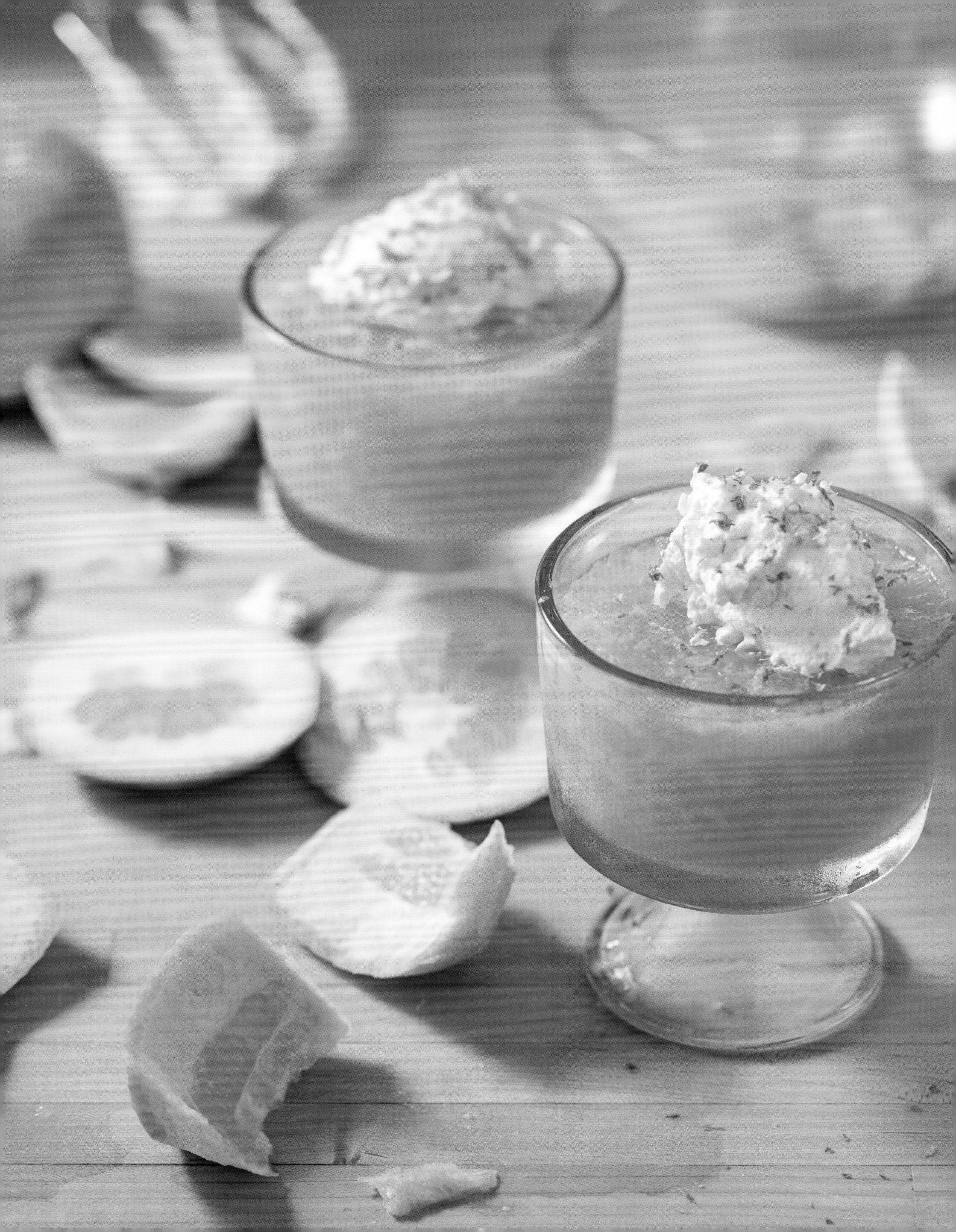

Golden Glow Salad

My body may be in its prime, but I've always been a bit of an old soul. I've always felt I would have been right at home in the bygone days, and I don't need a time machine to prove it. Classic sitcoms transport me back to a simpler era when dinner was on the table at six and neighbors randomly walked into the house without getting gunned down. No star of the small screen brought as much class and sass to her roles as the late, great Bea Arthur. So to commemorate my favorite golden gal, I whipped up this old-school gelatin dessert. Next time you throw a party, invite everyone you know and serve this wobbling wonder. Take my word, and everyone will thank you for being a friend!

One 11-ounce can mandarin oranges, drained, juice reserved

2 red grapefruit, segmented (page 128), juice reserved

One 20-ounce can crushed pineapple, drained, juice reserved, divided

Juice and zest of 2 limes

One 2¼-ounce packet gelatin

3 cups sparkling white grape juice, chilled

½ cup heavy cream

1 tablespoon sugar

1. Roughly chop the orange and grapefruit segments. Combine in a large bowl with most of the crushed pineapple, reserving ½ cup for the whipped topping.

2. In a 4-cup measuring cup, combine all the reserved juices with the lime juice (refrigerate lime rinds for zesting later). Pour 1 cup of the juice blend into a small saucepan, and sprinkle the gelatin over it. Let "bloom" for 2 minutes.

3. Heat on low until gelatin has completely dissolved. Stir gelatin mixture into remaining juice, and add enough sparkling grape juice (up to 3 cups) to bring the combined mixture up to 4 cups.

4. Divide fruit evenly among 6 dessert cups, and pour gelatin mixture over it, leaving about an inch at the top for whipped topping. Refrigerate for 1 hour, then stir to evenly distribute fruit. Chill for at least 3 hours more or until set.

5. When salad is set and ready to serve, whip the cream, sugar, and zest of 1 of the limes until stiff peaks form. Gently fold in the reserved pineapple. Put a generous dollop of topping on each salad, and garnish with more lime zest if desired.

JUST THE TIPS:
SEGMENTING A GRAPEFRUIT

Ever have the urge to eat a nice, nutritious grapefruit wedge, but can't handle all that stringy white junk left over after you've managed to scrape off the peel? Then, boy, have I got a trick for you:

1. First, cut both ends off your orb of citrusy goodness—grapefruit, orange, lime, it's all the same to me.

2. Stand up the fruit on one of its flat ends and cut down along the rounded side with your knife to remove a piece of the rind and pith. Repeat until all the rind and pith are removed. I guarantee that, when you're done, you'll be totally pithed off!

3. To remove the segments of flesh, cut along the interior of each membrane (yikes, that sounds brutal!) and pull the segments out. Make sure you're working over a bowl to catch all the juicy carnage!

4. Squeeze out the remaining juice in the membranes and throw 'em out. (What did they ever do for you anyway?)

5. Finally, marvel at all those fancy fruity bits you just let loose into the world!

FUN FACT: Did you know this technique is also called "supreming"?! Bet that li'l nugget of culinary wisdom will impress all the hot moms when you serve these perfectly sliced oranges at your daughter's next soccer game!

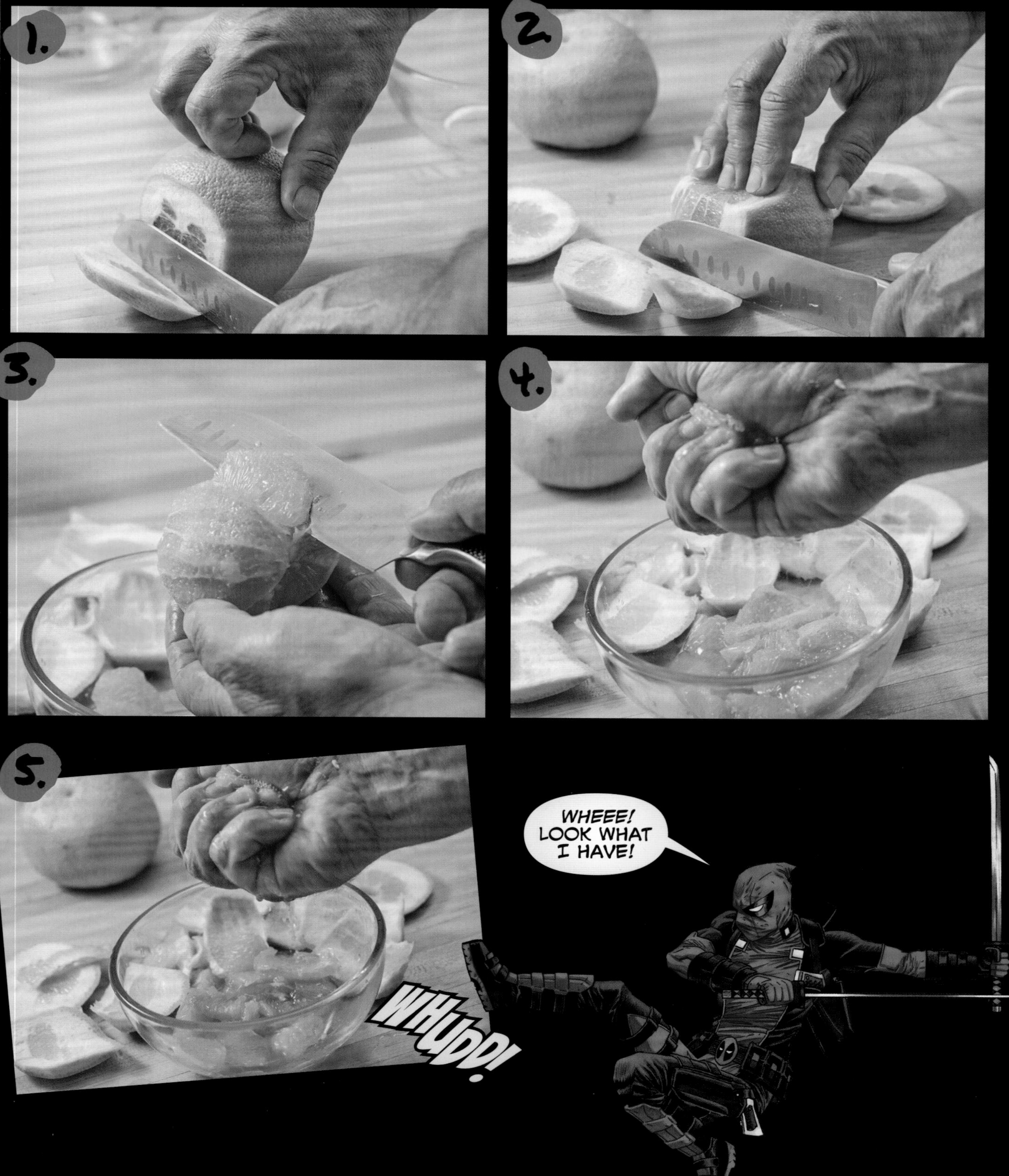

1.
2.
3.
4.
5.
WHEEE! LOOK WHAT I HAVE!
WHUDD!

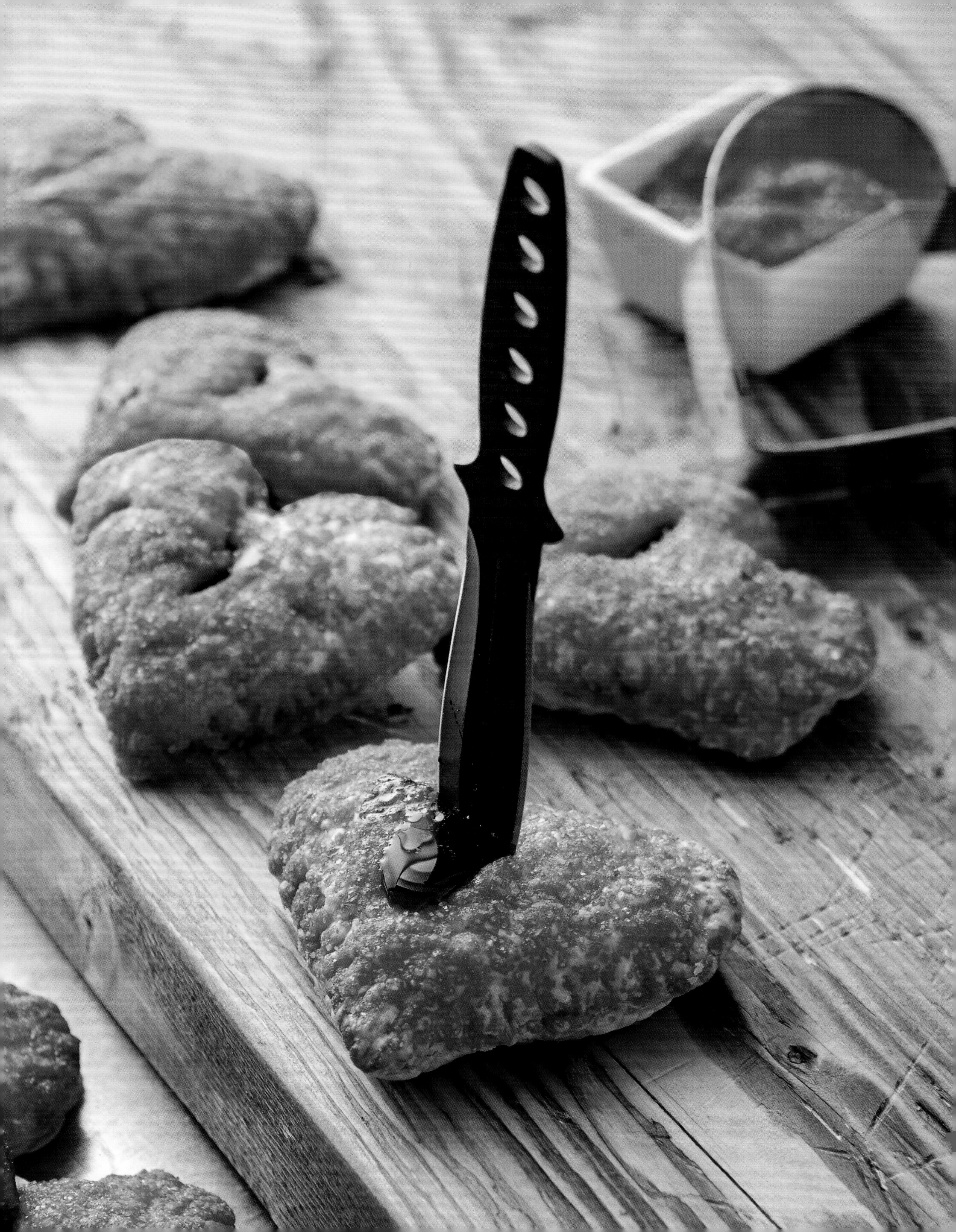

Bleeding Hearts

Yield: About 20 Hearts

My heart has been broken more times than I can count. And I'm not talking about the kind of broken that happens when you're punched in the chest repeatedly after mocking one of the X-Men for choosing the code name Strong Guy. (How was I supposed to know he would be so strong?) I'm talking about the kind of heartbreak that only happens when the love of your life moves on without you. Or, as in the case of my first true love, Vanessa, moves on without you but keeps finding ways to come back into your life and break your heart all over again. These little heart-shaped tarts are a lot like our love: piping hot and syrupy sweet but mere seconds away from being mercilessly devoured. (Make a big batch if you want to be a Copycat like her!)

FOR THE FILLING:

One 12-ounce package frozen cherries, thawed, with juice retained

1 tablespoon balsamic vinegar

½ cup sugar

¼ teaspoon ground cloves

1 teaspoon cornstarch

FOR THE EGG WASH:

1 egg white

1 tablespoon water

FOR THE PIES:

Flour for work surface

1 package frozen puff pastry, thawed according to package directions

Red sanding sugar, optional

SPECIAL SUPPLIES:

3-inch heart cookie cutter

1. To make the filling: Combine all the filling ingredients except cornstarch in a small saucepan, and bring to a simmer on medium heat. Keep mixture at a gentle simmer, stirring frequently, until the cherries are soft and the juices have begun to thicken. Remove a small amount of juice from the pot and mix rapidly with the cornstarch in a small bowl until smooth. Pour cornstarch mixture into pot and bring to a boil for 1 minute. Remove from heat, and transfer to a heatproof bowl or glass measuring cup. Refrigerate until ready to assemble pies.
2. To make the egg wash: In a small bowl, use a fork to combine egg white and water.
3. Preheat the oven to 400°F. Line two cookie sheets with silicone baking mats or parchment paper.
4. Roll out pastry onto a lightly floured surface until about a ¼ inch thick. Use the cookie cutter to cut out 40 hearts, using scraps if needed. Refrigerate the hearts on the cookie sheets for 15 minutes.
5. Working with 1 sheet at a time, place 2 or 3 cherries, lightly drained of juice, in the center of a heart. Cover with a second heart, and use a fork to tightly crimp the edges all the way around. Repeat until all the heart pies have been created and chill in the freezer for 10 minutes. Brush each heart pie with egg wash, and cut a slit in the center of each to vent. If using sanding sugar, sprinkle it on the hearts and bake for 12 to 15 minutes, until golden and puffed. Let cool before serving. Serve warm or at room temperature.

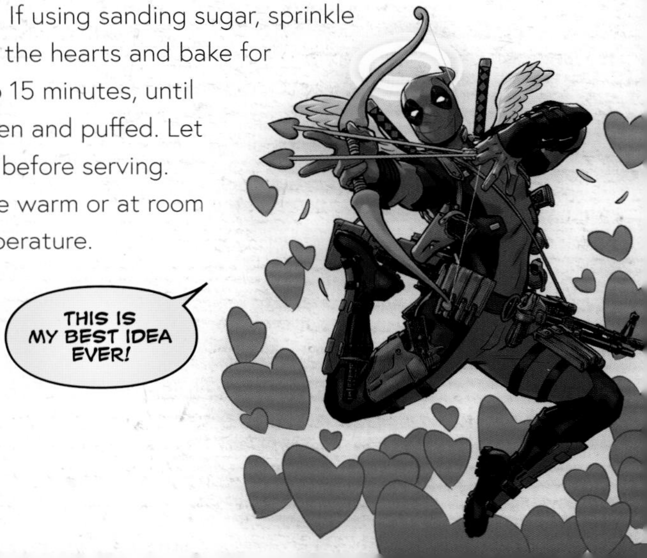
THIS IS MY BEST IDEA EVER!

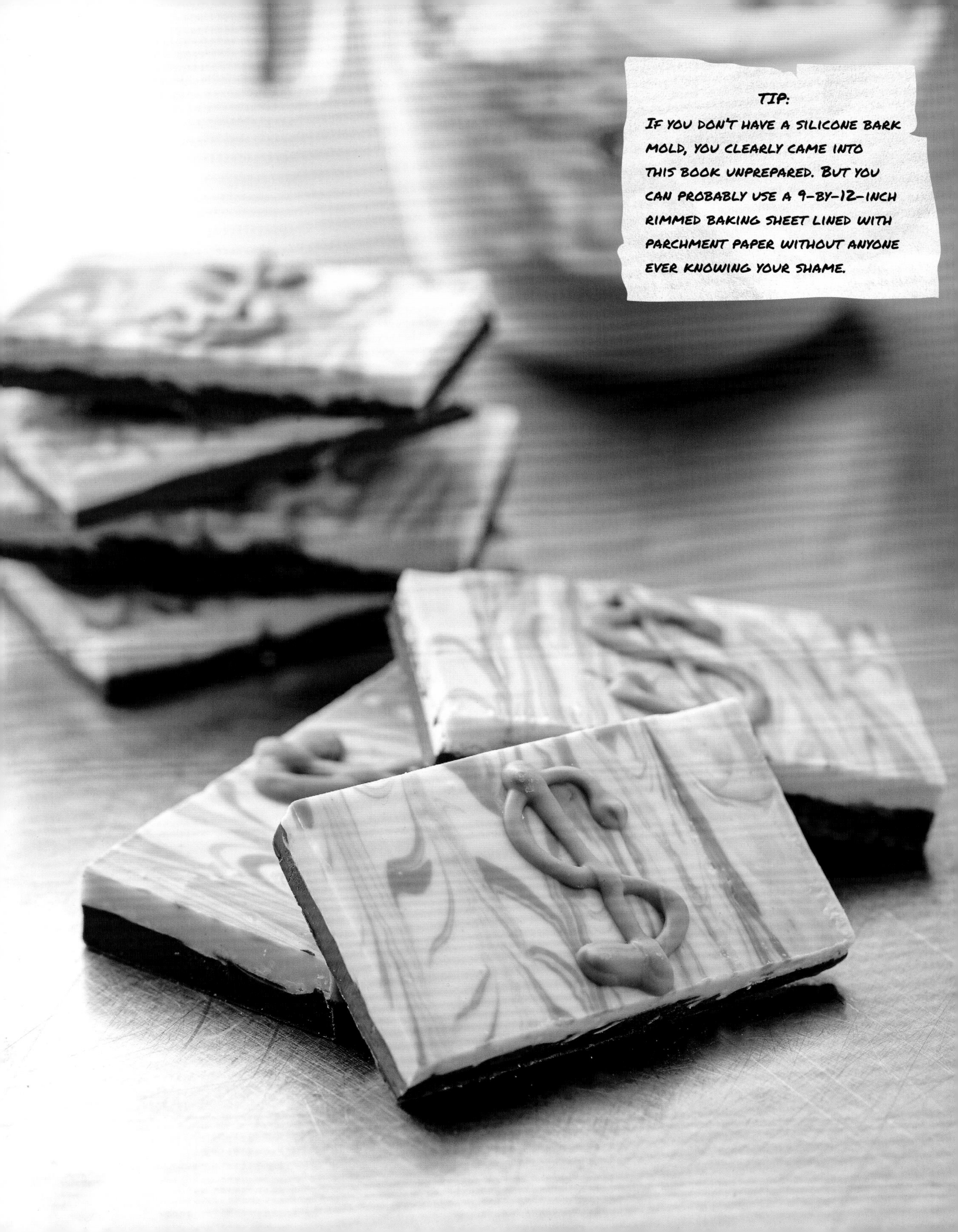

TIP:
IF YOU DON'T HAVE A SILICONE BARK MOLD, YOU CLEARLY CAME INTO THIS BOOK UNPREPARED. BUT YOU CAN PROBABLY USE A 9-BY-12-INCH RIMMED BAKING SHEET LINED WITH PARCHMENT PAPER WITHOUT ANYONE EVER KNOWING YOUR SHAME.

DEAD PRESIDENTS' BARK

I love money. And oddly enough, a lot of slang terms for money are derived from food, like dough, clam, cabbage, and cheddar. So if I were making a dish to express my infatuation with the almighty dollar, you'd think I'd choose one of those aforementioned ingredients, right? Wrong. Personally, when it comes to cash, I've always been a fan of the nickname Dead Presidents. Maybe it's because I got the chance to meet some actual dead presidents in person back when a rogue S.H.I.E.L.D. agent resurrected the deceased commanders in chief and turned them against the country they once benevolently served. Good times. Anyway, that mission inspired this batch of dollar-bill-themed chocolate bark. This treat tastes better than cabbage any day. (And thankfully smells better than Taft, too.)

18 ounces semisweet chocolate

1 tablespoon honey

3 tablespoons vegetable oil, divided

24 ounces white chocolate

2 teaspoons matcha green tea powder

1 to 1½ teaspoons ground ginger

SPECIAL SUPPLIES:

Silicone bark mold

Pastry bag

1. In a large microwave-safe bowl, combine 12 ounces of the semisweet chocolate with honey and 1 tablespoon of the oil. Microwave for 1 minute, remove from microwave, stir, and add about half the remaining semisweet chocolate. Continue stirring, using the residual heat to melt the chocolate. Heat in microwave for 30 seconds more, remove, add the last of the semisweet chocolate, and continue stirring. It is best to use the heat from the bowl as much as possible and avoid overheating the chocolate. Stir until completely smooth.

2. Pour the chocolate into the mold and spread it evenly, making sure it gets into all the corners. Bang mold on the counter a few times to release air bubbles and level out. Drag a fork along the surface of the chocolate in several places to give the next layer something to bond to. Refrigerate for 10 minutes while you prepare the white chocolate.

3. Place 12 ounces of the white chocolate and the remaining vegetable oil in a microwave-safe bowl, and microwave for 30 seconds to start. Repeat the same process used for the semisweet chocolate, adding white chocolate, stirring, and microwaving in short bursts (no longer than 30 seconds) until completely

smooth. Pour ½ cup white chocolate into a separate microwave-safe bowl and mix with the matcha powder. Add ground ginger (to taste) to the remaining white chocolate and stir until smooth.

4. Remove semisweet chocolate layer from the refrigerator, and pour the ginger white chocolate over it, spreading it to cover completely. Working quickly, drizzle about half the matcha chocolate in lines across the bark, vertically and horizontally, then swirl together using a fork or skewer. If chocolate begins to set, heat slightly in a 200°F oven for 1 to 2 minutes. Refrigerate for 20 minutes or until set.

5. Let chocolate come to room temperature. Remove chocolate from mold, and use a knife to cut it into dollar-shaped (rectangle) pieces. Heat the remaining matcha chocolate in the microwave 10 seconds at a time until melted. Pour matcha chocolate into a disposable pastry bag (or resealable plastic bag), cut a small hole in the tip, and pipe dollar signs in the center of each bill. Let set a few minutes, then store in an airtight container in the refrigerator.

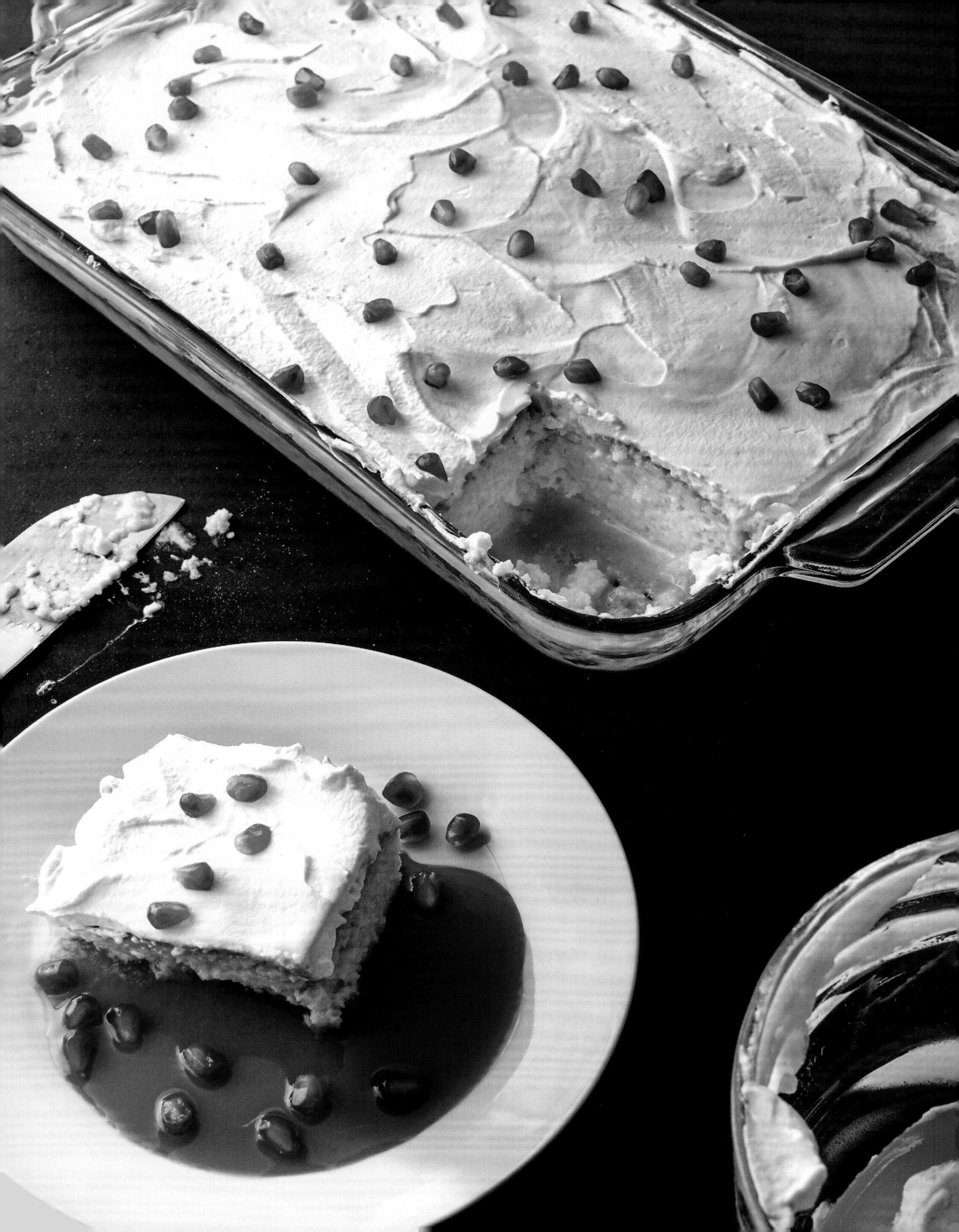

DULCE DE DEADPOOL

YIELD: 12 TO 15 SERVINGS

Here's something I bet you didn't know: Mexico has its own Deadpool. He calls himself Masacre, because apparently *Deadpool* doesn't translate quite right. The guy under the makeshift mask used to be a priest, at least until an extremely moving confessional from yours truly inspired him to trade divine justice for the vigilante variety. If the thought of me with a fancy accent isn't enough to make anyone swoon, Masacre also has a pet jaguar named Justicia! I hate to admit it, but Mexican Deadpool might actually be better than the original one. (And that's me!) Sadly, Masacre hasn't returned my calls since I stiffed him on his last paycheck when the Mercs for Money disbanded. But at least I got the recipe for his famous tres leches cake from him before that mucho macho merc said adios for good.

FOR THE POMEGRANATE SYRUP:

1 cup unsweetened pomegranate juice

1 cup sugar

1 cinnamon stick, halved

FOR THE CAKE BATTER:

3 eggs

1 cup whole milk

Zest of 1 small orange

2 tablespoons fresh orange juice

1 teaspoon vanilla paste
or vanilla extract

2¼ cups all-purpose flour

1¼ cups sugar

4 teaspoons baking powder

¼ teaspoon salt

¾ cup (1½ sticks)
salted butter, softened

FOR THE TRES LECHES:

One 12-ounce can evaporated milk

One 14-ounce can sweetened
condensed milk

½ cup whole milk

FOR THE WHIPPED CREAM FROSTING:

1 cup heavy cream

2 tablespoons sugar

Pomegranate seeds, for garnish

1. To make the pomegranate syrup: Add the juice, sugar, and cinnamon stick to a small saucepan. Bring to a boil on medium-high heat, stirring to dissolve sugar, and simmer for 2 to 3 minutes. Remove pan from heat, and let cool. Once the syrup is cool, remove cinnamon stick, and set aside.

2. Grease and flour the bottom of a 9-by-13-inch glass casserole dish. Set oven rack to lower third of oven, and preheat to 350°F.

3. To make the cake batter: Whisk 3 eggs in a medium bowl. Add 1 cup of milk, orange zest, orange juice, and vanilla. Set aside.

4. In the bowl of a stand mixer with paddle attachment (or in a large mixing bowl using a hand mixer), combine the flour, sugar, baking powder, and salt. Stir until combined. Add the softened butter, stirring on low until a coarse crumb mixture forms.

5. Reserve ½ cup of the egg mixture, and add the rest to the batter bowl. Mix on medium (or high if using hand mixer) for about 2 minutes. Stop the mixer, add the remaining ½ cup milk, and beat for 1 minute more. Stop the mixer again, scrape down the sides of the bowl, and mix about 30 seconds more. Pour batter into the dish. Bake 25 to 30 minutes or until a cake tester comes out clean.

6. Remove cake from oven, and let cool 15 minutes. Run an offset spatula or thin knife gently around the sides of the dish to loosen the cake and make it easier to serve. Using a long fork or skewer, poke a series of holes, in rows, all across the cake. Brush with a scant ¼ cup of pomegranate syrup. Let cake cool completely, about an hour.

7. To make the tres leches: Once the cake is cool, combine the evaporated milk, condensed milk, and whole milk in a large measuring cup or a medium bowl and pour over top of cake. Refrigerate for at least 3 hours, then brush with an additional ¼ cup of pomegranate syrup, and refrigerate for 1 hour more or overnight.

8. To make the whipped cream frosting: When ready to serve, in the bowl of a stand mixer, add the cream and sugar together and mix on high speed until stiff peaks form. Gently swirl ¼ to ½ cup of pomegranate syrup into the cream, until barely incorporated (you should be able to see streaks of pomegranate in the cream). Using an offset spatula or butter knife, frost the entire surface of the cake and sprinkle with pomegranate seeds. Serve each slice of cake on a pool of pomegranate syrup. Cake must stay refrigerated when not being served and will last up to 3 days.

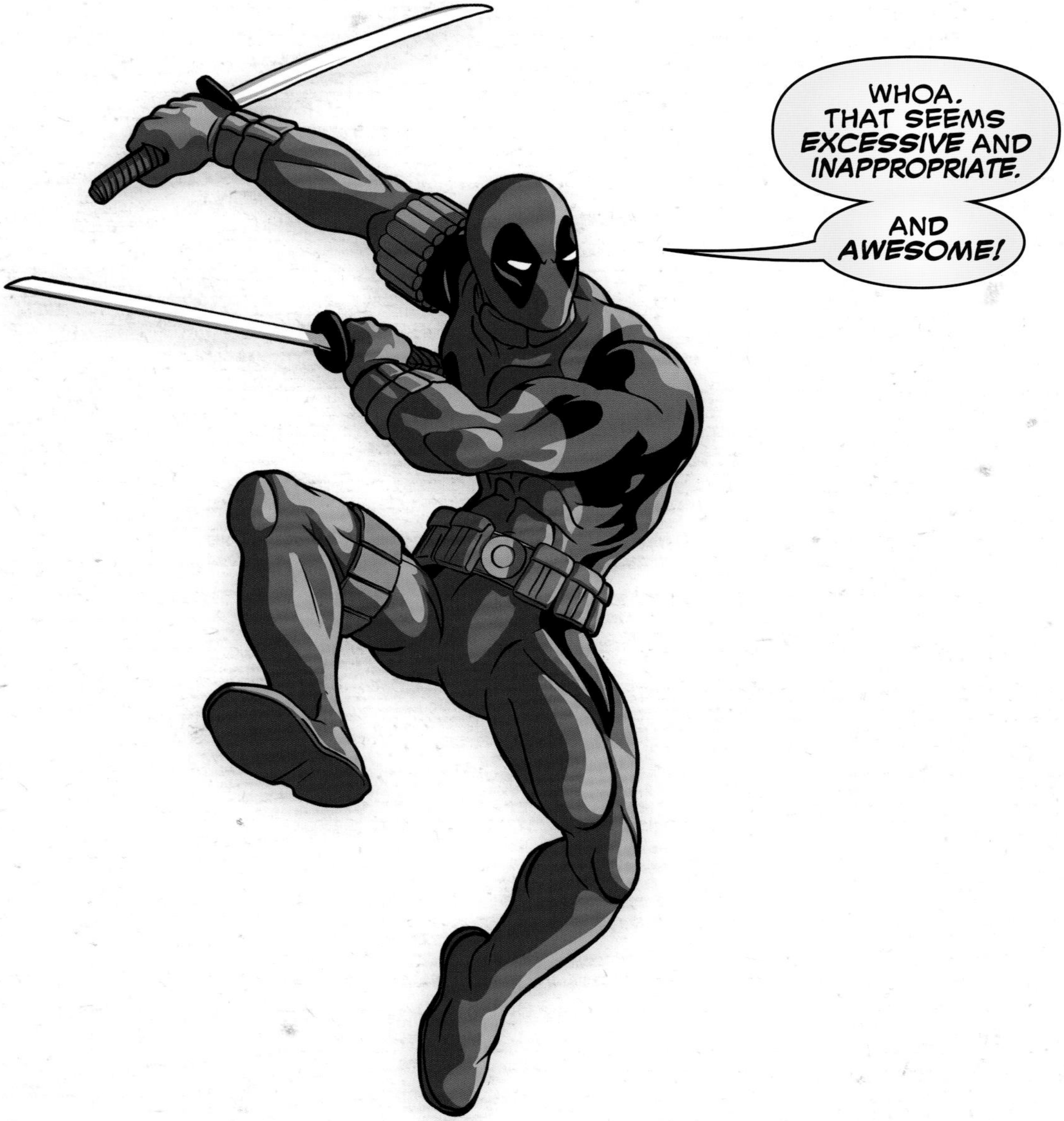
WHOA. THAT SEEMS *EXCESSIVE* AND *INAPPROPRIATE.*
AND *AWESOME!*

DOUBLE-SHOT CUPCAKES

I try to live a relatively clean life. I've had enough toxic chemicals involuntarily pumped into my bloodstream over the years that I'm not necessarily eager to poison myself any further. But being a hired gun requires you to stay awake for long periods of time while stalking your targets, so you occasionally need to run on more than adrenaline alone. That's where this beauty comes in. It may look like a simple chocolate cupcake, but it's got enough caffeine in it (thanks to a double shot of espresso) to keep you fully alert on even the longest of stakeouts. Please note: This dessert's name is in no way a recommended serving, so I'd have only one of these at a time if I were you. No use staying awake all night if your hand is too jittery to pull the trigger when the time finally comes!

FOR THE CAKE BATTER:

1½ cups sugar

1⅓ cups all-purpose flour

⅔ cups unsweetened cocoa powder

½ teaspoon salt

1¼ teaspoons baking powder

1¼ teaspoons baking soda

2 eggs

½ cup milk

1½ teaspoons vanilla paste or vanilla extract

6 tablespoons salted butter, melted

¾ cup hot brewed coffee

FOR THE FROSTING:

3 egg whites

⅛ teaspoon salt

½ cup water

1 cup light brown sugar

½ teaspoon fresh lemon juice

1½ cups unsalted butter (3 sticks), softened and cut in small pieces

1 teaspoon vanilla paste or vanilla extract

1 teaspoon instant coffee powder, mixed with 2 teaspoons of water

SPECIAL SUPPLIES:

Candy thermometer

1. Preheat the oven to 350°F. Line a cupcake pan with cupcake liners.

2. To make the cake batter: Sift together the sugar, flour, cocoa powder, salt, baking powder, and baking soda. Transfer to the bowl of a stand mixer with a whisk attachment (or use a hand mixer in a medium bowl), and blend briefly. In a separate bowl, whisk together the eggs, milk, vanilla, and melted butter until well combined. Add wet ingredients to dry, and mix on low for 3 minutes. Slowly add the hot coffee, and mix on low until just combined. Make sure to scrape the bottom of the bowl (batter will be very thin). Fill each cupcake liner just over halfway with batter, and bake for 15 to 20 minutes, until a cake tester comes out with a few moist crumbs.

3. To make the frosting: Add the egg whites and salt to the bowl of a stand mixer fitted with a whisk attachment (or a large bowl if using a hand mixer), but do not mix yet. In a heavy-bottomed saucepan on medium-high heat, stir together the water and brown sugar, and bring to a boil. When the sugar begins to boil, start mixing the egg whites until frothy. Add lemon juice to the eggs, and mix until soft peaks form. Stop the mixer.

4. Butter a 2-cup, heat-safe measuring cup. Put the candy thermometer in the sugar, and continue to boil until the temperature reaches between 238° and 242°F. Remove from heat and pour into greased measuring cup. Slowly add the sugar syrup to the egg whites in small amounts at a time, whisking after each addition. When all the syrup is added, beat the mixture on high until the meringue is completely cool (the outside of the bowl should be cool to the touch).

5. Add the butter one piece at a time, beating well on medium after each addition. Split the frosting into 2 bowls and flavor half with vanilla and half with coffee mixture. Use a large pastry tip or a small spoon to scoop out a small hole from the center of each cupcake. Fill each cupcake with the coffee frosting and frost with the vanilla.

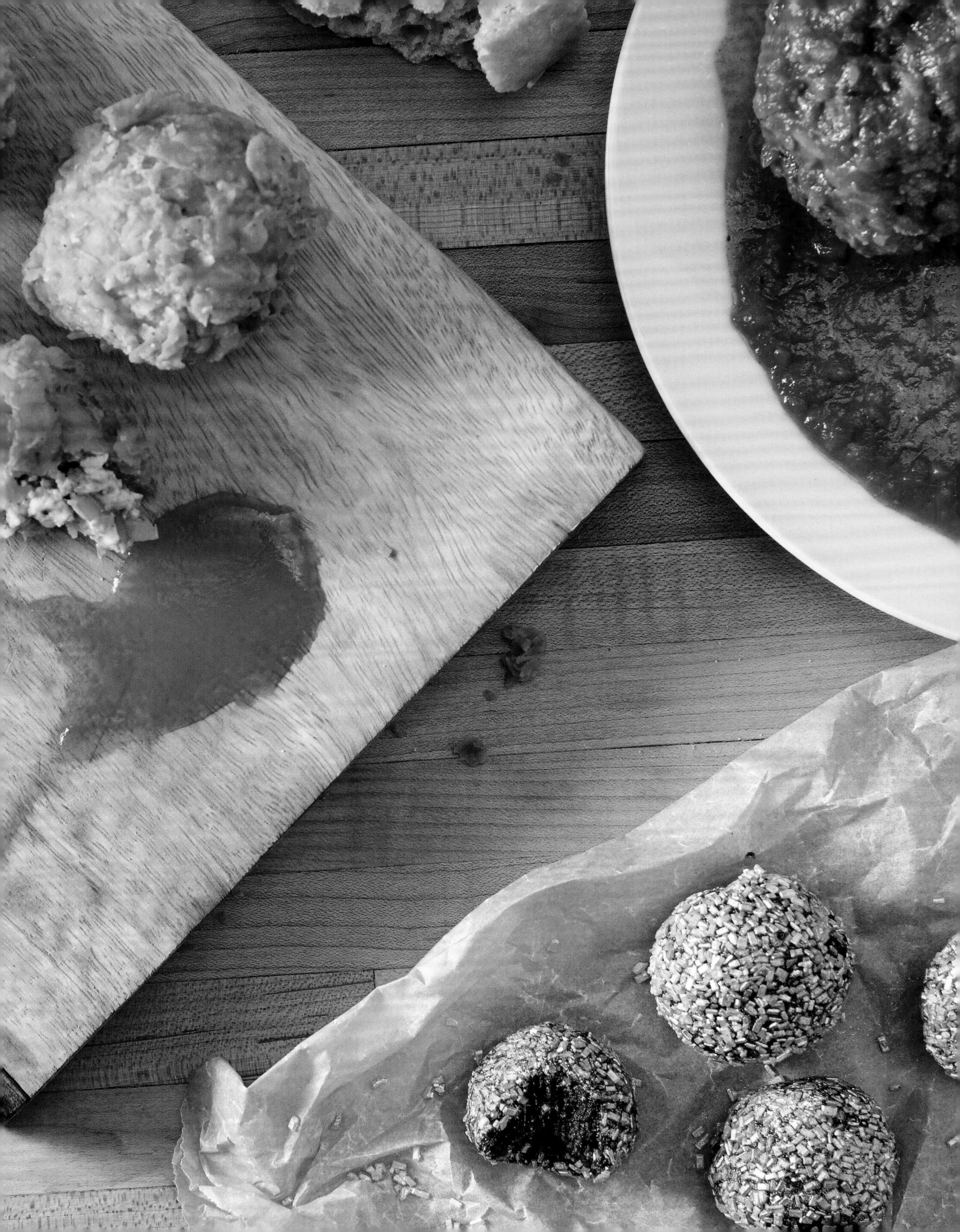

Menus

So, you've read through the whole book and still have no idea how to take a bunch of random recipes and combine them into a proper meal? Seriously? Do I really have to do everything for you? Okay, I will . . . but only because it's in my contract with the publisher.

In my opinion, pretty much everything in this book tastes great together. But there's bound to be some idiot who takes that statement so literally that they decide to drown their wheat cakes in nacho cheese sauce and then write me a nasty e-mail about their poor choices. So I guess it's best if I spell it all out a bit more clearly for you all.

With that in mind, here are some cleverly themed menus I whipped up using the dishes in this book. Hopefully, these spreads should impress just about any company you invite over. If not, let's be honest: It probably says more about your taste in friends than the taste of these dishes.

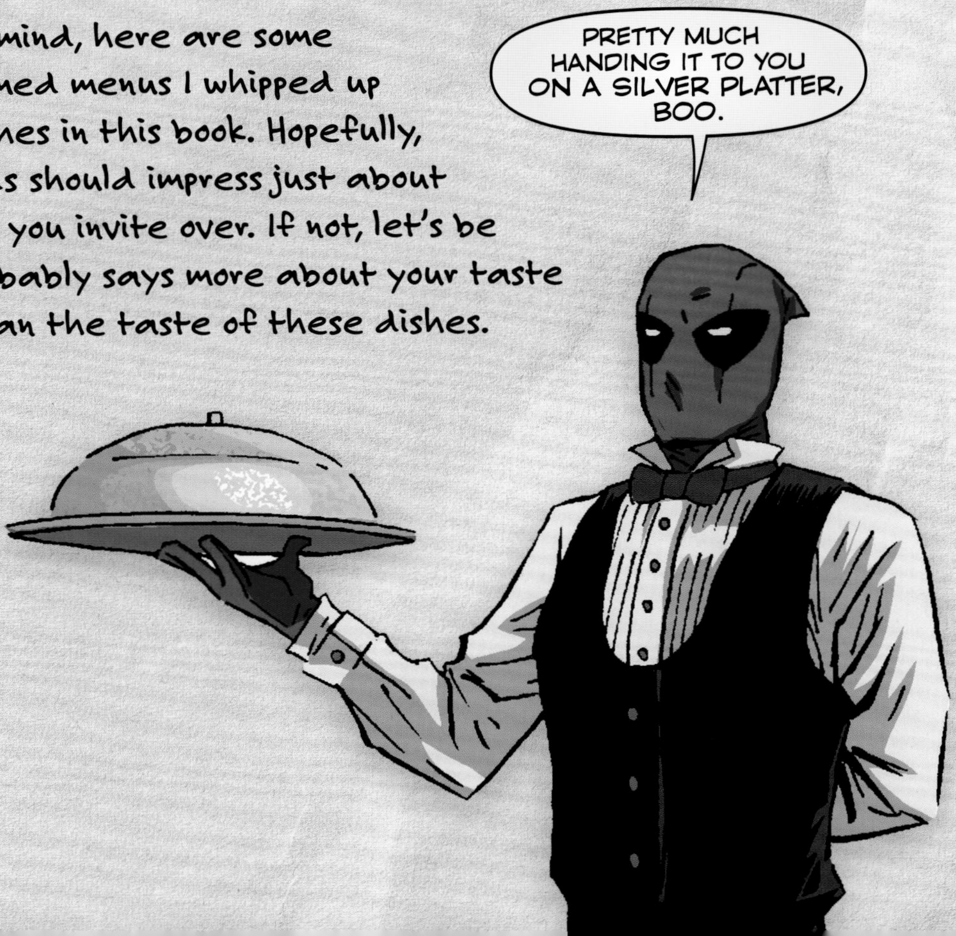
PRETTY MUCH HANDING IT TO YOU ON A SILVER PLATTER, BOO.

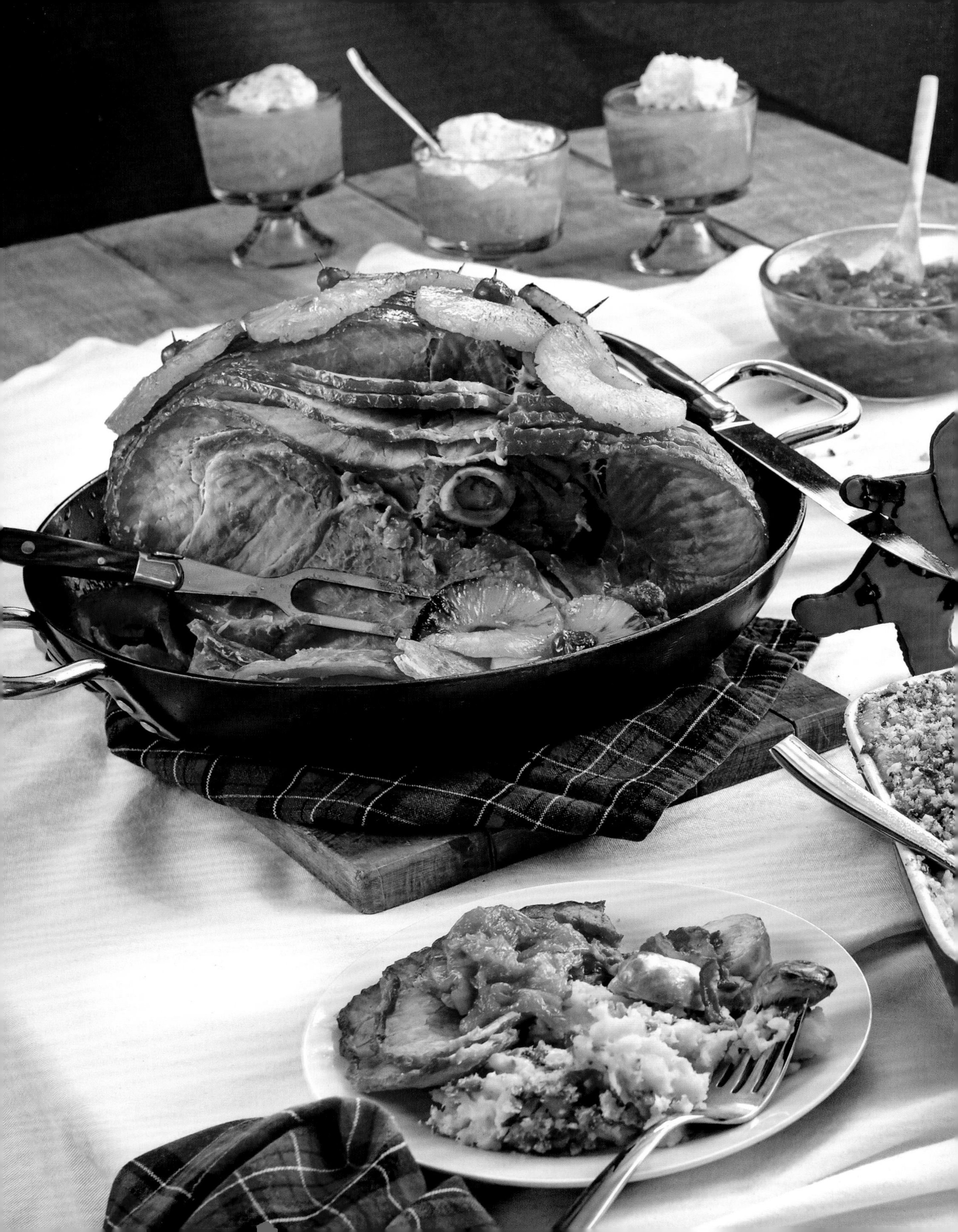

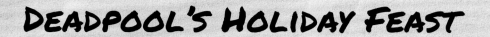

DEADPOOL'S HOLIDAY FEAST

Holidays are a special time, no matter what you're celebrating. Even if you're the one stuck slaving over a hot stove while everyone else is sitting around doing nothing, there's still no feeling quite as rewarding as getting all that gorgeous food onto the table and admiring your hard work—at least in the microseconds before it all gets devoured. Here are some recipes sure to please on any special day:

1. Main Dish: What a Ham

2. Served with: Make 'Em Sweat

3. On the Side: Mashed Stuff, and Brussels Sprouts Cockaigne

4. Complemented with: Boxing Day Bread—also great for leftover knuckle sandwiches!

5. Dessert: Golden Glow Salad

6. To Take Home: GingerPools

BRUNCH WITH WADE

Like I said earlier, breakfast food isn't just for the morning anymore, so this mix of sweet and savory dishes should help satisfy your cravings for early morning delights long after most restaurants have switched to their lunch menus. This combo is perfect for those days when you never want to change out of your pajamas . . . which for me, is pretty much every day!

1. Main Dish: Oh, Stuff It

2. On the Side: What's Shakin' Bacon?, with or without Muffin to See Here

3. To Drink: The Healing Factor

4. Dessert: Bleeding Hearts and/or Double-Shot Cupcakes

FIESTA FUN

If you ask me, every day should be Taco Tuesday. But while that might make sense to my stomach, it also throws the rest of the week into total chaos. So if we have to limit tacos to one day a week, why not make every other night "chimi night"? With all the different fillings and sides I taught you how to make, there's really no excuse not to have a full-on fiesta every night until Tuesday rolls back around again!

1. Main Dish: Choose a chimi or two, such as the Crab Rangoon and the Steak Fajita

2. Serve with: Black Ops Salsa, DP Dip, and/or Nacho Average Cheese Sauce

3. On the Side: Chips (I don't have to tell you how to make these, do I?)

4. Dessert: Dulce de Deadpool

A Well-Rounded Meal

I called this menu "well-rounded" because all the food included on the list is, well, rounded. (And for some reason I can't quite figure out, the censors wouldn't let me get away with just calling it "BALLS!" like I originally wanted to.) Whatever you call it, serving this selection of sumptuous spheres is bound to have you rolling in praise from anyone who pops these tasty balls into their—oh . . . now I see it.

1. Appetizer: Banh Mi Buckshot and/or Fireballs
2. Main Dish: Bozhe Meat
3. Dessert: Cannonballs

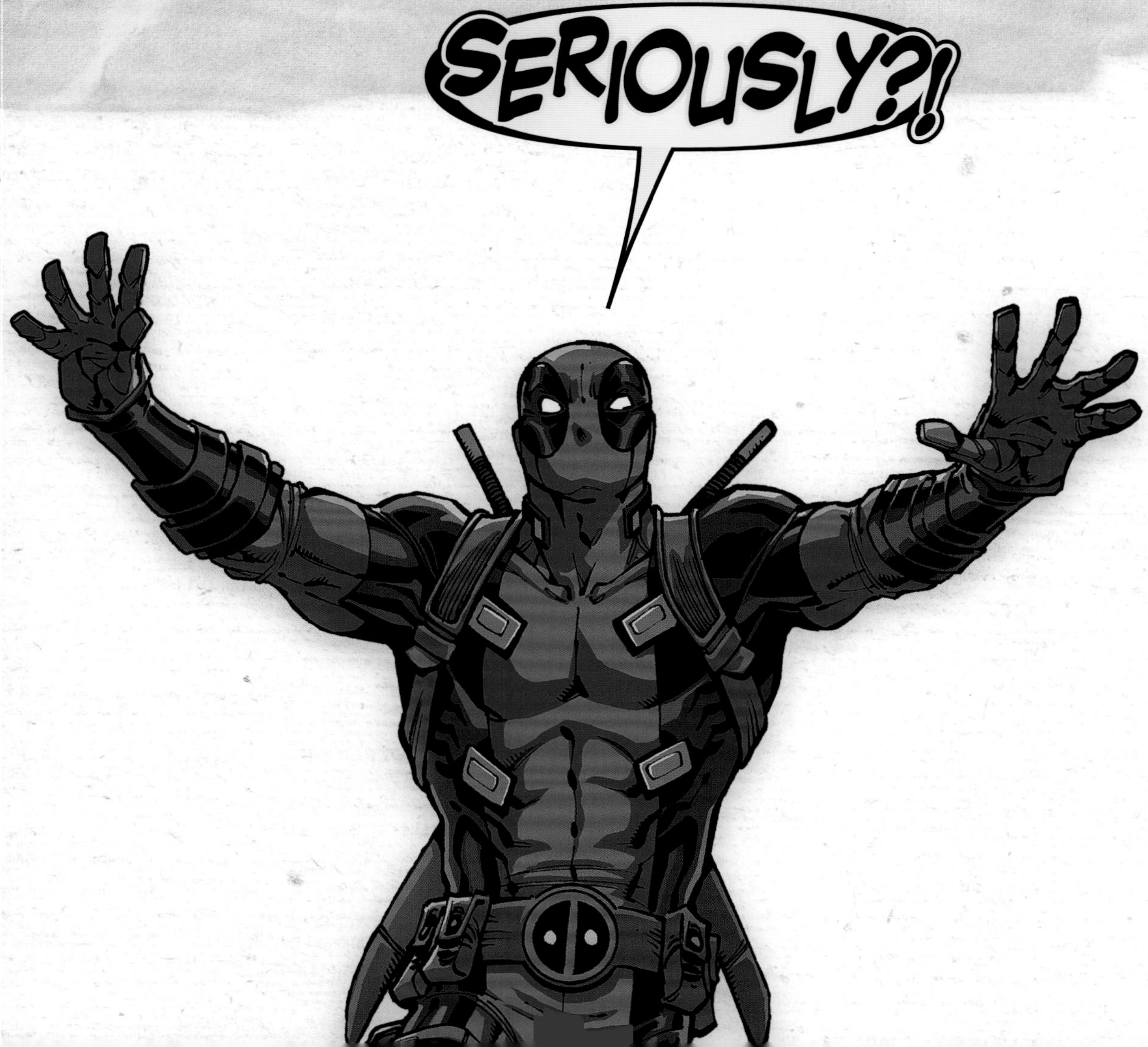
SERIOUSLY?!

PO Box 3088
San Rafael, CA 94912
www.insighteditions.com

f Find us on Facebook: www.facebook.com/InsightEditions

Follow us on Twitter: @insighteditions

All rights reserved. Published by Insight Editions, San Rafael,
California, in 2021.

No part of this book may be reproduced in any form without
written permission from the publisher.

Library of Congress Cataloging-in-Publication Data available.

ISBN: 978-1-68383-844-9

Publisher: Raoul Goff
VP of Licensing: Vanessa Lopez
VP of Creative: Chrissy Kwasnik
VP of Manufacturing: Alix Nicholaeff
Designer: Brooke McCullum
Editor: Hilary VandenBroek
Associate Editor: Anna Wostenberg
Managing Editor: Lauren LePera
Senior Production Editor: Elaine Ou
Production Associate: Eden Orlesky
Senior Production Manager, Subsidiary Rights: Lina s Palma

Photography by Ted Thomas
Props and food styling by Elena P. Craig

ROOTS of PEACE   REPLANTED PAPER

Insight Editions, in association with Roots of Peace, will plant two trees
for each tree used in the manufacturing of this book. Roots of Peace
is an internationally renowned humanitarian organization dedicated
to eradicating land mines worldwide and converting war-torn lands into
productive farms and wildlife habitats. Roots of Peace will plant two
million fruit and nut trees in Afghanistan and provide farmers there with
the skills and support necessary for sustainable land use.

Manufactured in China by Insight Editions

10 9 8 7 6 5 4 3 2

ABOUT THE AUTHORS

MARC SUMERAK is an Eisner– and Harvey Award–
nominated writer and editor whose work over the past
two decades has been featured in comics, books, and
video games showcasing some of pop culture's most
beloved franchises, including Marvel, Star Wars, Harry
Potter, Firefly, Ghostbusters, Back to the Future, and
many more. He lives with his wife and two children in
Cleveland, Ohio. Find out more at www.sumerak.com.

ELENA PONS CRAIG is a food and prop stylist and
recipe developer with more than twenty-five years of
experience in culinary design, marketing, photography,
and publishing. She has a deep love for pop culture
and for using it to have fun with food. She lives with
her family in Fairfax, California.

ACKNOWLEDGMENTS

Marc would like to thank Elena, Hilary, Insight Editions,
Marvel, and all the amazing creators who have put
words in Wade's (Merc-with-a-)mouth over the years.

Elena would like to thank Hilary, Insight Editions, and
Marvel, for this amazing project. Marc, for making it so
much fun. Ted, for gorgeous photography as always.
Her friends and family, for tasting, talking about, and
washing up after DP and her! Finally, thanks, DP, for
being her first . . . cookbook, that is.